Bringing technology home

Bringing technology home

Gender and technology in a changing Europe

Edited by
CYNTHIA COCKBURN AND
RUŽA FÜRST-DILIĆ

Open University Press
Buckingham • Philadelphia

Open University Press
Celtic Court
22 Ballmoor
Buckingham
MK18 1XW

and
1900 Frost Road, Suite 101
Bristol, PA 19007, USA

First Published 1994

A catalogue record of this book is available from the British Library

ISBN 0 335 19158 4 (pbk)   0 335 19159 2 (hbk)

Library of Congress Cataloging-in-Publication Data
Bringing technology home: gender and technology in a changing Europe
  / [edited by] Cynthia Cockburn and Ruža Fürst-Dilić.
    p.   cm.
  Includes bibliographical references and index.
  ISBN 0-335-19159-2   ISBN 0-335-19158-4 (pbk.)
  1. Sex role—Europe.   2. Women—Effect of technological
innovations on—Europe.   3. Housewives—Effect of technological
innovations on—Europe.   4. Technological innovations—Social
aspects—Europe.   5. Technology—Social aspects—Europe.
I. Cockburn, Cynthia.   II. Fürst-Dilić, Ruža.
HQ1075.5.E85B75   1994
303.48'3'082—dc20

                                                          93-32058
                                                          CIP

Typeset by Graphicraft Typesetters Ltd., Hong Kong
Printed in Great Britain by
St Edmundsbury Press Limited, Bury St Edmunds, Suffolk

Contents

Notes on contributors

M. Carme Alemany Gomez is a sociologist, specializing in the sociology of education, human resources and education policy and reform, and in the sociology of work. Her research in these fields has focused on the situation of women, particularly in science and technology. She is currently Director of the Centre for Studies on Women and Society (CEDIS) in Barcelona. Her most recent publication is *Yo no he jugado nunca con Electro-L* (*I never played with Electro-L*), Ministerio de Asuntos Sociales, 1992.

Katerina Arvanitaki studied German literature at Thessaloniki University. She has worked since 1977 in the National Bank of Greece, in various clerical positions on the front desk and in the back office. She is an active trade unionist, especially involved in women's issues and in trade unions' responses to new technology. She initiated a women's group in OTOE (Federation of Trade Unions in the Banking Sector) and is currently active in the Women's Secretariat of GSEE (Confederation of Greek Trade Unions).

Anne-Jorunn Berg is a sociologist (cand.polit.) and a researcher at the Institute of Social Research in Industry (SINTEF-IFIM). Currently working at the Centre for Technology and Society and the Centre for Women's Research of the University of Trondheim, her research is on feminist questions in the sociology of technology. Her particular interest is on users' domestication of telematics in everyday life and the construction of femininity and masculinity in this process. She is co-author of the book *I menns bilde: Kvinner-teknologi-arbeid* (Trondheim: Tapir, 1988).

Danielle Chabaud-Rychter is a researcher in sociology in the Group for Studies on Social and Gender Division of Work (GEDISST) in Paris, a laboratory of the French National Centre for Scientific Research (CNRS). Her research interests lie in domestic work and industrial work, and in the sociology and anthropology of technology. Publications include papers on 'the gender division of technologies' and 'the family as social actor' and she is co-author with others of the book *Espace et temps du travail domestique*, (Paris: Meridiens-Klincksieck, 1985).

Cynthia Cockburn is a researcher and writer in the Centre for Research in Gender, Ethnicity and Social Change of The City University, London. Her research interests include women and work, men and masculinity in relation to technological change, positive action for sex equality in employment and trade unions, and international links between women. Her books include *Brothers: Male Dominance and Technological Change* (London: Pluto Press 1983), *Machinery of Dominance* (London: Pluto Press 1985), *In the Way of Women* (London: Macmillan 1991) and with Susan Ormrod, *Gender and Technology in the Making* (Newbury Park, CA and London: Sage, 1993).

Ruža Fürst-Dilić holds an LLB from the University of Zagreb and an MS in sociology and social anthropology from Iowa State University of Science and Technology. Her main research interest has been women, family and youth in rural sociology and social demography, on which she has published extensively. As Scientific Secretary in the European Co-ordination Centre for Research and Documentation in Social Sciences she coordinated East–West collaborative research on women in science and technology, gender relations in a changing Europe, youth and new technologies, population policies and immigration. She is currently a freelance researcher.

Elina Haavio-Mannila is professor of sociology at the University of Helsinki, vice-president of the Finnish Sociological Association, and past editor of the Finnish Journal of Sociology. She has been a member of various Finnish state committees, including those on marriage and working conditions. Her major studies are related to gender roles in society: in the family, at work, in politics and in sexual life. Among her publications in English is *Unfinished Democracy: Women in Nordic Politics* (with others) (Oxford: Pergamon Press 1985).

Outi Huida is currently a researcher at the Finnish Institute of Occupational Health in Helsinki. She has a MSc in sociology. The research project reported here, 'New Technology and Gender', was the first in which she participated following her graduation from the University of

Helsinki, where she was a student of Prof. Elina Haavio-Mannila, one of the co-authors of Chapter 1.

Kaisa Kauppinen-Toropainen is a research scientist at the Finnish Institute of Occupational Health in Helsinki. She has a Ph.D in social psychology from the University of Helsinki where she is currently a senior lecturer. Her research has dealt with gender roles, family and work, and women's position in professional occupations. She is currently researching women's well-being and coping strategies in Russia and Estonia. Co-author with Elina Haavio-Mannila of *Women and the Welfare State in the Nordic Countries* (Westview Press 1992).

Vitalina Koval has a degree in history and a Ph.D in economics. She is a senior research fellow at the Institute of Political Sciences and Labour Problems, of the Russian Academy of Sciences, in Moscow, where she has worked since 1969. Her current research interests lie in women's issues in Russia in the transition to the market economy. Publications in English include 'Soviet women in science' in the book *Women in Science: Token Women or Gender Equality*, V. Stolte-Heiskanen (ed.) (Oxford: Oxford University Press 1991).

Andjelka Milić was born in Belgrade, first studying then teaching at Belgrade University where she obtained her Ph.D in sociology in 1976. She is currently Professor of Sociology in the Faculty of Philosophy. Her interests lie in family sociology, social anthropology and latterly in gender studies. She has published work, among other things, on the family, and on Marxism and feminism. Among her publications in English is 'Women and nationalisms in former Yugoslavia' in N. Funk and M. Mueller (eds) *Gender Politics and Post-Communism* (Routledge 1993).

Susan Ormrod is a lecturer in media and communication in the Department of Innovation Studies at the University of East London. Previously she was a full-time researcher at The City University, London, and the University of Manchester. She is co-author with Cynthia Cockburn of *Gender and Technology in the Making* (Newbury Park, CA and London: Sage, 1993).

Riitta Smeds is Associate Professor in Industrial Management at Helsinki University of Technology. She teaches courses in marketing and business simulation; her research areas are organizational evolution, technology management and the management of innovation and change in industrial enterprise. She collaborates as task leader and coordinator in several European research and development projects (EUREKA). She was also the leader of the Finnish cross-disciplinary research project reported here, funded by the Research Council for Technology at the Academy of Finland.

Maria Stratigaki studied economics and has a Ph.D in the sociology of work. She has done research on the gender division of labour, new technology and women's work in Southern Europe and has been active for many years in women's groups and left politics in Greece. Publications in English include (with others) *Women of the South in European Integration: Problems and Prospects* (1992), published by the Commission of the European Communities, Equal Opportunities Unit (DGV), where she is currently employed.

Introduction: Looking for the gender/technology relation

CYNTHIA COCKBURN AND
RUŽA FÜRST-DILIĆ

This book is about 'relations' of gender and technology, and it is itself
born out of a very particular set of relations. The nine chapters and this
introduction were shaped by five years of working together as a Europe-
wide group. That makes it very different from most edited collections.
The content is different too, because most of the empirical work reported
here is new work, done over this period specifically for our group project.
The meaning of our findings was hammered out between us in successive
group meetings.

We worked not just as a group but as a women's group. That does not
mean there were no arguments and some quite fundamental differences.
It means we felt our working relationship could and should be able to
deal with them creatively. An example of how what seemed to be 'friend-
ship' was given priority over what seemed to be 'work' is the case of
Yugoslavia. The onset of war threatened to cost us the participation of
Andjelka Milić and Ruža Fürst-Dilić, from Belgrade and Zagreb respectively. Research seemed suddenly irrelevant to them amid such horrors.
We saw the need to restructure the agenda of our workshop to talk about
what was happening in the former Yugoslavia and what they were feeling
about it. But of course it turned out that mutual support and work were
not after all separate things. The chapter on Yugoslavia that finally
resulted may well be the one that brings the most original thinking to the
project as a whole.

Our work began in Zagreb in the summer of 1988. The Vienna Centre
(European Coordination Centre for Research and Documentation in
Social Sciences) invited a number of women from different European
countries with known interests in gender and technology to a meeting to

consider a cross-national project. We would like to acknowledge the role of the Vienna Centre and thank them for their support.

Our meeting was hosted by Ruža Fürst-Dilić who as a Vienna Centre coordinator was involved throughout the subsequent group project. Those of us represented here are the ones that stayed the course, obtained funds or otherwise managed to set up a project in our countries, and brought it to a conclusion. We were sad to lose some on the way: Eva Sokolova from Bulgaria, Ewa Gunnarsson from Sweden and Gisela Erhardt from the former German Democratic Republic. But we also gained a late-comer, Anne-Jorunn Berg from Norway.

Cynthia Cockburn obtained funding from the Economic and Social Research Council of the UK to act as research link person, working from The City University London. We would like to thank both those institutions for their support. Between 1988 and 1992 we were enabled by the Vienna Centre to meet as a group a further five times: in the snows of Suzdal (one of the 'Golden Ring' cities of Russia), in the Mediterranean cities of Dubrovnik and Athens, on the Catalunyan coast and in the English countryside: the reader will notice how we suffered for social research.

The original proposal from the Vienna Centre was that we focus on 'the impact of new technologies on changing gender relations in Europe'. We agreed as a group quite early on to alter this to 'the mutual shaping of new technologies and gender relations'. But how to research that in a way that had meaning for all of us – from widely different cultures in Europe East and West, South and North? We knew we wanted both men and women in the picture, masculinities and femininities, the public and private spheres, work and home. In order to guarantee inclusion of the second of all those pairs, we chose to focus on *domestic technology*, each of us selecting a different innovation. But we would study our chosen artefact not only in use in the home but in its whole life circuit from design, through manufacture, marketing, sale, purchase and maintenance. In short, we opted for a technological trajectory from the drawing board to use and, in some cases, to disuse.

Our decision would give us varied 'levels' of technological sophistication, from mechanical engineering to artificial intelligence, and would involve both product innovation and process innovation. The range of technologies brought into the project's scope could give us different ways into 'the domestic' or 'everyday life' – through cooking, cleaning, communication. We chose: an advanced food processor, the microwave oven, a new model of washing machine, a centralized vacuum cleaning system, the personal computer and the Minitel telephone video system. Those had a clear artefactual presence and a bearing on domestic labour and leisure processes. We also however looked at 'smart house' prototypes. (A 'smart house' is a totalizing domestic technology in which many services and controls are integrated electronically by a 'housebrain'.) Two other technologies enabled a different perspective on domestic life: through consumption. One was computerization in the Greek banking industry, experienced in the home as a new spending practice: the deployment of the plastic credit card. The other was new technology in hosiery manufacture in Russia generating a commodity, panty hose, that was itself symbolic of women's new persona as consumers in a market economy.

All the researchers were alert to the circuit of social relations in which an artefact becomes a meaningful innovation, but in the event not all projects give equal weight to all parts of the trajectory. Those that touch on design, production, marketing, sale and use include Chapter 1 on the central vacuum cleaning system by an interdisciplinary team of four researchers from Finland: Riitta Smeds, Outi Huida, Elina Haavio-Mannila and Kaisa Kauppinen-Toropainen. Other accounts of this kind include the case study of the microwave oven made in Britain by Susan Ormrod and Cynthia Cockburn, reported in Chapter 2 by Susan; and that on the Greek bank credit card system by Katerina Arvanitaki and Maria Stratigaki from Greece (Chapter 3). Some projects give particular weight to the design–user link – Chapter 4 by Danielle Chabaud-Rychter on the French 'food robot' and Chapters 5 and 9 on Minitel and the 'smart house' by Anne-Jorunn Berg of Norway. Two projects prioritized production technology – that of Vitalina Koval (panty hose, Russia, Chapter 6) and that of Carme Alemany Gomez (the washing machine, Spain, Chapter 7), using the factory as a starting point in exploring the links between point of origin and point of use, women's lives at work and at home. The account from the former Yugoslavia by Andjelka Milić (Chapter 8) is in many ways a special case. She considers technology and education as aspects of modernization, and illustrates their expression in gender relations in the contrasted lives of agricultural housewives and highly-qualified women software engineers.

Comparative research?

We have often asked ourselves, and been asked by others, whether this project constitutes *comparative* research. There were doubts about this from the start. Stefan Nowak (1989: 34–56) wrote of cross-national research

> the more complex are the objects or phenomena in which we are interested, and the more they correspond to common-language categories – which usually means that they are in all their complexity socially relevant for the members of the population who perceive and define them – the less likely it is that such natural social objects will be explainable by a single explanatory theory.

Women, men and technology are just such everyday categories, and quickly proved to be laden with different meanings for each of us.

It has been suggested that cross-national research, truly speaking, is research that transcends national boundaries and *utilizes systematically comparable data* from more than one country (Kohn 1989). In this definition, the nation may be the object of comparison, the unit of analysis or the context of the comparison – or the study may treat of the nation as part of a larger system. By such standards our studies are clearly not directly comparable: we do not draw on similar statistical evidence and our domestic technologies differ widely in nature. Besides, our largely qualitative approach does not lend itself to direct comparisons: with studies so focused, our findings cannot be read as 'representative' of our countries. On the other hand, there is an underlying coherence in the subject of concern – technological and social innovation – and in our shared belief that technology and gender can both be seen as relations and as having something to do with each other. Perhaps we may see our different countries as a panel, rather like a panel on a television show, an array of participants each of whom may be questioned to produce a different account of similar phenomena.

As editors, we hoped for a while that, even if our research data were not comparable, we would at least be able to find our sociologies, our methodologies and approaches to be valid subjects for a cross-national comparison. In this respect, for instance, we might have been able to say something about sociology itself. Those of us coming from Western and Northern Europe, whatever kind of 'social scientist' any one of us personally may be, can draw on a long tradition of sociology that has flowered dramatically in the post-Second World War decades. Our Greek participants say by contrast that sociology as an academic discipline barely exists in their country even today, and they joined the project as feminist activists, without research funding or university backing. In the Soviet Union sociology was limited to state-sponsored descriptive studies, and in Russia today critical sociology is only now beginning.

We might also have compared methodological preferences. We all felt we needed statistics for some purposes – to describe the sexual division of labour, for example. We asked each other many times as we tangled with gender relations, 'Do numbers count?' We all, eventually, replied 'Yes. But numbers don't tell us everything.' As Anne-Jorunn Berg said, 'It depends what kinds of questions you want answered.' Some participants wanted to be able to check qualitative findings against more formally-generated data: the Russian and Finnish projects therefore combined methods, using written questionnaires in addition to qualitative interviews and observation. Others mistrusted 'positivism' and felt a more complex rendering of reality would emerge from qualitative processes of observation and open interviews.

Perhaps it would be correct to say that some of the researchers at the latter end of this spectrum – those from Britain, France and Norway for instance – were pleased to be able to use their projects to try out a new methodology and the theory closely associated with it. Those at the former end, of which Finland and Russia are instances, were more concerned to add new findings to those amassed from previous research using similar methods. Or finally, perhaps, as Susan Ormrod said, 'It's just that we look for our evidence in rather different forms.'

Any hopes of rigorous comparison of sociological approach in any case went out of the window as work progressed. We found we were changing each other in the process of our research relationship. For example, Vitalina Koval from Russia said,

When I began this project I had no idea what 'gender' meant. Then the Centre for Gender Studies was set up in Moscow. I began to see how gender can be thought of as 'relations' between the sexes in the social sphere. And each of our meetings gave me more impulse to think about gender. Without the meetings it would have been impossible.

So we were influencing each other. Anne-Jorunn Berg from Norway expressed delight at

getting out of my Anglo-American theoretical straitjacket . . . When I met up with the French tradition of technology studies it put me on my toes. At first I couldn't understand it. That an artefact can be an 'actor' along with human actors? Perhaps . . .

The mutuality spread. Vitalina asked Kaisa and Cynthia to be involved in planning her research and designing the questionnaires. Cynthia was introduced to Scandinavian feminist 'rationality theory', and so on.

If this contamination at first made us two, Ruža and Cynthia, as co-ordinators and editors, rather nervous, the anxiety quickly gave way to enjoyment: surely this is what group working should be about? Some of us might have said, 'Of course, if technology actors shape each other along with the technology, it's obvious that researchers must shape each other along with the research.' That, finally, is what we have to say on the subject of comparative cross-national research.

The remainder of this introduction will explore the similarities, differences and relationships of our theories and our findings. Instead of summarizing and introducing the chapters one by one, in the usual way, we shall move theme by theme and draw on the chapters to exemplify them.

Approaches to understanding gender

Differences about sex differences are expressed, of course, in language. Thus, English appears to be blessed with two terms, 'sex' and 'gender', the one applicable to biological difference (male and female), the other to cultural difference (masculine and feminine). French, Spanish, Norwegian and many other European languages have no such distinction. The French for instance say *rapports sociaux de sexe* when they want to say what the English mean by gender relations. These chapters are translations into English and therefore misleading in permitting the word 'gender' to seem a universal asset.

Perhaps however the difference between our lexicons is not as great as it seems. After all, anglophone feminists have only recently (Oakley 1972), in a political move, *chosen* to bring the grammatical and botanical term gender into everyday use to enhance a feminist concept, namely 'there's more culture than biology about women and men'. Language is deployed creatively, just like technology.

Besides, is 'gender' even an asset? Linguistic moves are contested and may be short-lived. No sooner had some of us from some cultures grasped happily at the notion that socially-shaped differences between women and men can be conceptualized as gender than the ground moved beneath our feet. Thus, Anne-Jorunn said at our final meeting 'I used to be jealous of you English who could make this neat verbal distinction between biological sex and cultural gender. But now I wonder if it's so good after all. What *is* sex? What *is* gender? Should we be making this distinction?' She did not mean that gender could again be reduced to sex but that sex might reasonably now be subsumed into gender.

As a group then we are spread out at different places on a spectrum. At one end is a practice of specifying sex difference as biology, in contrast to gender difference as social. 'Gender is relations between the sexes in the social sphere', said Vitalina. At the other, 'biology' was itself seen as cultural. 'Some of us are breaking down the naturalness of sex too', said Anne-Jorunn. We shifted our position as we went along. Sometimes it was painful. Carme, feeling herself edging towards this latter end of the spectrum exclaimed, 'I thought I knew something about gender. Now I wonder if I know anything!' There was, however, something we felt we did all 'know': none of us saw cultural differences between women and men as determined by biology.

Since we are all children of our time, it will not be surprising if we also experienced tensions in the group around the not unrelated dichotomy: structure/agency. Some of us felt easy enough using the terms 'society' and 'social structure'. Those who did, were also likely, when thinking of men's power and women's oppression, to introduce the notion of 'patriarchy'. For Andjelka, in the countries of the former Yugoslavia the power relations of patriarchy were still intact in family and state. Vitalina describes Russia as a society in which the attitude towards women is still based on old patriarchal traditions. Maria and Katerina use the adjective 'patriarchal' to qualify relations of authority and control. However, all these uses occur within a general understanding that social relations change historically. The Greek paper for instance refers to a shift in the control of women from the personalized power of husband to an impersonal but equally male power in institutions – in this case the Greek banking sector. It is evident that some manifestations of male power are more accurately termed patriarchal than others. Sometimes a less specific sense of the 'systemic' was preferred. Thus Elina Haavio-Mannila (Finland) said she found 'gender system' preferable, as being easier to relate to 'class system'; and it is the case that Carme (Spain), whose chapter is notable for its class awareness, also uses 'male power system'.

Too great a readiness to leap to structure, however, troubled some of us. One exchange went as follows. Riitta Smeds was defending 'structure' and 'system' against charges of stasis and timelessness.

Riitta: No. System has dynamism, it's in process.
Susan [suspiciously]: Do gender relations flow from it?
Riitta [confidently]: No. They develop in it.
Elina [amplifying]: The system includes elements and
  interactions – gender practices, for instance.
Susan [thoughtfully]: I don't understand this concept of system.
  The instances in our research don't flow from some system of gender
  relations in the background of action . . . I'd rather say factors aren't
  influential till they're brought into play.
Anne-Jorunn [helpfully]: Everyone in sociology now is trying to
  overcome this agency/structure dualism. As I see it, the empirical
  focus we all have should help us not to be trapped in it.

Nor were we, when it came to writing up. The contributors will be found to move fluidly from micro to macro phenomena, from the individual to the social context, and back again.

Approaches to understanding 'technology and . . .'

When Vitalina first found herself in pursuit of 'the impact of technology on gender relations', in her new-technology panty hose factory in Russia she looked around and found in the Russian literature few technology impact studies of any kind and none concerned with differential effects on women and men. The tradition, there, besides had been to see technology as 'a prime mover'. Whether this can be said to derive from the Marxist tradition in the Soviet Union depends of course on which position you take on the question 'was Marx a technological determinist?'

In sharp contrast, Danielle Chabaud-Rychter was the beneficiary of a rich French inheritance of sociology of science and technology. And in this the focus had long shifted away from 'impact' to innovation. She was already drawing on the 'laboratory studies' of Bruno Latour, Michel Callon and others (Callon 1989; Latour 1989) that others of us were encountering in English translation. She builds on available methodology to good effect here in a gendered ethnography of interactions and changing meanings surrounding the electric food processor.

Those of us who had been working in technology studies in English were already 'social constructivists', and shared with the Francophones (Danielle and Carme) a perception of technology not 'as having social aspects' but as 'being social in its very constitution' as Carme puts it (MacKenzie and Wajcman 1985; Bijker *et al.* 1990). There was a growing feminist literature that showed the constitutive 'social' to be gendered (Cockburn 1983, 1985; McNeil 1987; Cowan 1989; Harding 1991; Wajcman 1991). The social constructivist approach shifts attention away from the artefact as hardware to the knowledge and processes that together give a thing meaning. All of us inevitably consolidated around this approach because of the demands made by the concept of 'gender'. Gender was clearly social relations. To be able to see gender and technology shaping one another, technology had to be seen as social relations too.

There were however subtle differences. Some of us saw the artefact as a *vehicle* for understanding social relations. Thus Andjelka surmised that perhaps we were returning to an old anthropological tradition of trying to understand societies and their structures through the function of specific objects. And Riitta laughed and said perhaps it was more like archaeology, 'We're finding out all the things you'd never guess about the microwave oven if you were excavating a site 300 years from now.' For Elina the idea of studying sociology through a material artefact had been novel: 'To see it as a metaphor for social creativity – that's been important for me.'

Susan, on the other hand, exemplifies the approach that sees the technical and social as a 'seamless web'. The innovation that she and Cynthia had identified as the focus of their study had not been the microwave oven as artefact but the activity of microwave *cooking*. In looking at what was meant by engineering and cooking they had seen, she believed, the way the boundary between the technical and the social was drawn in discourse, and how the two were consequently differentiated and constructed.

There was therefore no identikit of theoretical tools in use in the group, although a toolbox was always there on the table between us. To it we added new theories, picked some out and tried using them. Some worked, others we handed back. 'I've thrown away many ideas through this process', said Danielle, 'I feel I'm *producing* ideas.' Maria (Greece) agreed, 'I found out how you can produce knowledge.'

There were moments when the imperialism of the English language, or Anglo-French hegemony, or some other such tyranny troubled us, but on the whole we were strong on diversity. On a bad day, Anne-Jorunn feared, 'all we have in common is our ethnocentricity'. And Vitalina sometimes despaired that anyone without a communist past could possibly understand Russian thinking. But she added 'I do understand your *willingness* to understand'. We were, Carme said, 'working towards affinities without obliterating differences'. As John Galtung writes of comparative research, to homogenize is collective suicide.

> Any effort to reduce this diversity is doomed to fail; underneath the repression resistance movements will form . . . There is a principle of variety at work here. Only by cultivating variety, not only among social scientists but also within us can we be mentally prepared to reflect and construct variety around us.
>
> (Galtung 1990: 96–112)

The mutual shaping of gender and technology

What can these studies, taken as a whole, show us about the mutual shaping of technology and gender? The two processes are difficult to distinguish because they happen simultaneously: they are in fact the *same* process read in different ways.

The first and most obvious shaping influence is the mode of production and its related power relations. In the capitalist countries of North, West and South Europe we saw plenty of evidence of technological decisions designed to enhance a company's control of markets or of labour. Anne-Jorunn, in Chapter 9, for instance, describes her prototype electronic homes-of-the-future as clear instances of 'technology push', a bid to grasp and shape the market, through standardization, for future company products. Carme, in Chapter 7, finds the new model of washing machine being developed for production in her Spanish company is intended not so much to improve its usefulness in the home as to enable new methods of production that will bypass labour resistance. The Greek credit card was certainly not introduced as a social service.

Andjelka's description of technological development in Yugoslavia (Chapter 8) is a terrible indictment of the self-interested political elite under which a hopeful socialist society was stultified and its technology misdirected. Her emphasis on the way creativity (or atrophy) results from sociopolitical structure is echoed on the micro-scale by Riitta and colleagues (Chapter 1) from Finland who argue that the organization of a company can encourage or suppress social and technological inventiveness. Perhaps the most dramatic evidence of social shaping, though, comes from Russia (Chapter 6). At our last meeting Vitalina said of the ossified society of those fading years of the communist state

> I can see so clearly how the implementation of new technology depends on the social structure of a society. In our country technology was used mainly for military purposes. I can see how technical genius was misspent – to ruin the achievements of humanity.

Gender relations of course are also powerfully shaped in and by these same macro-forces. The historical constitution of the male-headed nuclear family and the emergence of women into the waged labour force in the context of capitalist production and consumption is well understood (Barrett and McIntosh 1982 review some approaches; see also Bourgeois *et al.* 1978). Many of the differences between the lives of women in East/Central Europe and 'the West' can be explained in terms of the contrasted social systems of communist and capitalist blocs (Heinen 1990; Haavio-Mannila 1993). The effect on gender relations, and specifically on women's chances, of differing organizational structures, such as the business firm, has also been explored (Kanter 1977; Kvande and Rasmussen 1990). And Andjelka Milić shows in Chapter 8 how the very political and economic system that failed to deliver the creative promise of technological modernization in Yugoslavia also failed 'to generate new social actors, roles and relations'.

Our studies however were designed more precisely to show the gender/technology relation on the micro-scale, in the detailed interactions of what we came to think of as the 'circuit of technology'. Here we will focus on three clusters of activity in the technological trajectory: design and marketing, manufacture and sale, and use, consumption and domestic life. We piece together the story with illustrations from relevant chapters. In the interests of readability not every possible example is cited every time.

Male designers and imagined women

Taken as a whole the studies reveal an almost total absence of women from design engineering. There were no women among the qualified engineering professionals responsible for the food processor, for instance, (Chapter 4), or for the washing machine (Chapter 7), or the central vacuum cleaning system (Chapter 1). In this sense technologies can be said to be profoundly gendered. The 'smart house' (Chapter 9), for instance, is exposed as self-indulgent masculine techno-fantasy with no reference at all to domestic labour processes. 'Machines to aid housework?' say these architects and communications specialists. 'That's the job of the white goods producers.'

The white goods producers show a similar reluctance to get their hands down the toilet pan. To sell successfully, however, domestic appliances must correspond, even if only perfunctorily, to the needs of the person who does the housework. Our studies show, as we shall mention again below, that this person is still, even today, characteristically a woman.

The various accounts reveal in fascinating detail the way the all-male design teams contrive to introduce women, real or imagined, into their thinking processes. Danielle, for instance, found the male designers of the food processor commissioning marketing reports of the buying behaviour of abstract segments of the female population; imagining a woman's preferences by 'putting themselves in her place'; engaging women as testers to simulate women's responses; and enlisting the services of women on their own assembly lines who could 'stand for' the housewife. Carme found designers giving production prototypes of the new washing machine to male managers to take home for their wives to try out.

Only in the case of the microwave oven (Chapter 2) were women, in a team of home economists, in a position to make a serious input to decisions concerning the development of a microwave range. But, as Susan reports, when managers do introduce domestic skills to the firm they barely know what to do with them: the home economists were metaphorically relegated to a broom cupboard. The input of the male engineers was considered more important, they were paid much more and the women sometimes felt they were, as we saw in Spain and France, employed merely as stand-ins for all those women users out there, a device to 'keep the women out of the men's hair'. As one of Carme's male engineers admitted, there's 'a slight break-down of communications with the outside world'.

Despite the many devices used by some designers to imagine the woman user she remains, as Danielle says, 'Other' to the designer. And in other cases the designers' knowledge of women and women's work was surprisingly speculative (Chapter 2). There was a preference for keeping separate the public and private sphere, and a lack of interest in domestic life (Chapters 5, 7 and 9). Instead, the designers attempted to make their artefacts carry a message to the user about how she should behave. As Danielle points out, the artefact speaks to the user, but it is not very good at conveying messages back to the designer. Only when it breaks down does it say something about life beyond the design office. To avoid breakdown and ensure that appliances comply with safety regulations, male designers tend to project the worst-case scenario, which involves imagining a woman user who is careless, clumsy, absent-minded or dangerous in using appliances (Chapters 2 and 7). This deficit model of women is echoed in the findings that some men think women misuse the Minitel telephone directory (Chapter 5) and cannot be trusted with credit facilities (Chapter 3).

Here we have moved, of course, in the way we found ourselves doing continually, from an emphasis on the shaping of technology to an emphasis on the shaping of gender identities. For the design engineers and marketing specialists themselves slip imperceptibly from describing 'the user', 'the housewife', to configuring her. In Chapter 2 Susan shows how gender, as well as technology, is reinterpreted in the course of the circuit. As designers translate the microwave oven from simple pie-warmer to cooking-oriented 'combination oven', gender is enrolled and new gender subjects created. Design engineers have it in their scope, through the technologies they project into everyday use, to affirm the sexual division of labour, shape up the contemporary women and define their work. This regulation of women extends, as Carme (Chapter 7) and Katerina and Maria (Chapter 3) show, even to their bodies and their spending habits.

Advertisers and marketing personnel give a gender to the commodity they promote, whether this is an artefact or (as in the Greek credit card) a service. But in doing so they also tell us who we are. Riitta and friends (Chapter 1) show how the central vacuum cleaning system was represented as masculine for purposes of persuading the male-dominated hardware retail suppliers to stock this 'women's gadget'; then at times a gender-neutrality was sought when selling to the anticipated user; but again the image was masculine when the installer or maintenance technician was addressed. Gendered people are thus constructed too: men, we learn, are technically competent.

Manufacturing and selling artefacts, gendering people

Technology is also playing a bigger role as a criterion of differentiation in the sexual division of labour in production and distribution. We found very few women in technical management or in skilled technological occupations, whether concerned with the old technologies or the new. In Finland the supervisors, technicians and senior managers of the vacuum cleaner factory were male. It was rare to find a woman placed over a man, whatever the work. The same applied in the Spanish case and in micro-wave manufacture in Britain – as described elsewhere (Cockburn and Ormrod 1993). Andjelka (Chapter 8) found many women software engin-eers, the well-qualified products of a relatively egalitarian socialist higher education system. But she also found that ten years after graduating, equally qualified men had pulled ahead into positions of greater technical authority.

Maria and Katerina (Chapter 3) report on the results of the shake-up due to electronic innovations in Greek banking: men were in the jobs perceived as more technical or offering more prospects, women in routine, dead-end and technologically degraded jobs. We were all surprised at first to see women in leading management positions in Vitalina's Russian panty hose factory (Chapter 6) – until she explained that such positions in 'female' light industry have low status. And besides, the interesting jobs generated by new technology all went to men. In Russia, despite formal equality there was widespread informal sex discrimination. But even where, as in Finland, equality laws were normally observed, sex-segregation ensured women earned less. We found widespread evidence of men getting technological training or retraining at the expense of women. Men were now and then to be found entering 'women's' jobs, for instance on the assembly line (Spain and Greece), from which they would however quickly climb. There were few instances of women getting access to 'men's' jobs.

Those studies that followed the technology into the shops found a similar sexual division of labour there. Its organization around techno-logy was particularly striking in the British retail study, where the 'brown goods' department (televisions, videos, music systems) was considered technically interesting and therefore masculine, while the 'white goods' department (cookers, fridges, washing machines) was seen as a family sphere, predominantly female, and less important.

The rationales produced for the sexual division of labour were the familiar two. First, women are considered unsuited to do work with 'heavy' associations, as that of the Greek computer operators, or goods handling in the Spanish factory. As Carme (Chapter 7) points out, the designers do give some thought, superficial though it may be, to the gendered ergonomics of the knobs and switches on the appliance they manufacture. But they give no thought to designing production equipment to empower women workers in the factory. Femininity is here being shaped as deficient, not-normal.

Second, femininity is constructed in these workplaces as 'non-technical'. This is a self-fulfilling prophecy, since it leads to women being passed over for technical training and retraining. They have to prove their competence over and over again. Women, particularly older women, are vulnerable to technological redundancy. The two chapters (on Greece and Spain) that dwell on the trade union have equally dismal stories to tell of failure to represent women's interests in times of technological upheaval

(Chapters 3 and 7). The net result appears to be that, while new technology does not of itself disadvantage women, and some women experience it positively, men are gaining relatively more from technological change and as a result the sex gap is, if anything, widening. The gender gap of course – what is feminine, what is masculine – widens with it.

The process is terribly wasteful of women's creativity. Just as women's expertise in housework is neglected as a design resource, so is their capability undervalued at work. Even where women are equally or better educated relative to men this education may be squandered (as in Russia and former Yugoslavia) by the disadvantaging gender relations in which they live and work.

Technologies in use: domestic dramas

A significant proportion of European women work outside the home – though rather more in the former communist countries and rather fewer in the Mediterranean countries. Despite this, women are everywhere the sex that does most housework and maintains responsibility for care and the quality of family life. Carme for instance found women still doing the weekly wash for the household; Susan found them still having overall responsibility for feeding it. Even in Finland, where sex equality has long been promoted as government policy, women still do most of its cleaning. Several of us found that where men engage in certain tasks it is not to commit themselves to responsibility for the housework but to look after themselves or 'help' their partner.

Is new technology bringing any change in this respect? Other studies have shown that an increasing level of technology in the home has little effect either on the time devoted to housework or which sex does it (Cowan 1989). It may well be that few domestic innovations are in fact designed with the intention of reducing housework time, and fewer still with that of altering which sex does the work. The manufacturer's aim is rather to *enhance* the activity. None the less, in our study we saw one or two slender signs of change. The percentage of male partners sharing vacuuming increased by 10 or 15 per cent with the acquisition of a centralized system. Men do a little more food preparation in relation to the microwave oven. The marginally increased involvement of men, however, may be less connected with technology than with other social factors. Carme found age makes a difference: young men do a little more. Vitalina believed men's increased housework hours to be a (possibly temporary) response to the crisis situation in Russia: they have no choice but to do more if the family is to survive.

The 'smart house' projects are interesting for the continuity in gender relations they project. These technologies will save energy and defend property but do not promise to ease daily chores. The 'smart house' reflects men's perception of home as 'a place to put your feet up', but the work involved in turning such a house into such a home is invisible. Even the environmental consciousness the projects display does not speak of a woman's imagination. What about watering plants, feeding the fish, opening house to the sunshine?

Conversely, it is possible in some households to see gender relations shaping the technology. This depends on understanding a technological innovation as being complete only once the technology is in use. Invention is a beginning, but 'interpretive flexibility' may permit uses the designer never had in mind. This way women can be seen, even if late in the process, as genuine actors in the development of technologies.

Other researchers have shown how families make their technologies over to themselves, shaping them to 'the moral economy' of the household (Silverstone *et al.* 1992). Anne-Jorunn takes a similar approach in understanding Minitel, showing how this miniature video information unit attached to the telephone becomes what it is partly through the way the users fit it into the decor of their home and invent surprising knacks for using it. Susan likewise sees the British domestic cook's appetite for crisp brown dishes as influencing the designers' decision to develop ovens combining microwave with conventional heat. Some artefacts are bought and never used. Shoving the Minitel in the woodshed may represent a user boycott. But Andjelka's story from rural Yugoslavia, where new domestic appliances often sit unused for lack of water, roads and spare parts, is a reminder that a technology is more than an artefact. To become an innovation it depends upon a very large techno-social system.

More subtly, though, we found gender tensions being acted out through technology. Some of these artefacts – the washing machine and food processor for example – seem designed to find a use precisely within an established family household involving a married couple, perhaps with children. When they land there, they become pawns in women's struggle for autonomy and self-expression, men's need to define and control. In the Minitel story women use the electronic phone directory to learn more about their neighbours. Is this women's 'information work' or, as their menfolk say, sheer 'nosiness'? Susan and Cynthia found similar explosive tensions in the heterosexual couple over food and eating, with the microwave playing a part.

Women's bid for freedom is poignantly illustrated by their pleasure in owning a personal credit card. Katerina and Maria see the compulsive overspending some women card owners are drawn into as being a response to their oppression, similar to compulsive eating. Their husbands have reason to worry: here are their women controlling money and other men, bankers, controlling their women. The image of men-out-of-control culminates in the designers' nightmare scenario of the fallible technology of the smart house. The fear here is of the total seizure that may result if the central intelligence crashes: they call it 'the housebreak'. Your house going dead on you, your wife walking out – which is worse?

Having a focus on the home as well as the workplace enabled us to see the malign interaction, from a woman's point of view, between the two. Her domestic responsibilities mean she presents herself in the job market with one hand tied behind her. 'Tied hands' is part of what causes

Andjelka's women software engineers to fall behind in the career stakes. Women in Greek banking cannot take the jobs that mean roaming round the branches. We were reminded of the woman bank employee in 'Kentucky Fried Money', an essay on a similar technological innovation in Australian banking, who says 'The guys were asked if they wanted to go to New Guinea . . . I didn't want to go to New Guinea anyway' (Game and Pringle 1983: 42).

The home–work interaction works in reverse as well. Several studies show the relative position of women and men in job status and earnings to have an effect on gender relations in the home. The less power a man had outside the home the more he curbed his wife's freedom and sought to control the household's expenditure (Greece). And the better the job a woman had the more her husband helped with the housework (Finland).

Relative value, relative power

In the social relations of technological change, then, women and femininity are being reproduced as domestic, men and masculinity as technological. On to technology are mapped other qualities. It is represented as exciting, progressive and of high value. Domesticity, by contrast, is humdrum, repetitive and of low value. This is what gender is: an *ordering* process. The gender–technology relation involves the production and reproduction of a hierarchy, between women and men, the masculine and the feminine. Even, in a sense, between the 'technical' and the 'social' – and certainly within the various phases and faces of their interrelationship.

We were continually experiencing the put-down ourselves. We all met with smiles when we told people about our research. We felt abashed – 'I'm just a kitchen sociologist' – until we shared this with each other. Then we understood that the domestic, especially in relation to the technological, is not taken seriously as an academic subject because of this evaluation problem. Elina said 'It was a joke to study vacuum cleaners. Now I'm proud.'

In the research itself we found the knowledges of engineering and housework continually contrasted, the former carrying authority, the latter often colonized as the professionals developed a ventriloquist act, speaking for the absent woman. Only in the microwave chapter does domestic knowledge appear as codified, in the discipline of 'home economics', but the ambivalence remains even here. There is a kind of double-think. Women and their work are important: society cannot get along without them. Yet they are, as Vitalina said of Russia, second rate. She pointed out that the priority given in the Soviet Union to heavy industry, its failure to invest in commodity production, has been, in effect, an under-valuing of female domains of production and consumption.

Women's labour in the home is unrecognized – but what is more it is misunderstood. The producers of domestic appliances see them as commodities, they really do not understand them to be the tools of someone's labour process. They understand neither the meaning of that labour to the person who does it and the one who benefits from it, nor the social relations in which it is performed. If housework is acknowledged at all, it is seen as 'drudgery' – something to be evaded or made redundant. Women are not seeking to evade work. In a recent empirical study Jean-Claude Kaufmann found that a substantial group among French people of both sexes prefer washing up by hand to using a dishwasher. Some even get real pleasure from washing up (Kaufmann 1992). If women resent housework it is not so much for the labour involved, much of which they consider creative. It is for the time, the tie and above all the unfairnesss of unequal sharing. Besides, caring, taking responsibility, enhancing the quality of life, these are arguably the activities that most engage women in the household, and they are invisibilized.

To ascribe relative value, to say what is normal and what is not, to render visible or invisible, these are attributes of power. Money and technology, as many of the contributors here show in one way or another, are media or analogues of power. In the Greek banking study we see the circulation of money as the circulation of power. In the book as a whole we see the circuit of technology as a circuit of power. 'Technology', as Carme says in Chapter 7, 'presents itself as an instrument in the hands of men that dramatizes and augments masculine supremacy.'

The power everyone here reports seeing however is a somewhat Foucauldian power. This is explicit in one chapter, implicit in others. The power is not the simple downward pressure of domination but an encompassing, a sweeping in to social relations that most of the time seem natural, inevitable and even tolerable. Women may sometimes seem active participants in relations of gender oppression. Riitta, Outi, Elina and Kaisa find women are really hard on women, preferring male managers. Vitalina too finds women underestimating their own technical abilities and not going out of their way to get promotion. Andjelka finds it is not men, who we may guess have probably learned 'political correctness', but *women* who stereotype women and say they are less suited for some types of technical work in computer science.

It is these women software engineers in Belgrade, too, who themselves select jobs in sheltered backwaters. Just as in Chapter 3, Katerina and Maria find women are willing to trade career advantage for the possibility of evading exposure to direct personal patriarchal authority. Women often feel, 'well, the bed I lie on is the one I made'. The pressure from men to make it that way often slips out of view. Carme noticed how women in the washing machine factory voluntarily withdraw from public spaces, such as the canteen. But she surmises it is because men make the women feel uncomfortable there. A vicious circle is generated as women 'come to feel like intruders in spaces into which they seldom venture'.

A more general expression of the vicious circle is that the more women hide their 'difference' and their gender-specific needs, the more men's favoured discourse of gender neutrality is allowed to prevail, and the more it prevails the more invisible women's reality becomes. Several of us say in different ways 'they appear not to speak of gender, but the underlying reference point is men'. It applies as much to male managers' definition and evaluation of tasks in washing machine production, for instance, as to male designers' concept of the smart house. An unquestioned, unspoken male norm hides in the shadow of gender neutrality. Women are not, of course, so very different from men. But what makes us as different as we are is our position in the gender hierarchy – in particular men's exploitation of our difference. There it is again: the vicious circle we are continually fighting our way out of.

Women, technology and turmoil in Europe

The years of our group project, 1988 to 1993, have been turbulent ones for Europe. There has been profound recession world wide, with some European countries (Britain and Spain for instance) particularly badly affected, while none escaped depression. The withdrawal of the German participants from this study is a serious one, for we would have gained a different perspective from that vantage point.

For capitalism it has been a time of disintegration, with a high rate of bankruptcy and failure, in the midst of attempts to restructure part of Europe as a unified business community around a powerful central block (Germany and France), with political encouragement to companies to organize themselves as multinational Euro-firms. These currents are visible in our case studies. We see people in work, struggling to accommodate to technological change. Just out of sight, however, are the millions who have been 'shaken-out' in the 'labour saving' enabled by technological innovations or confirmed as unemployable in the same process.

We see examples of Japanese and US capital seeking manufacturing footholds in the Single Market, consolidation among European enterprises and local takeovers. We see the Southern supplicants adapting to the rules of the European Economic Commission. Design of new commodities, we find, is not only done by men 'for' women, but by dominant economies 'for' weaker ones. Among our studies alone we have Japan designing for Europe, France for Norway, Sweden for Spain and Italy for Russia.

By 1989 however the self-concern of Western Europe was swept aside by events in the East. Who could have imagined that Vitalina who joined the project in 1988 as a Soviet colleague would before its close be a citizen of something again called Russia, or that her centrally-planned economy would have been exchanged for the frightening inflation of an unmoderated market system? Who could have supposed that Yugoslavia, a country widely respected for its creative adaptation of communism and its cultural diversity, would be tearing itself to pieces in secession and war? A war that, as Maria pointed out, brings its technologies of destruction right into the home. The collapse of communist regimes throughout East and Central Europe and the Soviet Union has freed us all from the grip of Cold War. Released from that deadlock however the nation states now stagger in disequilibrium, and many communities in Europe feel danger in the air. The political and economic disturbances have a social corollary: huge movements of population, new forms of work, disintegration of public services, and new challenges for mutual tolerance.

Technology is a mute actor in this drama. At one moment it is a guarantor of our unity. Environmental pollution disregards national borders: one woman's nuclear disaster contaminates another's breast milk. The penetration of foreign capital into the new market economies means we may soon all use the same electrical gadgets and wear the same clothes. The standardization emanating from Brussels is itself a technology and shapes others.

At another moment, however, technology divides us. The abused labour of poorer countries produces commodities that the protected consumers of richer countries are persuaded they need. And why speak of countries, when classes will do? The women labourers who manufacture panty hose frequently go bare-legged. Computer and electronic technology are seen as the mechanism for renewal of growth. Some would say epochs of boom and collapse are characterized precisely by the scrapping of one technological paradigm and the triumph of a new one (Coombs *et al.* 1987). But the revolutions of this wheel carry some to the top and crush others beneath.

The lives of women are changing. Women who thought they could rely on a welfare state and relatively full employment are finding that even the most social democrat countries are not immune to the wave of conservatism and monetarism. Women who thought the transition from communism to the market would bring nothing but gain now find the new freedom has been purchased at a high cost. In Russia and the countries of East/Central Europe women's unemployment is well over half and in some cases three-quarters of total joblessness because services such as canteens and clincs are being lost and nurseries are closing (Einhorn 1993; Enloe 1993).

Women are subject to, and swept up into, an ideology that sees women again as defined by their biology, that would have them return to their 'natural' duties. Even women in countries with a long tradition of women in the labour market suddenly find they can no longer assume they have a right to a job. And, besides, with a withdrawal of supportive services and an increase in the burden of housework and care, many women are ready to throw in the towel and stay home if they can. In the older capitalist countries women are finding that 'women's issues' are no longer legitimate items on the social agenda. The 'social' has to fight for its life against the 'economic', not only in the Single European Market, but throughout Europe.

Should we feel optimistic or pessimistic about the gender–technology relation? The picture presented in this book is not, despite the overall context described above, one of unqualified gloom. For Vitalina, to see new production technology invested at last in a 'female sector' and long-dreamed-of commodities coming into women's hands – that is a plus. Women working and obtaining control of their own earnings, as we see in Greece, is a step forward. There is evidence that technological change can improve things for everyone within a defined sphere: it is just that men gain more than women and so another notch is racked up on the cogwheel of inequality.

Some of our chapters speak explicitly of optimism. They are the ones that introduce a theory designed to get us away from determinism – 'technology is running away with us', 'women are doomed by their biology' – and allow for a certain interpretive flexibility, scope for manoeuvre, 'as it happens', by creative users and creative livers. We would probably all affirm that approach, theoretically. But in practice our research has given us different experiences and many of us have seen the creative potential, 'as it happens', aborted. It is not only in Yugoslavia that the hopes of modernizing social relations, through technological innovation, have been disappointed.

Yet the women's movement is far from spent in Europe, and in some places it is only now coming into being. There are clear pointers here to a feminist strategy on technology. We want in conclusion to suggest four aims.

First, we need to defend women's right to healthy, sustainable, paid work. That means we need new process technologies that will ease and enhance our jobs rather than intensify or routinize them. It also means, in circumstances of technological change, resisting redundancy and defending our right to technical training and retraining.

Second, there should be more women in technological design. We have a right to share in the activity of design because it is creative and rewarding. But, more importantly, it is only when enough women have advanced technological skills that a feminist critical analysis of technological innovation and production will become a reality.

Women are also needed in design because we can help, with men, to generate a more holistic perspective on human needs and the technological possibilities for meeting them. Women's particular skills, knowledge and creativity should also be acknowledged and valued in the circuit of technological innovation in other ways wherever women are: as production workers, sales staff, women in the home.

Third, all women should have the supportive domestic technologies they need to make housework pleasant: that means appropriate housing and equipment available on the market, the household income to buy them and the infrastructure to support them. We also however need supportive and sharing relationships in the home – and successive waves of domestic technological innovation have shown that to be a matter with little direct relation to technology. It does not follow from technological change so much as from women's struggle. Without both, the right technology and the right social relations, we will be unable to satisfy our wish to combine a public with a private persona, fulfilling paid work and a fulfilling home life.

Fourth, and finally, we must fight not just for ourselves as women, but for the re-evaluation of the domestic, the private and the relational. Engineering should be put at the service of the 'unimportant' everyday activities, instead of being allowed to master and deform everyday life. Indeed the concept of 'technology' itself is due for a rethink. A good deal of what goes on in everyday life – cooking, cleaning, washing, caring and spending – should be recognized and valued as technology too.

If our studies have one particular message it is that technology relations and gender relations affect and shape each other. Technological innovation cannot fulfil its creative promise when it is shaped in relations of dominance, whether of nation, class or gender. And it is hard for individuals and communities to create themselves in new liberatory forms while powerful techno-social systems perpetuate old oppressions.

References

Barrett, Michele and McIntosh, Mary (1982) *The Anti-social Family*. London: Verso.

Bijker, Wiebe E., Hughes, Thomas P. and Pinch, Trevor (eds) (1990) *The Social Construction of Technological Systems*. Cambridge, MA and London: MIT Press.

Bourgeois, Françoise, Brener, Jacquline, Chabaud, Danielle *et al.* (1978) Travail domestique et famille du capitalisme [Domestic work and family in capitalism], *Critiques de l'économie politique* [*Critical Economy Review*], No. 3, April–June, 3–23.

Callon, Michel (1989) *La Science et ses Réseaux* [*Science and its Networks*]. Paris: La Decouverte.

Cockburn, Cynthia (1983) *Brothers: Male Dominance and Technological Change*. London: Pluto Press.

Cockburn, Cynthia (1985) *Machinery of Dominance: Women, Men and Technical Know-how*. London: Pluto Press.

Cockburn, Cynthia and Ormrod, Susan (1993) *Gender and Technology in the Making*. Newbury Park, CA and London: Sage.

Coombs, Rod, Saviotti, Paolo and Walsh, Vivien (1987) *Economics and Technological Change*. Basingstoke: Macmillan.

Cowan, Ruth Schwartz (1989) *More Work for Mother: The Ironies of Household Technology from the Open Hearth to the Microwave*. London: Free Association Books.

Einhorn, Barbara (1993) *Cinderella Goes to Market: Citizenship, Gender and Women's Movements in East Central Europe*. London and New York: Verso.

Enloe, Cynthia (1993) *The Morning After: Sexual Politics at the End of the Cold War*. Berkeley and London: University of California Press.

Galtung, Johan (1990) Theory formation in social research: a plea for pluralism, in Oyen, E. (ed.) *Comparative Methodology: Theory and Practice in International Social Research*. Newbury Park, CA and London: Sage.

Game, Ann and Pringle, Rosemary (1983) *Gender at Work*. Sydney and London: George Allen and Unwin.

Haavio-Mannila, Elina (1993) *Women in the Workplace in Three Types of Societies*. Ann Arbor: University of Michigan.

Harding, Sandra (1991) *Whose Science? Whose Knowledge? Thinking from Women's Lives*. Milton Keynes: Open University Press.

Heinen, Jacqueline (1990) Inequalities at work: the gender division of labour in the Soviet Union, *Studies in Political Economy*, No. 33, 39–61.

Kanter, Rosabeth Moss (1977) *Men and Women of the Corporation*. New York: Basic Books.

Kaufmann, Jean-Claude (1992) Les deux mondes de la vaisselle [The two worlds of washing-up], in Gras, A. and Caroline, M. (eds) *Technologies du Quotidien: La Complainte du Progrès* [*Everyday Technologies: The Lament of Progress*]. Paris: Editions Autrement.

Kohn, Melvin L. (1989) Cross-national research as an analytic strategy, in Kohn, M.L. (ed.) *Cross-national Research in Sociology*. Newbury Park, CA and London: Sage.

Kvande, Elin and Rasmussen, Bente (1990) *Nye Kvinneliv: Kvinner i Menns Organisasjonen* [*New Women's Lives: Women in Men's Organizations*]. Oslo: Ad Notam.

Latour, Bruno (1989) *La Science en Action* [*Science in Action*]. Paris: La Decouverte.

MacKenzie, Donald and Wajcman, Judy (eds) (1985) *The Social Shaping of Technology*. Milton Keynes: Open University Press.

McNeil, Maureen (ed.) (1987) *Gender and Expertise*. London: Free Association Books.

Nowak, Stefan (1989) Comparative studies and social theory, in Kohn, M.L. (ed.) *Cross-national Research in Sociology*. Newbury Park, CA and London: Sage.

Oakley, Ann (1972) *Sex, Gender and Society*. London: Temple Smith.

Silverstone, R., Hirsch, E. and Morley, D. (1992) Information and communication technologies and the moral economy of the household, in Silverstone, R. and Hirsch, E. (eds) *Consuming Technologies: Media and Information in Domestic Spaces*. London and New York: Routledge.

Wajcman, Judy (1991) *Feminism Confronts Technology*. Cambridge: Polity Press.

1

Sweeping away the dust of tradition: Vacuum cleaning as a site of technical and social innovation

RIITTA SMEDS, OUTI HUIDA,
ELINA HAAVIO-MANNILA AND
KAISA KAUPPINEN-TOROPAINEN

Technology is the systematic know-how people use as an extension to their natural abilities. It is a part of human culture that has strongly affected social development in industrialized countries (Smeds 1985). The nature of a society, however, is not determined by its technologies, since technologies are developed, produced and used in a social context. We are specially interested here in the way gender relations and technology shape one another.

Innovations are ideas or inventions that are successfully implemented so as to become new products, processes or practices. In this study we focus on one technological innovation – somebody's brainchild that has now entered hundreds of thousands of households worldwide. It is the *central vacuum cleaning system* (CVS).

The central vacuum cleaning system has been developed to make vacuuming easier, less noisy, more hygienic and more comfortable. The central unit and the piping are permanently installed into the house, with the effect that the person doing the vacuum cleaning needs only to handle an 8-metre long suction hose. The exhaust air is vented outdoors through the piping, so that microdust does not circulate in the indoor atmosphere. The CVS is thus recommended by the Allergy Federation in Finland. With its system character and the theme of increasing home comfort, a house with the CVS is a step towards the 'smart house' concept (see Chapter 9).

The development, production, marketing, distribution, use and maintenance of the CVS, as of any other innovation, bring together a large network of interrelated actors, which we call an *innovation network* (Figure 1). We are interested in the roles women and men play in the different functions of the innovation network, at work and at home. One of our research questions therefore is: have the gender roles remained traditional, or has the CVS, a technological innovation, helped to change them?

It will become clear however that we see technological and social innovation as similar kinds of *creative* process, both involving *organization* – whether on the large scale of society, the mid-scale of an enterprise or the micro-scale of a family household. Our study therefore asks the more far-reaching question: how does gender feature in these creative processes of change? What kind of organizational relationships, whether in the firm or the family, encourage technical and social innovations? All our questions are situated within a general interest in the three-way relationship between innovation, organization and gender relations.

Theoretical perspectives

The three theoretical perspectives applied in this study are: the concepts of location, representation and disposition; the distinction between technical and responsible rationality; and a typology of gender equality discourses.

Locations, representations and dispositions

The *gendered pattern of locations* signifies the positions women and men hold in a given society, at work, at home and elsewhere. That is to say, who does what, and how. *Representations* are what people say and show. It means the verbal, gestural, symbol-using and meaning-making practices that – among other things – sustain or challenge a gender regime. Representations can be studied by reference to thinking, telling, writing, enacting, hinting, suggesting, portraying; in other words, symbolic meanings, discourse and images. By *dispositions* is meant the historical and social structures and cultural patterns (long-lived and widespread, although not immutable) that lie behind the observed behaviour and attitudes of the members of a society. They tend to prompt outcomes, but do not determine them (Cockburn 1992).

The gendered pattern of locations, suggested by dispositions and expressed in and shaped by representations, arranges the activities of women

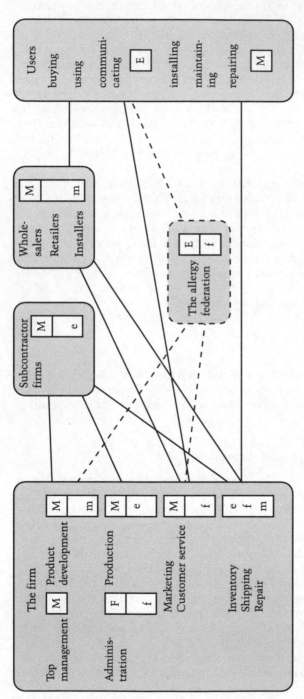

The locations of men and women in the innovation network:

M/m = male majority in managerial positions/as workers,
F/f = female majority in managerial positions/as workers
E/e = equal numbers of men and women in managerial positions/as workers

——— = business relationships
- - - - = communication

Figure 1 The CVS innovation network

and men. For instance, in Finland, women and men are differently located in relation to home, with women still carrying the main responsibility for housework. In 1987 men spent on average 108 minutes and women 209 minutes daily in domestic work (Babarczy *et al.* 1991). Gender segregation also prevails in Finnish work life. In 1990, 44 per cent of all gainfully employed people worked in occupations in which the proportion of one sex was over 90 per cent (Kandolin 1993).

One factor supporting the gendered pattern of locations is homosociality, which Jean Lipman-Blumen (1976) defines as a preference for the company of persons of one's own sex. Especially at work, men show a somewhat greater homosocial tendency than women do (Haavio-Mannila 1988). Another factor is male domination in the field of technology. For example, only about 10 per cent of Finnish academically trained engineers are women. The figure is slowly increasing, with the proportion of female students in the technological universities today standing at about 20 per cent (Pöyry 1989).

Men more than women have traditionally participated in decision-making around developing and producing new technologies. Technological know-how mainly belongs to the masculine sphere. If we see occupations as distinguished from each other vertically (by grade) and horizontally (by function), we can say that the higher positions in the former case and the production occupations in the second are masculine.

Different rationalities

In industrial production, a key concept is *technical rationality*, with efficiency as its basic value. *Economic rationality*, getting the largest possible profit for the least possible input, is also important in commodity production. *Bureaucratic rationality* aims at an administration that combines both technical and economic rationalities. Scandinavian researchers (Sørensen 1982; Waerness 1984; Ve 1992) have suggested that technical, economic and bureaucratic rationalities are limited. Including as they do the tendency to instrumentalize and make use of human emotions, they cannot be said satisfactorily to encompass human rationality. Care workers, in working for and with human beings, have developed a rationality different from that prevalent in the production of goods. This *responsible*, or *caring rationality* emphasizes that people cannot be used as means to achieve ends which are alien to them.

Society and its organizations need technical, economic and bureaucratic rationalities in order to function efficiently. However, these rationalities should be applied responsibly, in an ethical way that does not negate the intrinsic human value of the people concerned. This *holistic rationality* is achieved through combining the different rationalities in decision-making and action. The input of both women and men is needed: women are instrumental actors in the same way as men, but Norwegian feminist scholars (for example Ve 1992) have found a greater tendency among women than among men to think in terms of responsible rationality.

	Gender differences noted:	
	Yes	No
Equality actively promoted: Yes	Gender sensitive	Gender neutral (Gender blind)
No	Gender stereotyped	Gender insensitive (Individual-centred)

Figure 2   Gender equality discourses

Discourses of gender equality

A third predisposing factor is gender equality discourse. To illustrate the different types of discourse prevalent in gender issues, we developed the frame of reference shown in Figure 2. It has two dimensions: 'gender differences are noted' (yes/no) and 'equality is actively promoted' (yes/no).

In the *gender sensitive* approach, gender differences are accepted and equality is actively promoted. Individual differences and the different viewpoints of women and men are appreciated. This approach is gaining currency in scientific discussion.

The *gender neutral* approach is embedded in the Nordic gender equality ideology. According to an international comparison (Hofstede 1983), Finland and the other Nordic countries rank high in gender equality, and also in equality between superiors and subordinates in working life. Though equality is actively promoted, however, gender differences are not noted; equality signifies 'sameness'. This implies hidden discrimination, for, despite formal equality provisions, society continues to be based on male norms.

In the *gender stereotyped* approach, gender differences are noted, even exaggerated, but equality is not actively promoted. An example exists in the former Soviet Union (Rimaschevskaya 1991), where women were treated as 'the weaker sex', a special group in need of protective legislation. Despite this, women often work in hazardous conditions.

Gender insensitivity is an individualistic approach: gender differences are not noted, nor is equality actively promoted. Inequality is explained not by gender but by differential access to other resources, such as money, power and technological education. The fact that more men than women control such resources is overlooked.

These different approaches to gender equality have a shaping effect on the new technologies developed and used in a society. Unless equality is promoted, women are often excluded from the process of developing new technologies: women can be stereotyped as inadequate to this 'male sphere', or ignored on the basis of individual characteristics such as lack of formal technological training. Under conditions of gender neutrality, the outcome of technological development is assumed to be unaffected by whether the people involved in the process are male or female. By contrast, a gender sensitive approach allows both sexes to enrich the development process by contributing their different viewpoints. Diversity is valued as a source of technological and societal creativeness.

In Finland, the dominant gender ideology has, as we saw, been one of gender neutrality, but emerging discourses increasingly stress gender sensitivity. Formal equality is reflected in many practices: women are half the labour force, and national policy supports their participation by such means as long maternity leave, a law guaranteeing communal day-care arrangements for every child under three years and official encouragement to men to share domestic responsibilities.

Nevertheless, the norm of gender equality in Finland has in some respects remained at a level of principle. A gendered pattern of locations still exists both at work and at home. Women earn less, have less authority in society, and do more housework than men. There are still several psychological and structural processes inhibiting the equality-in-principle from becoming an equality-in-fact.

Aims in the study

In this study of the interrelation of gender and technology, we look first at the locations of women and men in the innovation network developed around a small firm, a producer of the CVS (Figure 1). Second, studying the level of representations, we try to get access to people's gender equality discourses in order to learn what they think and say about both gender and technology, and how they interpret the existing pattern of locations. We also study the types of rationalities that women and men apply in regard to new technology, both in the organization producing the CVS and in the homes using it. Third, we search for the interrelations between new technology and the cultural patterns – dispositions – in the innovation network. Does the firm take into account the special qualifications of its female employees in designing and producing new labour-saving machines that have traditionally been used by women? Does this new household technology increase gender equality at home and at work? Do men participate more often in cleaning at home if there is such technological equipment as the CVS available?

Innovations in working life

The firm: a short history

The idea of producing the central vacuum cleaning system in Finland was rooted in an individual entrepreneur's interest in new technology, combined with his miserable experiences in vacuuming with the family's old 'hoover'. He wanted to equip his new house with the most advanced technology, and therefore imported a CVS from the United States in 1977. Since the system aroused interest among his neighbours, friends and relatives, a business idea formed in the entrepreneur's mind. In 1982 he got together with two of his earlier business acquaintances, men who were experienced in marketing and developing electronics and other technological equipment. They founded a firm located in central Finland.

In its early days, the firm had a 'family' culture, its product development and marketing strategies were clear and its profitability was good. The organization grew rapidly. In 1988, by which time it employed 44 people, the firm was acquired by a privately owned high-technology concern. At this stage, the founders left the firm. The only one of the pioneers who remained was the office manager, a woman who had held that same position since the founding of the firm.

In the next three years the firm saw rapid change. Its new parent company merged it with two other small firms to form an autonomous subsidiary. The firm also extended its market into Sweden by buying its CVS agent there. Some of the marketing department's functions were transferred to the capital, and the rest of the firm moved into a new building in its home town. The mergers and the relocations were not the only causes of turmoil, however. During this period the firm experienced three different managing directors. The management strategy became production-oriented, with a strong drive for efficiency, but it lacked a clear vision and development strategy. Despite the formal autonomy of the firm, decision-making was centralized in the parent company's head office. Organizational relations became entangled, characterized by distrust and suspicion between the managers and the other employees.

Product image

On the retail market, the CVS is usually grouped with heating, plumbing and air conditioning systems, rather than with ordinary vacuum cleaners. It is typically sold to the public through hardware stores, which, by long standing, have male staff and managers. At first, in the marketing process, the CVS was consciously given a male character in order to fit it, as the company president put it in interview, into 'the macho-culture of men'. The first television advertising campaign for CVS featured Superman. The idea was successfully sold to the male-dominated retail chains and to male customers. A television advertising campaign in 1992 therefore presented a gender neutral product image: in a cartoon, the CVS chased dustball figures out of the apartment. In brochures, the users of the CVS are mostly shown as women, though men are featured too. The advertisers have thus tried to modify the traditional gender pattern of location among *users* of the CVS – but *only* among users. In the installation instructions, the illustrative characters have remained all male. So far, there has not been a campaign to involve women in installing the system. Rather, women are seen as leaving that task to their partner or to professional installers.

Our research subjects in the firm

Our empirical study took place in 1991, during the difficult transition phase in the firm. Despite this nearly everyone participated: of the 60 people on the company payroll we saw 55: 19 men and 16 women on the shopfloor, and 10 people of each sex in the office, filled out our question-naires and participated in individual interviews. Most of them also took part in group interviews.

The functions on the shopfloor were production, shipping, inventory and repair. The office included management, administration, product development, marketing and customer service (see Figure 1). There was only one, day-time, shift. As is typical in Finland, both the women and the men were employed on a full-time basis.

The average age of the women on the shopfloor, as of those in the office, was 35 years. The men on the shopfloor were younger than the women with an average of 28 years, whereas those in the office were older, with an average of 39 years. The level of formal schooling and vocational training was not very high among the employees. None held an academic degree. On average, the men had more formal schooling and vocational training than the women. On the shopfloor, most of the women had received no vocational training at all, whereas most of the men had some. In the office, too, more men than women had a college level education.

In Finland as a whole, the average level of vocational training is slightly higher among women than among men (Lehto 1991). However, male industrial workers usually have more vocational training than their female co-workers. This is often due to the fact that female industrial workers have ended up in their jobs by chance; they have not striven after them. If they do have vocational training, it has usually been acquired from some other field of traditional women's work (Kevätsalo 1992).

Division of labour on the shopfloor

The firm had approximately 10 subcontractors supplying metal, plastic, electronic parts and painting services. The main task on the company's own shopfloor was thus final assembly. Most of the work tasks were performed manually, although everyone at certain times used some technical tools and appliances. Women and men mostly had similar work tasks. Along the assembly lines were small working groups consisting of both sexes. In addition to assembly, such groups took care of testing and packaging the products. Group members collectively decided on the division of work, and most tasks were rotated. In the storeroom too, both women and men were employed. Several employees of both sexes were deployed flexibly, doing 'a little bit of everything', depending on the situation.

A few tasks were performed only by men: assembling the biggest ma-chines for industrial use, processing pipes, controlling the computer-based inventory, and handling the tasks in the repair shop. In addition, all three supervisors were men. Packaging of pipes and despatch of finished products were tasks assigned to women. Occasionally however some of the men participated in these tasks too, especially during busy hours.

Whenever possible, the work was organized into piece-work mainly on a group basis. When it was impossible to apply the piece-work system, as for instance in the case of storeroom workers, wages were paid on an hourly rate. The supervisors had monthly salaries. On average, the monthly earnings of the men (FIM 6,200) were higher than those of the women (FIM 5,600). When the (male) supervisors were excluded however there was no difference between the average wages of women and men. Equal wages are not the norm in the Finnish metal industry: in 1989, women's average wages were 81 per cent of men's. In recent years, however, the gender wage gap has been diminishing, not only among metal industry assembly workers (Kevätsalo 1992), but also more generally between all full-time employed women and men in Finland (Kandolin 1993).

The employees for the most part accepted without question the fact that certain jobs were occupied only by men, explaining this by the demands these jobs made on physical strength or technical training. Both women and men tended to say that what was significant was not gender, but rather the person's ability to cope with the tasks. The women in fact expressed this acceptance more often than did the men. The women were relieved that they did not have to perform the heaviest tasks in the production process, and they were not always interested in the most technical jobs. Said one, 'If I had been interested in electronics, I would surely have gone to school and got the training for it.' Only two women had slightly mixed feelings about the situation: they assumed that the men's wages were higher than their own, which, according to the data acquired through our questionnaires, was not the case.

Some of the men expressed a willingness to share the tasks with women even more equally than at present. 'I don't think my job has any features that would mean a woman couldn't handle it', said one man on the shopfloor. They thought besides that further job rotation could improve both the productivity and the atmosphere in the workplace.

Division of labour in the office

In the office, the division of labour between the men and the women was more traditional. The men were managers in product development, production, marketing and sales. They were also the ones to create new contacts with the outside world, with wholesalers, dealers and sub-contractors. The women carried out mainly the clerical and support tasks, such as handling the paperwork, calculating salaries and wages, consulting customers and maintaining contacts with suppliers and retailers. There were only three men without direct subordinates, whereas only one woman held a managerial position, as office and finance manager.

Here in the office the difference between the monthly salaries of the

men and the women was considerable. On average, the women's salaries
were less than half the men's monthly earnings (FIM 6,600 as against FIM
14,300). These figures cannot be compared directly, since most of the
men were in managerial positions and the only female manager did not
answer the question regarding her salary.

Although neither the men nor the women regarded the gendered
pattern of locations in the office as good or justified, it was not much
criticized. The men usually referred to the early practices of the firm: the
founders were men, and men had been in charge since the beginning. The
top managers' descriptions of how they came to work for the firm explained
the persistence of the gender division in the office: the founders and their
successors had used their network of mostly male business acquaintances
when recruiting people to the top positions.

The women however evaluated the situation in a wider social context.
They referred to the stereotype which includes the roles of a man as a
manager and a woman as an assistant. They often pointed out that the
situation in the firm was not exceptional: similar features were common
at other workplaces, too. However, the women did not express great
dissatisfaction with the gendered pattern of locations, and none of them
brought up the issue of salary differences. They merely wished that the
superiors would give them a chance to use their potential. 'I'm probably
using only 50 per cent of my capacity', said one.

Equality in the workplace

General attitudes about how women and men cope with work-related
matters were explored by asking if there were gendered differences in
learning technical skills or in supervisory skills. Generally, equality was
promoted: women and men were said to be equal and skills were ultimately
regarded as dependent on the individual's interest and abilities. Rather
more of the men expressed this gender neutral view. Rather more of the
women linked skills, particularly supervisory skills, with the masculine
gender.

Learning new technical skills was seldom considered a gendered ability. 'It's completely up to your own wits', as a male shopfloor worker put
it. The experiences of socialization from early childhood were however
held to be important: boys play with technical toys more than girls do,
and their interest in technology is encouraged. Later, boys choose to
acquire further training in the technical field with which they already
feel familiar. Therefore, in the beginning of the process of learning new
technical skills at work, men have a certain advantage over women, who
usually need more thorough instruction.

In the firm, the men's technical experience and expertise was most
evident when technical problems arose. The men tended to solve them
in collaboration with other men, seldom turning to their female co-
workers. When women needed assistance in technical matters, they chose
to turn to a man as often as to a woman. For the most complicated

technical issues, a supervisor had to be called in – and, as we saw, they were all men.

Regarding supervisory positions, masculinity was generally not considered a guarantee of good performance. Only a few of the male and female employees had a stereotyped image of male supervisors as having more authority and credibility. One man in the office did not believe that the male-dominated retail chains were ready to deal with a female managing director. It would, he said, 'be such a shock to most of our clients [in the retail trade], it'd take years to overcome it'. On the whole, however, the principle of equality was evoked in most answers. Ultimately, individual abilities and personality were considered the most significant factors.

Despite this gender neutral attitude to supervisors in general, one-third of the women said they actually preferred male superiors to female ones. Their reasons revealed stereotyping. One woman for instance said 'I think women are more envious, men can concentrate more on the matter in hand.' They considered male superiors easier to get along with, since 'they say what they have to say more clearly and they don't talk behind your back'. These opinions were often borne out by their experiences of female managers and supervisors.

Similar suspicious attitudes on the part of women towards female superiors were also evident in another study of Finnish industrial workers (Kevätsalo 1992). Both however are in contradiction with what we know of opinion in the Finnish labour force at large. According to both women and men, female superiors are seen as creating a pleasant and supportive atmosphere at work (Kandolin and Kauppinen-Toropainen 1993).

On the whole, attitudes in the firm supported gender equality. A previous Finnish study also shows that neither women nor men working in the metal industry consider inequality a big problem at work (Kevätsalo 1992). The management in particular emphasized equality as a norm. However, since they were aware of the special interests of our study, our research subjects may have tended to give us an image of an ideal workplace. A certain politeness towards us as researchers was observable. Yet even on the shopfloor, where the gender aspect of the study seemed to be less clearly understood, we found the men mostly speaking of the women as equals. However, we should consider the possible effect the interviewers, being young female researchers, had on the answers. It would have been interesting to find out whether a male interviewer would have obtained a different view of gender attitudes in the firm.

Workplace atmosphere

The sharp distinction between the shopfloor and the office was characteristic of the firm. The physical and functional separation was reflected in the unofficial relations, with a feeling of distance between employees of the two levels. This distance between blue-collar and white-collar workers is not unusual in Finnish firms (Kevätsalo 1992). Notwithstanding the general workplace equality in the Nordic countries mentioned earlier, a certain class difference still prevails in Finnish working life.

Due to lack of social cohesiveness, several mini-cultures had emerged in the firm. The shopfloor was the largest homogeneous cultural unit. The atmosphere was friendly here, since most of the employees were young and shared the same work tasks. Togetherness was enhanced by their critical opinions of certain supervisors and managers. In the office there were more cliques and disharmony, and the different functional units had difficulties in communicating with and understanding one another. Each employee had, however, seemingly found his or her place within the mini-cultures, since nobody felt left out of the work community and everyone had co-worker friends. The friendships were not strictly gendered, although there was a tendency to have more same-sex than opposite-sex friends.

Career possibilities

Working in this small firm was not considered a vital career opportunity, but in the office both the women and the men were satisfied with their positions. The men had nowhere to go from their top positions, and, though some women did remark that they could manage the work better than the male managers, no one actually expressed a wish to be promoted. Instead, what worried the women in the office was the increasingly routinized character of their work.

On the shopfloor, the male workers likewise expressed no interest in promotions. They had noticed the difficult situation of the supervisors, located between the managers and the shopfloor workers. The women for their part had come to work on the assembly lines without any special hopes for advancement. Due to the stagnant situation in the firm, and lacking female role models, they did not consider their dead-end work situation as a problem worth discussing.

Innovations in the firm

Ideas stem from the variety and diversity of creative individuals. It is known that ideas are most likely to be implemented and become innovations in an organization with active formal and informal networks, and a culture and management style that nurture creativity (Tushman and Nadler 1986). Also, champions of change are needed if informal networks are to be built in the organization and new ideas 'sold' within them. A champion is someone with the power, the resources and the support to bring about changes (Kanter 1983).

The management style in this firm did not support innovation, although the problems caused by the critical transition period needed creative solutions. Being dependent on the parent company, the management were unwilling to risk their own positions. They therefore ignored ideas coming from their subordinates. They were defensive, trying to hold on to existing practices. 'Making sharp turns', as one male manager put it, did not fit into their schedules. They explained their defensiveness also as arising from the apprehension that some employees might try to present their co-workers' initiatives as their own, hoping to be rewarded. This kind of activity would cause conflicts and damage social relations.

That managers were not responsive to the creative potential of employees was partly due to their lack of vision and power to steer development. It also illustrated the communication gap between the managers and other employees. The employees did not make new inventions in order to get a reward but to remedy defects in the production process, facilitate their own tasks and make their workday more pleasant.

It was generally believed by non-managers that the organizational position of the initiator of an idea was crucial: suggestions coming from 'the wrong person' were seldom accepted. To put forward an idea of one's own therefore seemed as futile as tilting at windmills. Informal social relations could perhaps have generated sensitivity to different ways of thinking, but networking between the different mini-cultures or units was rare.

The men in product development had the best possibilities of realizing their innovative ideas. They usually experimented with product ideas they themselves found interesting, without paying too much attention to the opinions of their superiors. As one of them said, 'we go on with our experiments even though the boss wouldn't agree with us. Until we need money – then the situation has to be reconsidered.' They also used their creativity in improving their own working conditions. For example, they had succeeded in acquiring a computer, something that seemed impossible through the formal channels.

The product developers expressed a degree of gender sensitivity. They mentioned the lack of female colleagues as a defect. Women as well as men, after all, were using the final products so (as one put it) 'it would do no harm at all to have some female insight into the development process'. They gave no sign however of actively seeking this 'female insight', even by trying to involve the firm's female employees in these processes.

The other employees, male or female, were not encouraged to bring up their own ideas, even though many of them were using such products at home. Women on the shopfloor did not even try to contribute to the process of product development. Some of the men on the shopfloor occasionally came up with small technical product changes that could facilitate their own tasks in the production process. In addition the men working in the repair shop and the women taking care of customer service often noted customers' complaints and ideas, which they put forward to those responsible for product development either directly or through their superiors. Whether or not these ideas were realized or even tested, however, depended entirely on the preferences of the product developers.

In the group interview, the latter remained indifferent towards the ideas coming from the shopfloor. They regarded those dealing with marketing, the customers and the subcontractors as their most important sources of feedback. But they disregarded even these information sources if they seemed to threaten their own creative autonomy. As a result, the product developers were not always familiar with customers' needs nor with the restrictions and demands of production engineering. Thus, some of their creations, though innovative, were practically useless.

Although the other employees' innovative ideas were usually rejected by the managers and the product developers, they had not given up. As champions of change in their own work they had developed small-scale improvements to facilitate work performance.

Innovative ideas about the work environment and working practices varied not according to the subject's gender but to her or his position in the organization. In the office, the men had better access than the women to the sources of money and power in the firm. It was therefore possible for them to plan new acquisitions or other changes in working practices. For example, many of the men had been planning the acquisition of new computers and computer programs, while the women had ideas about how, as the users of computers, they could execute their tasks more efficiently. On the shopfloor, the one evident difference between the women and men was the way in which they managed to realize ideas that called for technological know-how. The men generally had more technical skills than did the women, and usually made adjustments to their machines and tools themselves. Some of the women, on the other hand, had utilized the men's experience in support of their innovations by enlisting the help of a male co-worker with the required technological knowledge.

Despite the problems at the workplace, managers and employees had one thing in common: everyone was convinced of the usefulness of the central vacuum cleaning system. In fact, all managers and one-third of the employees had acquired a CVS for their own home.

Innovations in the domestic sphere

Our subjects in the home

In 1991, about 65,000 Finnish households had a CVS, most produced by the firm under study. In June 1991, we obtained names and addresses from the company's warranty file and sent a questionnaire to 512 of these households. We wanted to find out about the division of household tasks and about the decision-making processes in the family in connection with this piece of new technology. We sent two questionnaires to each household, one for the person who had filled in the warranty card, the other for her or his partner, should such exist. We received answers from 101 men and 107 women in 122 households. Thus, in most cases both partners participated in the study.

The subjects demonstrated a variety of social backgrounds, income groups and educational levels. Their ages ranged from 21 to 72 years, the average age for both sexes being 42 years. Most, however, were employed on a full-time basis, married or cohabiting, had children and lived in detached houses. On many questions no statistically significant difference was found between the male and female respondents. Our overall description of respondents' attitudes therefore only differentiates where it is relevant to do so.

Most respondents felt positively about bringing new technology and automation into their home, though some had difficulties in defining their relation to these things. There were two kinds of reason for being interested in technology: a willingness to learn new things and keep up with technological development, and a desire to speed up and facilitate housework. The men expressed both reasons equally, the women more often the second.

The households studied were pioneers in introducing new technologies into their homes. We found, by comparing our results with those of a survey conducted by the *Reader's Digest Eurodata* (1991), that our CVS owners tended to have more technological equipment (such as compact disc players and microwave ovens) than the average Finnish family.

Reasons for buying a CVS

The more expensive a household machine, the more likely are partners to make the decision to buy it together (*Suomalainen nainen* 1989; *Suomalainen mies* 1990). Since the CVS costs four times as much as an ordinary vacuum cleaner and its installation calls for building work, it is considered to need joint approval. Four-fifths of our respondents had made the decision to buy the system together with their partner. In the remaining cases the decision had been made as often by a man as by a woman.

When buying the CVS, the subjects (women even more than men) most often paid attention to its technological characteristics. The price of the equipment was the second most important factor. The design and the colour of the central unit was not considered important, since it is usually placed out of sight in a basement or cupboard. One of the product developers with whom we spoke in the manufacturing firm had assumed that men would pay more attention to technological factors, women to the looks and the colour of the machine. Our finding diverged completely from his presumption. The interests of women and men proved similar. The stereotype, it seems, does not correspond to the reality in Finnish families.

In order to find out why people had replaced their ordinary vacuum cleaner with a CVS, several possible reasons for buying the equipment were put forward in the questionnaire. The most common reason given for buying a CVS was hygiene, the elimination of microdust from the indoor atmosphere. Many families stressed this and more than one-third of the respondents reported 'dust allergy, asthma or an equivalent illness in the family' as one of their reasons for buying the CVS. A quarter of those giving this reason, however, reported that cleaning with the new equipment had not in fact reduced allergic symptoms. Though some reported some improvement, only a few families felt they had gained considerably in this respect from using the CVS. As a counsellor of the Allergy Federation pointed out in an interview, simply owning a CVS does not make a difference; it has to be used appropriately. A device that keeps the home dustless without human intervention is still no more than a dream.

'Making vacuum cleaning easier' was the second most frequently mentioned reason for buying a CVS. This was important for both women and men when thinking of themselves as the one who has to do the vacuuming at home. When they were thinking of their partner's performance, the answers were slightly different. Of the respondents living with a partner, the men were more concerned about making vacuum cleaning easier for their wives, than the women were about making the task easier for their husbands. This can be interpreted in the light of the locations of women and men in housework: though (as we shall show) men have increased their participation in this task, women in Finland still vacuum clean more often than do men. The men perhaps implicitly hoped that the machine would liberate them from further obligations in vacuuming if the women found the task easy to perform.

Although most of the respondents were interested in technical equipment and favoured home automation, 'keeping up with technological development' had not been a particularly important reason for acquiring the CVS, when set against the expected practical advantages. And not many respondents had been disappointed: both the men and the women were generally satisfied with their CVS. And, despite the absence of female input to the creative processes of designing the CVS, the complaints of the women in our study about the system did not differ from those of the men.

Both women and men, it seemed, often applied *holistic rationality* in buying a CVS, since their answers illustrated both technical rationality and responsible, caring rationality. We interpreted a concern with microdust extraction and ease of cleaning as technical rationality. Such reasons for purchasing the CVS were as frequently found among women as men.

In expressing a hope however that the CVS would ease the partner's performance in housework duties and diminish the allergic symptoms of family members respondents were manifesting caring rationality. In contrast to other researchers cited above, we did not find more women than men applying responsible rationality. In fact the counsellor in the Allergy Federation said that among the people she encountered it was the men who had the more holistic approach to technology. 'Maybe men' she said, 'ask more questions about things in the long run, about the maintenance and the spare parts [of the CVS], and for women it is usually enough to know what it costs and where you can get it.'

The CVS at home

In the homes of those living with a partner, we found the gendered pattern of locations to persist in many areas. Repair and maintenance fell mainly in the male domain, while doing laundry and taking care of clothes, for instance, were mainly female responsibilities. The CVS, a piece of new technology, had, however, gone some way towards equalizing the participation of women and men. The proportion of families in which vacuum cleaning was shared by the partners was 40 per cent before acquisition, 46 per cent after, according to women's replies. Men's responses also suggested an increase in sharing, from 34 per cent to 43 per cent. (These figures only include those respondents who were already living with a partner before acquiring the CVS.) But, again, technical tasks, such as installing and repairing the CVS or emptying the dust canister, were mainly performed by men; this illustrates men's more holistic approach where technical equipment is concerned.

A practice of sharing vacuuming was related to a high educational and income level on the part of the woman. In families where both partners were employed, the greater the male advantage in earnings the more likely was the woman to be vacuuming unassisted. The man's participation increased as the income gap narrowed. In those families in which the man was the one who mainly took care of vacuuming, the woman had usually acquired a higher educational level than other women. Our research therefore confirms earlier studies in showing that the absolute and relative educational and financial resources of the partners are important determinants of the division of labour in the family (Haavio-Mannila 1984; Kauppinen-Toropainen and Kandolin 1991).

The partners' participation in vacuum cleaning was in line with the division of tasks in the household generally. Those who seldom participated in vacuuming, often also left other household tasks to their partner. On average, the women carried a heavier load of housework duties than did the men. This explains the women's interest in new technology as a facilitator of housework. The most burdened women in this respect, those who took care of vacuuming and had to do most of the other housework tasks too, were the least satisfied with the division of housework in the family. Those women whose partners participated equally in vacuum cleaning were more likely to be satisfied with the division of labour. Interestingly, there was no further increase in the incidence of women's satisfaction in cases where the husband assumed the *main* responsibility for the task. For women, it seems to be sufficient if men share housework equally with them. They do not expect them to take it over entirely.

Towards greater creativity and gender equality

Returning now to the concern with the three-way relationships between innovation, organization and gender relations that we stated at the outset, it is possible to detect certain pointers in this case study and make some generalizations.

We have presented evidence that technological change can bring change to gender relations. Buying new technological equipment, the central vacuum cleaning system, was followed by a more equal sharing of the task of vacuum cleaning between women and men in the home. Such a social innovation in the wake of a technological innovation was enhanced by structural features of the family household. For what also affected the gender practice of vacuum cleaning – and also housework in general – was the relative economic and educational status of the partners: the greater the woman's 'clout' in the family, the more actively her partner participated in family life. We might also expect that another factor encouraging innovation here was the holistic rationality that appeared to operate among many couples – responding creatively to principles both of efficiency and care.

However, men showed more interest in technology than did women, both at home and at work. When the particular skills of women and men complement each other, the division of labour creates mutual dependence and cohesiveness. But multiple skills would help women as well as men to operate more independently in different spheres of life. Men become multiskilled as they participate more actively in the 'female' household tasks. Women, on the other hand, still often leave the technical tasks to men. The increasing importance of technology in everyday life however challenges women to become more skilled in the 'male' sphere: to take steps towards getting more involved in the use of technology.

The effect on gender relations of technological change may be less direct in worklife than it is in the home sphere. The firm manufacturing CVS, though actively developing and producing new technology, was in many respects stifling creativity. Gender equality was endorsed in principle by both management and employees, but the unchanging gender pattern of locations, including a traditional sexual division of labour and a self-reproducing masculinity in decision-making, characterized the firm as quite conventional. The stagnant situation in the firm, defensiveness in management, a closed structure, a lack of informal networking and of communication between different organizational levels, all deprived creative individuals of either sex of opportunities to innovate. Women, due to their disadvantaged position, were doubly deprived of such opportunity.

The traditional division of labour that still prevails in many hierarchical work organizations today faces several challenges on the individual, organizational and societal levels. Attitudes favour equality, and new technology seems to support change towards a more equal sharing of tasks at home. Official policy in Finland actively promotes gender equality in all spheres of life. Furthermore, during times of economic recession and accelerating competition, organizations must continually improve their performance. 'Lean' organizations, in which hierarchies and rigid divisions of labour are replaced by flexible, multiskilled group working, can be both efficient and creative (Smeds 1994). We also know that flat and flexible organizations are most responsive to women's ideas (Kanter 1983). Lean organizations take the fullest advantage of the innovation potential of both women and men; simultaneously they can promote equality in worklife.

References

Babarczy, Agnes, Harcsa, Istvan and Pääkkönen, Hannu (1991) *Time Use Trends in Finland and in Hungary*. Studies, No. 180. Helsinki: Tilastokeskus [Central Statistical Office of Finland].

Cockburn, Cynthia (1992) *Gender and Technology: Mutual Shapings: Two Lectures*. Technology Assessment Texts No. 6. Copenhagen: Technology Assessment Unit, Technical University of Denmark.

Haavio-Mannila, Elina (1984) Perhe hoiva- ja tunneyhteisönä [The family as a caring and emotional unit], in Haavio-Mannila, E., Jallinoja, R. and Strandell, H. (eds) *Perhe, työ ja tunteet* [*Family, Work and Emotions*]. Helsinki: Werner Söderström Osakeyhtiö.

Haavio-Mannila, Elina (1988) *Työpaikan rakkaussuhteet* [*Love Affairs at Work*]. Helsinki: Werner Söderström Osakeyhtiö.

Hofstede, Geert (1983) National cultures in four dimensions, *International Studies of Management and Organizations*, Vol. XIII, No. 1–2, pp. 46–74.

Kandolin, Irja (1993) Women's labour force participation and sex segregation in working life, in Kauppinen-Toropainen, K. (ed.) *OECD Panel Group on Women, Work and Health. National Report: Finland*. Helsinki: Ministry of Social Affairs and Health and Institute of Occupational Health.

Kandolin, Irja and Kauppinen-Toropainen, Kaisa (1993) Female leadership and work community dynamics, *Life and Education in Finland*, No. 1, pp. 2–5.

Kanter, Rosabeth Moss (1983) *The Change Masters*. New York: Simon and Schuster.

Kauppinen-Toropainen, Kaisa and Kandolin, Irja (1991) Perhevalta: puolisoiden palkkaero ja vuorovaikutuksen laatu [Family clout: income differences and interaction between partners], *Työ ja ihminen* [*Work and People*], Vol. 5, No. 3, pp. 313–24.

Kevätsalo, Kimmo (1992) *Eriarvoisuuden arki metalliteollisuuden työntekijätehtävissä* [*Everyday Inequality in the Metal Industry*]. Helsinki: Metallityöväen liitto [The Finnish Union of Metal Workers].

Lehto, Anna-Maija (1991) *Työelämän laatu ja tasa-arvo* [*Worklife Quality and Equality*]. Studies No. 189. Helsinki: Tilastokeskus [Central Statistical Office of Finland].

Lipman-Blumen, Jean (1976) Toward a homosocial theory of sex-roles: an explanation of the sex-segregation of social institutions, *Signs*, Vol. 1, No. 3, Part 2, pp. 15–31.

Pöyry, Sirkka (1989) Technology is part of everyday life, *European Journal of Engineering Education*, Vol. 14, No. 4, pp. 339–49.

Reader's Digest Eurodata (1991) A consumer survey of seventeen European countries. The Reader's Digest Association Ltd.

Rimaschevskaya, Natalia (1991) Socio-economic changes and position of women in the Union of Soviet Socialist Republics. Paper presented at the Soviet-Finnish Seminar on The Impact of Social Changes on the Status of Women. Moscow, June.

Smeds, Riitta (ed.) (1985) *Man in 2000: Technology, Values and Society*. Porvoo: Suomen Teknillinen Seura [The Engineering Society of Finland].

Smeds, Riitta (1994 forthcoming) Managing change towards lean enterprises, *International Journal of Operations and Production Management*, Vol. 14, No. 3. (Special issue covering the 4th International Production Management Conference. London, April 1993.)

Sørensen, Bjorg Aase (1982) Ansvarsrasjonalitet [Responsible rationality], in Holter, H. (ed.) *Kvinner i Felleskap* [*Women Together*]. Oslo: Universitetförlaget.

Suomalainen mies [*The Finnish Man*] (1990) Kerava: A-lehdet.

Suomalainen nainen [*The Finnish Woman*] (1989) Helsinki: A-lehdet.

Tushman, Michael and Nadler, David (1986) Organizing for innovation, *California Management Review*, Vol. XXVIII, No. 3, Spring, pp. 74–92.

Waerness, Kari (1984) Caring as women's work in the welfare state, in Holter, H. (ed.) *Patriarchy in a Welfare Society*. Oslo: Universitetsförlaget.

Ve, Hildur (1992) Gender differences in rationality: the concept of praxis knowledge and future trends. Paper presented at the International Conference on Gender, Technology and Ethics. Luleå, Sweden, June.

2

'Let's nuke the dinner': Discursive practices of gender in the creation of a new cooking process

SUSAN ORMROD

The microwave oven has come to stand for quick, convenient and spontaneous eating. It is however a technology in which unseen electromagnetic radio waves bombard the food, challenging the everyday homeliness of conventional cooking, with its longer and more visible processes. So, when Roseanne (the central character in a US television comedy series) quips 'let's nuke the dinner', she neatly sums up the contradictory fears and misunderstandings that surround the microwave oven. No one expects too much from it in terms of cuisine, but its sheer practicality allows life's other domestic traumas and comedies to go on around it. It has reduced enormously the time and physical effort of cooking, but it is still a woman (Roseanne in this instance) who makes the decision what to cook and how to cook it, while her family carry on without even acknowledging it has been done.

Of course, too much can be made of an instant on television, but its humour would not work had it no cultural referents. It is these which, for the two of us from Britain, made the microwave oven a promising choice for study.[1] As a kitchen appliance it enabled examination of an encounter between masculinity and femininity. By that we did not simply mean that the microwave oven is engineered by men and then used by women in the home, but rather that it takes its place within each different site, from design through to use, where women and men interact. Masculinity and femininity are too often seen as separate spheres, or as concentrations of either one sex or the other. As this account of microwave cooking will show, women and men are brought together in *specific relations* of gender and technology, and identifying these can lead to new understandings.

A circuit of gender–technology relations

Technology studies are usually either of innovation or of use. The aim in our research was to include both, and the spectrum of activities in between.[2] We wanted to explore the connections around this circuit, by tracing the particular networks of meanings, relations and practices constructed within it.

Taking a cue from the 'social shaping' literature, we understand technology as comprising artefacts, knowledge, and processes or activities (MacKenzie and Wajcman 1985; Bijker *et al.* 1989). We see technology and social relations as a 'seamless web' where a number of elements, human and non-human, are combined in *networks of meanings and practices* (Callon 1986, 1989). In this chapter, then, I make no assumptions about what is social, what is technical, but examine how it is that these are constructed and differentiated. It is the organizing of the boundaries between people and machines, between 'social factors' and 'the technical', that is the subject of exploration. These are the dynamics of gender and technology relations in interaction.

It is important to specify that gender too is seen here as *processual*, as socially produced in an active process in which all kinds of forces are at work. Gender identities, like technologies, are achieved rather than given. The mutual implication of 'the social' and 'the technical' in such achievement is not simply additive, but crucially interactive. Nor is the interaction simply a matter of neatly separable variables that can be traced in some linear fashion. There is no clearly identifiable outcome as a result of two (or more) clearly identifiable factors interacting. The interaction is complex and continuous and all the elements combined are transforming of, and transformed by, each other.

As a relation of differentiation, gender *orders* relations within both organizations and everyday life, the workplace and the home. The order it produces is hierarchical. However, as Rosemary Pringle points out, women and men are not automatically and passively inscribed into existing power relations (Pringle 1989). The order does not straightforwardly produce relations, it is also always being produced by them. To take the case of the microwave oven, gender relations must be negotiated, accepted, created and re-created as part of the process and management of manufacture, distribution and use if the circuit for the microwave oven is to be successfully established.

If gender differentiation is to be understood in a way that can account for changes that occur in gender relations over time, then analysis must avoid seeing discourses of gender as mechanically repeating themselves (Hollway 1984). If it does not, feminism will be unable to challenge *successfully* the dominances now being achieved in their distinctively modern form. It will simply be locked into an apparently timeless 'battle of the sexes'.

This attention to the processes by which gender relations are reproduced has resonance with an approach to science and technology that likewise emphasizes the dynamic: science/technology relations in action

(Callon 1986; Latour 1987). The account that follows uses two particular concepts from the work of Michel Callon and Bruno Latour. The first is that of an 'actor-network'. The development of a technology necessitates the forging of networks of alliances between various actors, including individuals and groups, 'natural' elements and artefacts. Establishing networks means 'enrolling' actors and activities. That is to say some actors seek to bring others behind a project by persuading them that they have a solution to their particular problem, or that they have common interests.

The second concept is that of 'translation'. Translation is the *interpretation* given by the builders of artefacts (or facts) of their interests and those of the people they wish to enrol in the project. It results from the discursive moves, combining people and machines, in which actors attempt to enrol each other. Translation is useful for recognizing the *inconstancy* of the actors (whether people, ideas or artefacts) as they are mobilized in the construction of a network. They are not simply diffused in the project, they themselves undergo changes in the process. Moreover these changes are not simply a matter of adaptation but involve a transformation of the very understanding and content of what is translated.

These theoretical perspectives on gender and technology are politically radical in the way they counter any sense of determinism (biological or technological) and force us to question the content of categories that are usually taken for granted as 'social', 'natural' or 'technological'. We are obliged to accept that no categories are pre-given, that we have to consider the power relations at work in their emergence and their reproduction.

In short, the artefact with which we were concerned in the research – the microwave oven – we saw neither as an end in itself nor as an outcome, but as a means through which to examine social relations – the production of gender and technology. We were concerned not so much with the microwave oven as artefact as with *microwaving as a new cooking practice.* Central research questions were: How do transformations in cooking practice come about? Who and what are the forces or relations which achieve such a transformation? What part do women and men play in such a process? How does gender influence, and how is it influenced by, technology?

The particular representation of the research in this chapter concentrates on attempts made by various actors during the late 1980s to *redefine microwave oven technology.* It was already in widespread use as a reheating tool, accepted in a mature market. Now the aim was to develop it into something with a great deal more culinary sophistication. I shall show how this redefinition of the technology hinges on processes of *subjectification,* in which actors across a number of associated industries combine to promote various constructions of themselves and their interests. It also hinges upon processes of *objectification,* in which some actors configure others – those in the industry, say, configure the end-user of the microwave oven.

The chapter focuses on the combination of two sets of processes: processes in which the microwave oven is redefined around gender, and processes in which gender subjects are reconstituted. They are not separable: the construction of gender is every bit as important to the 'success' of the project (of transforming microwaving as a cooking practice) as is the addition of, say, enhanced timing mechanisms. Gender is actively produced here, as it is elsewhere in a multitude of ways, by the assumptions and stated facts about women and men and their use of technology.

From pie-warming to home cooking: the construction of new cooking practices

Microwaving gradually became established as an alternative cooking practice in the United Kingdom during the 1970s and 1980s. By the time of our research in 1991 a microwave oven was to be found in well over half of all homes. In the latter half of the 1980s however steps were taken to enhance the microwave oven. The shift was from the microwave as a take-it-or-leave-it, state-of-the-art technology to something developed to meet the perceived needs of the user, something that compromises with everyday life in the home and responds to the diversity of local cuisines. In this section we shall see four different faces of this transformation, namely changes in: the *selling* of microwaves; in the *organization of design*; in the *product* itself and its anticipated *purchaser*; and in *marketing* and the configuration of a *user*.

This overall change has been taking place during years of economic recession. Microwave ovens, often an optional extra in the home, supplementing a conventional oven, have been hit harder than some other white goods. They have faced competition from other forms of cooking, now sporting innovations such as halogen heating and stand-alone hobs. The 'first sale' market was by now almost saturated and manufacturers were increasingly seeking the replacement market. Concerns over food safety emerged, with incidents of poisoning by listeria bacteria and salmonella in inadequately heated food. In a series of 'scares' that had widespread media coverage the finger of public concern was pointed at the microwave oven. Microwaving was challenged to match up to higher specifications and more reassuring standards.

These were the problems confronting the promoters of microwaving, calling for some response. One answer has been the redefinition and enhancement of the microwave and microwave cooking on which we are focusing here, with the effect of locating it more firmly within an understanding of domestic cookery in a European context. The various moves this involved crucially depended on assumptions about gender and the home. These assumptions, perhaps, had not been articulated so clearly when the microwave oven was first introduced. Their articulation, as we shall see, now took place across all spheres from manufacturing, selling and use of the artefact, to consumer advice, food products and kitchen design.

Selling the microwave/gendering the microwave

One of the changes vital to this transformation of microwaving occurred in the late 1980s in *sales strategy*. It was a shift from selling the ovens as 'brown goods', a category that includes televisions, videos and music systems, to selling them as 'white goods', among the conventional ovens, fridges and freezers. It was an occurrence that demonstrated clear understandings and assumptions about gender.

We made a particular study of a retail chain we call Home-Tec,[3] a group with many hundreds of high street and out-of-town electrical appliance stores. It incorporates two distinct chains, run in parallel but each with its own identity, sales mix and target customers. The first chain, Arrow, has a masculine image, is closely identified with hi-tech brown goods, and sees its most significant customer group as young men aged 16–25 years old. Home-Tec's second chain, Bunnett's, sells both brown and white electrical goods. It has a family image, and sees itself as selling to 'couples' across a much broader age range. Interestingly, the existence of these two marketing approaches allows for variation in masculinity (men feature alternatively as 'young men' and as 'family men'), but little in femininity (a woman has only a family persona).

The two chains, we found, operated distinct selling styles. Bunnett's did not exactly play down technology, but they did feel it should be rendered understandable. An effort was therefore made to present products in terms of their 'features and benefits'. So for instance, a recent display in Bunnett's had sought to explain how different microwave ovens were suitable for different kinds of cooking. Indeed, the main challenge in promoting the microwave oven to the customer was seen as counteracting the intimidating effect of new technology. By contrast, it was precisely the 'gizmo' quality of technology that was hyped in the Arrow stores. Here, no attempt was made to 'unpack' and make intelligible the various product features. On the contrary, CD players, for instance, carried labels which were incomprehensible except to the *cognoscenti* (such as '4 × Oversampling').

When the microwave oven first entered the retail market it was seen as being so revolutionary that it was not at first identified with kitchen appliances. As one marketing manager explained, 'It was electronic, it was gadgetry.' Microwaves were even sold in Arrow stores. In 1988 however Home-Tec's marketing strategy changed significantly. Microwaves were removed from Arrow and henceforth sold only as a white good in Bunnett's. How might we examine the processes by which it became established and identified as a kitchen product? How might we explain its change in identity from a relatively masculinized commodity to a more feminized one?

The change in Home-Tec's marketing strategy responded to several factors. First, the microwave oven's profit-making performance per square foot of shopfloor space came under competition from a new commodity, the camcorder. This prompted a clarification of its ambiguous nature, simultaneously hi-tech brown good and mundane white good. It was, besides, around this time that microwave oven sales suffered a sharp decline partly due to economic recession and partly due to the safety scares already mentioned. It was felt the two chains should cease competing for diminishing microwave sales. These factors were enrolled as rationales in the firm's decision to relocate the microwave unequivocally within Bunnett's stores as a kitchen product.

This repositioning of the microwave by Home-Tec as part of a changing sales strategy was, to use the concept introduced above, a *translation* of the oven from hi-tech brown good to domestic white good. The gendered distinctions made by the firm between its two chains of stores and two categories of goods came into play and contributed to redefining the meaning of the microwave. The translation involved a change in what the product was for and who it was targeted at. Technologies are as gendered as human subjectivity.

This shift in the identity of the microwave contributed to the reproduction of gender hierarchy in technology relations. The microwave was enrolled in the maintenance of masculine dominance around notions of the greater sophistication and knowledge-content of 'the technical' in contrast to the family as a feminized domain with its everyday domesticity. This example makes visible the construction of the boundaries between the social and the technical. As the oven is actively redefined from brown to white goods, the difference between technical and social and the unequal value of the two spheres, is reaffirmed.

Similarly, the stereotypical characterization of men as having a distance from cooking has been *remade*. During its stay among the brown goods in Arrow, the microwave in no way challenged stereotyped notions of masculinity – for it was presented as a technologically-interesting pie-warmer, and had no association with serious home cookery. When the microwave was reconstituted as a purely white good in Bunnett's, women were brought to the fore as its supposed users. Men were still present among the customers, but now seen as members of families, in which a woman conventionally takes responsibility for food and cooking.

If it can be transformed in this way by relations of gender at the point of sale, the artefact has no inherent constancy. It may be polished and well-packaged when it comes out of the factory, but it is not *finished*. The identities of 'the social actors' enrolled as users by the retailers are also inconstant: the attribution to men of technical competence, once highlighted, is now played down. As it happens, this particular instance demonstrates the reproduction and strengthening of conventional gender relations around cooking and technological competence. Rather than simply assuming conventional relations to be reproduced, however, the actor-network approach allows us to see the dynamics by which it occurs.

Producing the microwave/producing gender

The gendering of machines and people extends beyond the selling of existing models of microwave oven and into the areas where models are planned and designed. We found two significant changes in Electro's (the manufacturer) organization of its design processes. Each tended in the same direction as that described above. That is, they worked to further the translation of the microwave oven and its cooking process into more feminized versions. The first was a delegation to regional centres of some aspects of product design. The second was the employment of women home economists.

Until 1990 almost all design for the European market was carried out in the Corporation's head office in Japan. Then a decision was made to devolve more responsibility for design on to Electro UK. At the time of our research the first more or less British-designed oven had just been produced.

Microwaves manufactured in the United Kingdom to Japanese specifications had not always been successful in the UK and European markets. A pink and blue model, for instance, considered, as a Japanese engineer put it, 'very beautiful' in Japan, had hardly been appreciated here. More importantly, though, the microwaving principle itself had shortcomings in Europe. Simple ovens with microwave cooking only are suitable for Japan where the cuisine involves much steaming and thawing – of *sushi* for example. In Europe however the microwave was being criticized for producing soggy food. In European cuisine, which involves a good deal of baking, roasting and 'gratinee' dishes, the browning and crisping properties of conventional ovens are highly valued. Faced with some local market resistance, then, technical developments were needed. The answer has been the combination in a single small oven of microwave energy and a conventional energy source – often accompanied by features such as the rotisserie, grill and enhanced controls. Speed and simplicity of cooking had of course been the microwave's original attraction. 'Combi' cooking was slower, but it was more controlled and versatile. Above all it enabled a wider range of foods, with national cultural variations, to be incorporated into the microwave's repertoire. The new mode also partly dealt with safety fears. With the emphasis on the intervention of the cook, responsibility for safe and thorough cooking, the avoidance of 'hotspots' and 'coldspots' in food through stirring and monitoring, was passed to her.

These decisions around design were not neatly organized. Indeed, within the Electro Corporation there were a number of design efforts paralleling each other at several international sites while some tasks were carried out solely at head office in Japan. Despite these organizational variations, the design functions everywhere had one thing in common: a gender distinction. Design engineering and production engineering functions, which represented the company's technical innovation, were distinguished from functions concerned with the market or the end-user. In a sense this was a male/female distinction. The former appeared more important, more decisive, to the company and its products than the latter. Engineers had relatively higher status and pay. More than this, however, in deciding who should be employed in these various functions, Electro was putting boundaries around the functions themselves and establishing their relative importance.

One distinction in particular was significant in the overall design process: that between the design engineering department and the product planning department's test kitchen, staffed by home economists. Electro's introduction a few years previously of teams of home economists at head office and in regional companies highlighted the mobilization of gender and of traditional national cookery practices in the microwave project.

The relation of the the home economists' unit to design engineering can be seen as framed by gender and framing of gender. Both sections were in practice equally necessary to ensuring that Electro's microwave ovens would sell and work. We found however, and the home economists themselves complained, that their professional input was not widely perceived as having an equivalent value to that of engineering. Organizationally they were separate and unequal. The test kitchen was small and staffed by women. Design engineering was bigger, and employed exclusively male engineering staff. Moreover, the conceptual boundary between the two functions was drawn along a traditional dividing line. The engineers in the design engineering department were seen as doing 'technical' work, while the home economists in the test kitchen – despite the scientific nature of their procedures – were not. 'Cooking' was 'non-technical'. So tensions arose from the test kitchen's simultaneous incorporation into and exclusion from the design process, manifest in conflicts over this boundary.

We found the sharing of work in design to be as follows. The outline specifications for each model were mainly (though to a lesser extent than before) devised by the Japanese parent company. Design engineering were responsible for detailed design of the electrical and electronic components and the overall build of the ovens. The home economists for their part were responsible for testing the ovens' performance. Using standard loads of different kinds of foods, they tested the prototypes and production samples at each stage of their development. They also contributed to the design of cooking programmes and controls, and prepared or commissioned recipes for use in instruction books.

The tensions arising between these different dimensions of the design process were visible as much in the physical locations of the staff, however, as in how their responsibilities were described. The two home economists at head office, Isobel and Tammy, worked in the test kitchen, separate from the rest of the design team and closer to marketing and sales. Jackie, the home economist at the manufacturing plant, had two desks, one in the design engineering office and the other located in the general management office. There was some confusion over where she 'belonged'. Both the product planning and design engineering departments when prompted said she was their responsibility but neither included her when formally listing for us the members of their department. Jackie explained that in practice she had two bosses but that her main work group was the engineering team. This department was all male, but she felt accepted and respected by her colleagues.

I had sort of feedback from the girl who was working here on place-
ment ... One of the Senior Engineers was telling her, you know, 'go
and spend some time with Jackie next week, but you'll be surprised
at what she does as well, it's *not just cooking'*. Which was nice for
me to hear because they wouldn't tell me that, but they say it to
other people. (emphasis added)

There was acknowledgement here of the complex nature of the home
economist's job. The compliment was a back-handed one, however, inad-
vertently revealing how unimportant, relative to engineering, 'just cooking' was held to be.

The home economists were employed on a lower scale than the 'technical' grades of their engineer colleagues. Yet informally they were perceived to be an equally valuable part of the design process. Isobel and
Tammy in the test kitchen debated whether their work was regarded
seriously by their engineering colleagues.

Isobel [to Tammy]: Japan listen to you don't they?
Tammy: Oh yes.
Isobel: You have the final say don't you?
Tammy: Well, yeah, you do actually have the final say.

The surprise and hesitancy which characterized this exchange said something about their ambivalent status.

Tammy worked in liaison with 20 colleagues based in Japan, some in
engineering and some in home economics. There, too, the engineers were
male and home economists female. Tammy felt however that despite
such divisions her work was treated by both Japanese and British senior
colleagues in product planning as being as important as that of the engineers. This extended to training provision. Both Jackie and Tammy anticipated long-term training, including training in test procedures, at the
parent company in Japan.

In summary, the distinctions and elisions between engineers and home
economists demonstrated competing discourses, a discourse of equality
and a more traditional gender dichotomy. On the one hand the home
economists signified the manufacturer's link with the consumer and cook,
the household and the domain of women. Here the microwave was
experienced as the development of new cooking processes. On the other
hand, the engineers' microwave was a product in isolation from use, an
achievement of electrical engineering, a domain dominated by men from
which women were almost excluded.

Both types of knowledge and skill, domestic science and engineering
science, are crucial to the successful design of microwave ovens as products that will sell. Domestic science transgresses the boundaries erected
within technical discourses. Those senior staff in product planning and
design whose responsibilities spanned both areas openly acknowledged
this. None the less, a discourse valorizing 'the technical' was being used
by the company to organize and employ workers on unequal terms, in

contradiction with the alternative discourse of equality they sometimes deployed. In any case, recognition of the importance of the home economists in the design process at Electro represents a very restricted notion of equality. Equality is couched in terms where the reference point is men, and is belied by masculinist definitions of 'the technical'.

Enhancing the product, enhancing the customer

The introduction in the 1980s of home economists into the design process indicates the value placed, increasingly over time, upon the microwave oven as a *versatile cooking machine*, rather than a limited, if hi-tech, gadget. Originally microwaves had entailed eating commercial ready-meals or simple one-step dishes such as baked potatoes. The models now increasingly favoured, partly through the intervention of the home economists, a combination of conventional heat sources with microwave energy, and the addition of features such as rotisseries and grills. In the 'combi' oven, cooking-speed was stressed far less and the control of the cooked product brought more firmly within the hands of its operator. The operator was to select discriminatingly between different programmes, keying-in essential data so that the sensors could do their work. Responding to popular fears over 'hotspots' and 'coldspots', users were now implored to stir and check foods. Even the simple job of heating a can of soup became something that microwave ovens might fail to do properly without the intelligent intervention of the user.

Clearly the designers have in mind an 'operator' who spends more time at home; someone whose sense of identity, responsibility and enjoyment is already strongly associated with food preparation: a woman. If the microwaved meal of the future is to include home-baked bread, cakes and the traditional British Sunday roast dinner, a key assumption is that there is someone there, 'the housewife', who wants and is able to spend time actively cooking. The home economist Isobel put it this way:

> You have to put the pleasure back ... And we went back two years ago and we have, I hope, put that pleasure back into cooking with microwave. We took it away I think from *her*, in the beginning. By showing her these wonderful jacket potatoes – I like a jacket potato but you can't say there's any pleasure in producing a jacket potato with baked beans on the top. And [ironically] we showed her *wonderful* things to cook – the scrambled egg in 50 seconds in the morning! But we actually took away the skills and the pleasure that go back for generations that are in a house. (emphasis added)

If the combi oven was an innovation specifically geared to the 'serious cook', principally identified as the housewife, its promoters now had to enlist her traditional skills and enrol her into new microwave cooking practices with an extended repertoire. A number of resources were mobilized to achieve this. First, the home economists developed recipes and produced cookery books. The home economists' role in product development also included, for a couple of years during the boom sales period of the late 1980s, the provision of microwave cookery schools around the country. At the time of our study Electro employed a team of consultants to demonstrate their different models of microwave oven to customers in retail stores. That they were all women was not incidental: they could identify with the customer, and be identified by her as someone like themselves. Electro's team of sales staff, by contrast, who dealt direct with retailers' buying staff, were almost all men. As a sales manager explained:

> We decided that salesmen are salesmen because that's what we're paying them to do. We don't want the housewife badgered by salesmen. We want the housewife to choose her own oven. We want the housewife to feel comfortable and confident. If she chooses an oven . . . then she's bought it for the benefits that she will get for herself and her family, not because she's been pestered by some salesman. So by keeping them totally separate and devoid from each other, we maintain that very important role.

Neither was it incidental, of course, that the home economists – Jackie, Isobel and Tammy – were women. The sales manager said 'we've always had a microwave kitchen operated by ladies, *housewives themselves*' (emphasis added).

It is not surprising that when home economists had to imagine a customer they said they first thought of themselves. They were intended to do so. Women home economists played a key role in representing the user in the design process and development of new models. They felt, however, their 'standing in' for women users to be inadequate as a design resource. They expressed frustration that Electro UK did not itself conduct research into microwave use but relied on an agency whose concern was confined to monitoring sales of different models.

Home economists did at least often discuss and speculate about the customer. The engineers claimed not to, dismissing that as a marketing concern. When pressed, they admitted that, given women have traditionally been the main cooks in most households, the user was in all likelihood a female. Clearly, however, in the engineers' part of the design process, she was but a shadowy figure.

This lack of interest in acquiring detailed knowledge about the consumer/user of microwave ovens was not just confined to Electro. Home-Tec's head office marketing staff (male and female) likewise commissioned only general market research information about their customer base. 'Shopper profiles' substituted for detailed analyses of the consumers/ users of specific product groups. They none the less felt able to state boldly enough that their microwave oven customers were 'women, straight families, A down to C2'.

Instead of seeking concrete data on customer needs and preferences, and how they might differ by gender, Home-Tec relied on a proactive sales technique. Different approaches were deemed appropriate for

Arrows and Bunnetts, responding to the different customer bases and identities of the two chains, as the company perceived them. Bunnett's sales staff were trained to explain carefully to customers the 'features, advantages and benefits' of the various products *in use*. This was represented as being relevant equally to male and female customers, approached not as sexes but as 'individuals with specific lifestyles'. In Arrow stores, by contrast, customers were projected as being technically informed men and the emphasis in training was on equipping sales staff to satisfy them with information on products' technical specifications.

The features-and-benefits (FAB) approach to selling microwave ovens thus dates from around the time when the group moved microwave ovens firmly into the white goods sector of the Bunnett's stores, which as we saw amounted to a transformation in the meaning of the commodity from a technical novelty, a 'magic box', to a workaday domestic appliance. FAB appropriately played down the technology and highlighted the product's utility within a domestic setting. It explicitly attempted to overcome a suspected psychological block about technology in the female user. Despite their lack of concrete evidence about their microwave customers, many retail managers saw 'techno-fear' as a sales challenge. One said 'We do try and get them [the staff] to simplify because we do feel, perhaps for a woman for instance, that there is some slight technological fear.'

Some of the features highlighted by FAB responded to concerns over food safety and radiation hazards. A turntable, for example, could be presented as a precaution against uneven cooking ('coldspots'). A larger volume and power output could be presented as an effective safeguard (ensuring speedy but thorough heating) when cooking large quantities for families.

'Techno-fear' is clearly seen as a female deficiency. We found retailers addressing it not only in women customers but in their female sales staff, seen as clinging timidly to white goods, dismayed by the hi-tech complexities of videos and camcorders. Special training programmes were being developed to help give women sales personnel the confidence to sell brown goods.

It was no longer, then, simply a matter of presenting the microwave oven as a practical tool, but rather of emphasizing how a specific model in a range could meet the differentiated needs of the customer, as a unique individual or family group. Further, it was felt to be important to address the traditional and commonplace gendered divisions of cookery knowledge and skill in sales situations. A manager explained to us how a male customer, lacking cooking experience, might have difficulty understanding the sales pitch. If he was to be successfully enrolled, whether as an independent customer, or as the 'cheque book holder' accompanying his female partner, then the features-and-benefits sales technique must be deployed to this end:

> When you're training sales staff you have to teach them to identify
> the needs of the consumer and then understand the benefits of a

range of ovens. Sales staff can expect to be talking to a man who may come in to buy an oven for his wife, or come in with his wife. And sales people if they are male are not cooks themselves. We can't assume that we can put in a sponge cake and say that it'll cook in 15 minutes as opposed to 25, and expect them to have any conception of what that means. They have never cooked a sponge cake in their life. They don't understand that you would normally have to pre-heat the oven, and that it takes 25 minutes in a conventional oven. They won't know what it's like to turn on an oven and wait for it to pre-heat. You have to really spell it out for them.

Configuring a gendered user

Given the very different levels of cookery knowledge among both customers and sales staff, a key resource in the building of a successful microwave network was *education*. Only education of consumers by means of advertising, the media and the consumer associations could achieve microwaving as a widespread cooking practice.

Manufacturers and retailers of microwave ovens are not the only actors that join in the dual process of educating and configuring the microwave user. Related industries participate in the network, including the producers of purpose-made microwavable foods. A recent television advertising campaign for a line of 'wet ambient' foods – that is ready-meals with a long shelf-life at room temperature – demonstrated the way in which education of the consumer is also a process of configuring a user.

The campaign was an attempt to raise awareness of the product's existence and desirability. We were told by one of the firm's senior marketing executives (a man), that the promotion was aimed at the woman consumer – in particular the 'housewife'. He explained

> It's not so much a woman I think – we're directing it at the family, but it would be folly to present a commercial probably, where, if the woman was present, she was not the one doing the work in the kitchen. Because if a bloke was doing it and she wasn't, then it just wouldn't be credible, because, you know, it's an area of excellence, which they are meant to understand – the woman is meant to understand ... I think unless the housewife says 'it's safe' to the family, the family won't believe it, that's the point. So, you've got to convince her first, she probably convinces her family, and then is prepared to let her family take over as and when. The bridging of that gap is still very much in her hands, so we're still educating her.

Men are, none the less, seen as having an important role to play in the introduction of this new food product.

> Men are great experimentalists, seen as that, I think, in cooking – they're more likely for example at the shelves on a shopping trip to pick up things ... I think they are relatively experienced in the shopping, but not in the cooking.

These sentiments were reproduced in the company's latest television commercial which implied: 'Some microwave foods, unwittingly selected by men who know little about food, are so bad even the microwave oven rejects them. Women know our make of ready-meals is best.' The advert, relying heavily on humour, showed a man and children putting (un-labelled) packet foods into the microwave, which spontaneously spat them out and threw them across the kitchen. The wife/mother then selected the advertised brand of ready-meal from the cupboard and inserted it into the microwave with a knowing smile and glance to camera. The joke, however, was on her, since the microwave oven appreciated this food so much it appeared to eat it. The door remained shut and the electronic display flashed the words 'yum yum'.

This advert can be seen as reproducing a traditional discourse of gender around natural difference, with some slight competition from a discourse of equality. The man is now represented as having a new location in the home: he can be seen in the kitchen and will use the microwave oven. But he is naive, and uses it 'mechanically'. The woman is still the one with knowledge of taste and responsibility for nutrition. Of course the advert may also be read as lacking any equality discourse and simply reshaping that of natural difference: now the woman takes responsibility for serious eating while the man plays around with experimentation. Such a reading is certainly borne out by the senior marketing executive's perception of his consumers.

What is particularly striking about these assorted members of industry busy attempting to enroll 'the consumer' in microwaving is the highly speculative nature of their thinking on consumers. In the main, reliance is placed not on empirical market research evidence but on personal hunches and identification with the consumer (including gendered stereo-types). While detailed evidence is sought about sales and analyses made of what sells, when and where, such analyses do not extend to *who* and *why*. The female manager responsible for 'recipe dishes' in a major 'qual-ity' food retailer explained:

> It's *hypothetical*, but yes, basically it's the woman who has no time any more. Families may buy recipe dishes but they won't buy the same thing for the whole family . . . What cook-chill does is offer even a family the choice of having separate and different meals. You can have the choice to differ from your partner for instance. A couple will come into the shop and he'll say 'tonight, I'll have this', and she'll say 'I'll have that' for our supper tonight.
>
> We do speculate, we have meetings where we sit down and talk about it. But you probably know that [in our company we] actually shun these techniques of market research and so on. We all assume we know our customers. (emphasis added)

There is a slippage between the reasons marketing suggests to consumers when promoting its products and the projection of users in this process. The effect is to foreground, for both consumers and producers, idealizations rather than actual practices. Consumerism becomes the opportunity 'to buy into' identities through projected lifestyles that are sold along with 'the goods' (Featherstone 1991).

In summary, the 'success' of microwave ovens in terms of sales, and of microwaving in terms of cooking practices, calls for a range of activities across a number of areas working together to achieve the innovation. However, little concrete evidence about the use of microwave ovens in the home is gathered or accumulated. Instead, assumptions are made and consumers idealized. The principal user is configured as 'housewife' through the particular objectifying strategies of industry actors. An idealized notion of domesticity is enrolled, in which women largely take responsibility for food and sustenance.

Attempts are made to introduce this idealized notion of domesticity into the technology so that the product will sell and meet user requirements. 'Success' depends on playing down aspects of the microwaving that might be considered 'technical' and highlighting the oven's domestication. There was the response to women's supposed 'techno-fear'. There was the decision-making role projected for the 'family man', first enrolled as writer of the cheque that buys the appliance and subsequently as the open-minded experimenter prepared to try out the novel foods with which it is associated. It is this series of enrolments and representations that constitute the actor-network of 'microwaving as serious cookery'. Relations of gender, it will be evident, are crucial to its fabrication.

Negotiating the meaning of gender and technology

To conclude, then, the approach in this chapter has allowed an examination of how gender relations are enrolled within relations of technology and vice versa. Technology and gender have been specified as social processes whose boundaries and content are not pre-existing but negotiated. The boundaries between what are considered to be the 'technical' and the 'social', as well as the boundary between genders (forms of masculine and feminine), are arrived at as a result of observable social processes. These include the enrolment of ideas which allude to tradition, to precedent, to the natural, normal and usual. These are not however simply structural factors that determine subsequent events. Rather they are used dynamically, 'at the time', in the construction of contingent, specific networks. We have seen how gender is a thread running throughout the manufacture, distribution and configured use of the microwave oven, and how the attempt to enrol the notional 'housewife' has been a critical element in the project of enhancing microwave practice from 'pie-warming' to cookery. Despite all these efforts by microwave's promoters however, there is as yet little evidence to confirm success, even in terms of sales. Perhaps we must await the end of the economic recession before we can see whether people are really upgrading their microwaves as manufacturers and retailers hope, and whether, having acquired new facilities, they actually use them.

This is, therefore, a story of interpretive flexibility, a story where the role of gender and the role of the microwave oven continues to be negotiated. We have seen how the meaning of each has varied over time and in accordance with where actors stand in the network. In this case study, as it happens, the (temporarily stabilized) outcome of the negotiation is the preservation of politically conservative relations of power for women and men. What is important however is that such outcomes are not given. The relations of technology and gender are never a simple repetition of pre-existing patterns, but rather processes of modification. Seeing them this way we can see too the possibility of political strategies for change.

Acknowledgements

Particular thanks to Anne-Jorunn Berg, University of Trondheim, and David Rea, University of Plymouth, for their comments on earlier drafts of this chapter.

Notes

1 The research was funded by a grant from the Economic and Social Research Council and carried out in the Centre for Research in Gender, Ethnicity and Social Change at The City University, London, between 1990 and 1992. We would like to thank both organizations for their support. Cynthia Cockburn was the principal investigator, I carried out most of the interviewing and together we have analysed the findings and written up the results. The project is reported in full in Cockburn and Ormrod (1993).

2 We carried out the field research in a number of different sites across design, manufacture, marketing, distribution, servicing and use. Qualitative interviews, 90 in all, were conducted within: two major UK Japanese owned microwave manufacturers; two major UK electrical retail chains; and 20 households using microwave ovens. We also interviewed consultant engineers, trade and consumer associations, kitchen designers, microwave cookery experts, home economics teachers, advertisers and managers in related industries.

3 While interviews were conducted with more than one electrical retailer and microwave manufacturer (see note 2) the project concentrated on major case studies of one of each. The research material used here draws upon these case study organizations that we call, respectively, Home-Tec and Electro Corporation. In the interests of the anonymity requested by our informants, substantial details have been changed and all names, both those of companies and those of individuals, are fictitious.

References

Bijker, Wiebe E., Hughes, Thomas P. and Pinch, Trevor (eds) (1989) *The Social Construction of Technological Systems*. Cambridge, MA and London: MIT Press.

Callon, Michel (1986) Some elements of a sociology of translation: domestication of the scallops and the fishermen of St Brieuc Bay, in Law, J. (ed.) *Power, Action and Belief*. London: Routledge and Kegan Paul.

Callon, Michel (1989) Society in the making: the study of technology as a tool for sociological analysis, in Bijker, W.E., Hughes, T.P. and Pinch, T. (eds) *The Social Construction of Technological Systems*. Cambridge, MA and London: MIT Press.

Cockburn, Cynthia and Ormrod, Susan (1993) *Gender and Technology in the Making*. Newbury Park, CA and London: Sage.

Featherstone, Mike (1991) *Consumer Culture and Postmodernism*. London: Sage.

Hollway, Wendy (1984) Gender difference and the production of subjectivity, in Henriques, J., Hollway, W., Urwin, C. *et al.* (eds) *Changing the Subject: Psychology, Social Regulation and Subjectivity*. London: Methuen.

Latour, Bruno (1987) *Science in Action*. Milton Keynes: Open University Press.

MacKenzie, Donald and Wajcman, Judy (eds) (1985) *The Social Shaping of Technology*. Milton Keynes: Open University Press.

Pringle, Rosemary (1989) Bureaucracy, rationality and sexuality: the case of secretaries, in Hearn, J., Sheppard, D.L., Tancred-Sheriff, P. and Burrell, G. (eds) *The Sexuality of Organization*. London: Sage.

3

Computerization in Greek banking: The gendering of jobs and payment practices

KATERINA ARVANITAKI AND
MARIA STRATIGAKI

In this chapter we explore the way new money technology introduced into the banking system interrelates with the social construction of gender, particularly as a power relation, both in the workplace and at home. Those with economic interests in banking intend their technical revolution to reduce labour costs, accelerate the rhythm of money circulation and optimize credit policy. For many bank employees, however, the principal impact of the electronic representation of money, involving first electronic data processing and then on-line/real-time systems, has been the transformation of their work processes. In addition, since one effect has been the issue of personal plastic cards to bank clients, the new technology has affected their private life too, by modifying payment practices in private consumption.

We shall look at technological change as it affects the individual (woman and man) and the sexes (female and male), both as producers and consumers, as employees and as members of households. Banking and money technology, we found, illustrates with pleasing clarity the interrelation between the public and the private, work and home: money circulates, each stage in its circuit entails social relations, and those of one stage bear upon the next. The employees of the bank are the very kind of people, with secure salaries, whom the banks readily allow the privilege of credit cards. In particular, the banks' new employees – women – are often the new working wives who have this innovatory autonomy, their own bank account and plastic card. Some of the men are married to women very like those they now work with. Some however are the breadwinners for 'housewives' with a different relationship to family income, savings and expenditure.

The National Bank of Greece (NBG) and its own credit card, the 'Ethnokarta', were an interesting field for our Europe-wide gender and technology study, because the bank's technological investment and marketing policy and consumer behaviour were very much shaped by Greece's accession in 1981 to the European Economic Community (EEC). The creation of a Single European Market required member states, among other things, to deregulate banking, to internationalize systems of payment and credit facilities and homogenize consumer goods. These processes all intensified in Greece following 1987, the date from which the country was obliged to conform to EC banking policy as set out in the Second EC Banking Directive (Zavvos 1989).

Retail banking and consumer support services are relatively new in Greece. During the 1960s and 1970s government policy had seen banking's role as lending to manufacturers to promote industrial investment and stimulate production. Consumption was not yet within its scope, the greater part being financed independent of the banks through privately-held savings, which had been accumulating fast in the economic growth of the 1960s. Greece therefore lagged behind other European countries in banking technology (Hellenic Banks' Association 1987). At the time of writing in 1992, the system known as EFTPOS, or Electronic Fund Transfer at the Point of Sale, had only just started to be introduced in the Greek market. Besides, since the advent of automatic teller machines in large banks is also very recent, cash cards are hardly known. Even the use of credit cards, in existence for 20 years, is by no means widespread.

As the NBG can be seen as representative of Greek banking, so the people in our study may stand as representatives of a significant new group of consumers – employees in the service industries. Greece's integration into Europe carries the country along a trajectory characterized by a growth in this kind of salaried employment at the expense of self-employment, an increasing engagement of women in service jobs and significant changes in credit policies.

Greek credit card holders are commonly households consisting of one or two low-income salaried employees, typically in the service sector. Often, when the woman is employed as well as her partner, the couple will have two accounts and two cards. When the woman is a housewife the couple is more likely to have a single account and a 'family' credit card, used by both partners.

A disproportionate number of card holders, female and male, in fact work in banks, introduced to this new product by the employer. Bank employees have a further business relationship with their employer: usually such salaried employees will have their salaries credited directly to their bank account (a practice fairly new to Greece, even for large companies), and those with secure positions often have loans advanced to them by the bank.

The first part of this study, then, focuses on the workplace, using material gathered in field research late in 1990 (Stratigaki 1992). Thirty-five thematic interviews, tape-recorded and transcribed, were carried out in the National Bank with women and men (in roughly equal numbers) working in a range of jobs related to computer technology. The second part looks at the introduction and marketing of the credit card. It draws on further interviews, desk research and analysis of the magazines used to market credit cards. The third part, dealing with the home, uses material gathered through 14 in-depth interviews made towards the end of 1991 with women and men (seven couples) one or both of whom were employed in this same bank.

Computerization, gender and the organization of work

In the 1980s. Greek bank employees enjoyed secure job tenure, integrated salaried scales, favourable social security programmes, a well-developed internal labour market and strong union organization. The National Bank of Greece was one of the first to employ women – as typists and cleaners. Until 1982 most staff were recruited by public competition. There were two pass lists, one for women and one for men, with equal numbers of recruits drawn from each. This effectively disadvantaged women, who almost always performed better than men in the written exam and who could therefore have expected a higher proportion of posts.

It was not until 1984 that Greece, obliged to harmonize Greek law with European Community directives, introduced a principle of sex equality in employment – and with it a single list for both sexes. This nominally instituted for employees of the banking industry, as of other industries, equal opportunity in recruitment, career development and pay. As a result the proportion of women among bank personnel increased. For example, women had been 33 per cent of bank accountants in 1976. Ten years later they were 44 per cent. The increase was particularly great lower down the hierarchy – from 39 per cent to 57 per cent of the four lowest grades.

Women had always had a good presence in these lower grades where promotion was exclusively by seniority. A seniority system had been a trade union demand to limit the influence of subjective criteria such as personal relations or political clientelism, and in the single salary scale established in 1982 basic salary levels are directly linked to seniority. Above grade 7 in the 11-grade hierarchy however a selective procedure has persisted, in which bias against women has been able to operate.

Despite the formally guaranteed equality of opportunity for women and men in the NBG, gender differences are reinforced in various ways. Even the apparently objective seniority system in promotion involves in-built discrimination against women. Whereas compulsory military service is counted as bank service, parental leave, which can be up to two years, is not, and leave due to pregnancy-related problems longer than one month costs a six month delay in promotion.

The most important source of sex inequality within the bank however is the evaluation of jobs by criteria that play into gender difference, legitimizing inequalities between women and men in career opportunity, salary and job enrichment. The aspects of content that are taken into account in grading jobs include money management, responsibility for subordinates, direct contact with clients (front or back office), type of client (private individuals or companies), contacts abroad (speaking foreign languages), use of equipment (telex, computer terminal, typewriter), branch size, branch location (central, in Athens, provincial), overtime and travelling.

Gender characteristics, it will be apparent, can be read into such criteria to create implicitly female and male jobs within the bank. 'Female' jobs are those involving repetitive tasks, low professional status and intensive operation of equipment. They are jobs that do not involve travel or deal with important company accounts. They are considered low skill jobs deserving low grades and low rewards. Some jobs are so clearly woman-specific that even trade union documents use the feminine article in referring to them.

The gendering of jobs is further deepened by the process of skills development. Given that basic training in banking is received on the job, a worker tends to assimilate the gender of her or his job and its related training opportunities. A totally mechanical job is evaluated as making but limited contribution to the employee's banking knowledge, so impeding her or his access to positions of responsibility. The in-house training scheme through which the bank generates specialized personnel for its various departments also has a gendering effect. Training programmes take place during work hours but often call for extra study at home. Participation in such programmes presumes a personal career strategy and disposable leisure time corresponding to a male model. Not surprisingly, fewer women participate than men, and as a result fewer have banking specializations. For example, the many women found in the rather high-grade import/export field are where they are, not because they have received training specific to this job, but because they had gained competence in foreign languages prior to recruitment.

The union, it must be said, has contributed to this state of affairs. To retain job opportunities for its membership, particularly for a nexus of older, more experienced employees, it has espoused a strategy of reinforcing the internal labour market, dissuading the bank from external recruiting, and rationalizing job evaluation (Sakellis 1984), of which job-gendering is an unfortunate effect.

Nimble fingers, clever minds and smiling faces

New technology entered the National Bank of Greece in the shape of two systems, Electronic Data Processing (EDP) which arrived in the 1960s, and the 'on-line/real-time' computerized system introduced between 1975 and 1985. EDP involved a kind of mass production in the data field. It resulted in the creation of a specialized Organization Department whose jobs had little resemblance to those traditional in banking. Here was centralized the processing of information previously carried out in the back offices of the bank's many branches. The economy of scale thus achieved effected a considerable labour saving in the bank.

If EDP tended to fragment jobs, the on-line/real-time system that followed had a rather different effect. In linking the bank's 500 scattered branches by instantaneous transmission of information from the many counters in the network to the central data base, and vice versa, it tended to integrate labour processes, in both a spatial and temporal dimension (National Bank of Greece 1956–90).

These successive developments produced four important new jobs. They were those of keyboard operator in data entry; computer console operator; programmer/systems analyst; and teller. It is interesting to see how the gendering of these jobs changed over time as the technology progressed.

Keyboard operators in data entry

In the beginning, during the early 1960s, data entry was a job for women. This was a political context, in and outside the bank, that emphasized discipline and obedience to superiors. At first workers and their unions had little knowledge of the content and conditions of data entry work. Besides, women's subordinated position in society minimized the likelihood they would react against the bad conditions.

Later, computer technology began to take on an aura of prestige and seemed to promise an upgrading of the human tasks associated with it. The unit expanded fast and keyboard operators were particularly featured in bank recruitment schemes. By the beginning of the 1970s the work of the unit was demanding round-the-clock operation. Since night shifts were prohibited for women, the management was obliged to recruit some men to the unit. A supervisor said in interview:

> We recruited men, we watched them, we saw they weren't really falling behind. A man may be slower in the fingers, but he sits there in front of the machine and he *works*. Women think a lot about their responsibilities, their children. They have other preoccupations. Anyway, the men were a success. And now we have some men who are really good operators. But it's true that if you compare a good man with a good woman, she would be quicker than him. It's obvious from their scores.

So men came into the Data Entry Unit and could not immediately leave, since their terms of employment obliged them to stay for a certain period. Their complaints about working conditions won special compensatory benefits, including productivity bonuses and overtime rates. Keyboard operators were thenceforth granted the possibility of transfer to the mainline jobs in the bank branch network after a minimum stint of six years in data entry.

When the internal labour market of the bank was strengthened at the beginning of the 1980s, and competition for specific posts was replaced by a general competition, this job became a 'sink' for reserve list candidates. It was a device for filling what were unpopular posts. In effect the bank resorted to blackmail: candidates on the reserve list could choose between settling for data entry or postponing their recruitment to the bank. Fifty per cent of the recruits were men. The demand for benefits to compensate the unfavourable working conditions increased accordingly. The obligatory period in the job was reduced to four years and opportunities for well-paid overtime increased. It was men these changes appealed to, for they were the ones in a position to make use of them.

Eventually, however, as the health hazard in the job was recognized, working hours were reduced and the money advantage was eroded. The new shorter hours, in two shifts, appealed to women and served to make the job more 'female', with the result that 70 per cent of keyboard operators today are women. Although recruitment is sex-equal, the men use the assimilation possibilities and enter the main bank grades. Few women are willing to risk transfer into the branch network and, if they do not succumb to health problems, instead 'choose' to stay in data entry, hoping eventually for a supervisory position. Their chances are slight: there is only one supervisor to 35 or 40 operators.

What is noteworthy here is that the female character of the data entry job is constructed *inside* the NBG. Unlike other Greek banks its recruitment to the job is sex-balanced. It is the organization of work, the job content and the working conditions that tailor data entry to women's daily lives. Women are the ones obliged to trade enjoyable work at a less intense pace, normal hours and a promotion scheme for the possibility data entry offers them of coping with those other demands on their energies – childcare and housework.

Computer console operators

Computer console operators were from the start men, first because a 24-hour shift system had been necessary in all phases of the technological development, and second because the job was already heavily gendered in the external labour market. Through socialization, education and training schemes, men were more familiar with technology of all kinds. Besides, the huge size of the old mainframe computers contributed to the masculinity of the job. The 'machine room' as a result was and remains the men's place, where they feel free to swear and 'use language' just as they wish, and to pin up pictures of naked women over their control panels. 'It's no place for women. The work's tough. It makes you swear at times. How could women afford to work in the machine room?' said one of the younger computer operators.

One feature of the job associating it with masculinity is the high social and professional status it enjoys, due to the control it affords over the bank's expensive technological equipment. This status bestows a crucial bargaining advantage on operators. The job is defined as both 'skilled' and unhealthy, and elicits extra pay on both scores.

Computer operation therefore continues to be a male job despite reduced career opportunities and degradation of job content caused by recent developments in technology. The operators strive to defend their status – by, among other things, keeping women out. An important tactic has been to create a work environment closer to that of the army than a bank. 'We must be soldiers ready to do battle', they said.

Programmers and systems analysts

These too are predominantly men. Women's participation in these computer science jobs in the bank is little over a quarter (26.5 per cent). None the less, it is higher than that in the wider labour market – only 14 per cent of the membership of the Greek Association of Computer Specialists is female.

Programmers and systems analysts have high status in the social and professional hierarchy of the bank, similar to that of mechanical engineers in an automated production plant. Control of new technology is the strongest bargaining counter a group of professionals can have. Satisfying the bank's crucial need for software for its computers and solving its EDP problems are therefore held to be masculine jobs.

The selection process whereby candidates were chosen for computer training already imposed certain male-biased criteria. Programmers for instance had to be available to work on stand-by, to come in at short notice any time of the day or night. Systems analysts had to be prepared to work far from home. Between 1975 and 1985, as the on-line/real-time system was installed in the bank's many outlying branches, most systems analysts were moving from branch to branch for a month at a time. Only the few women with what was thought of as a 'masculine' brain, with high-level scientific training and no family responsibilities could possibly qualify. Around 1985, however, as developments progressively integrated many of the tasks of programmers and systems analysts into the hardware and abolished any distinction between the two functions, they were merged into a new job category: programanalysts. This evolution dramatically reduced the career opportunities for programmers, who had to seek analytic skills in order to extend their professional scope. The new specialism of programanalyst reflects a degradation of both component jobs. As a consequence more women succeeded in entering them.

Tellers

The National Bank of Greece was later than some smaller and more flexible banks in introducing the on-line/real-time system to a range of banking services. Only deposit accounts, in drachmas and foreign exchange, had been put on the system prior to 1992. Before the autumn of that year, when the bank began to install some automated teller machines (ATM), all transactions were made through human tellers.

Tellers are basic bank functionaries who, sitting at a computer terminal, provide clients with all banking services, such as money transfers to and from their accounts. The tellers' job integrates on computer a great deal of the work that used to be carried on manually in the back office of the branches, as well as much of the data entry work performed, in the first phase of the new technology, in the EDP unit. Despite the computer, the dependence on human tellers produced an accelerated rhythm of work for the staff and long queues at the counter for the client. There has been continual tension for all concerned as the tellers attempt to juggle customer demands with the constraints of the computer.

Until 1991 the teller's job was unpopular, so that bonuses and promotion possibilities had to be offered as inducements. At first, the job had masculine overtones due to its descent from a male job, that of cashier, and its association with computer technology. That it was seen this way is confirmed by the fact that bank managers described the existence of women tellers as an important achievement in sex equality.

There were, none the less, very practical reasons for choosing women, to which the managers also admitted. Women are ideal representatives of the bank at the front desk. They communicate better than men, behave more politely, smile a lot and look good. They also react less angrily than men to problems arising during transactions with customers. 'They are more competent than men, better negotiators, and more polite. That's why they are placed in key posts', said a personnel manager.

Women are therefore now preferred as tellers. They are the sex that copes best with the increased demands of the job, handling growing tension, stress and psychological pressure that might crack the self-control of men. The proportion of women tellers is now 41.5 per cent, and will increase yet further when a law of 1991 becomes effective that will break the time-honoured resistance of the union to part-time working in the bank. In the circumstances, however, if women come to predominate in telling it will scarcely be a sign of sex equality.

Women have their own reasons for accepting these jobs. A young woman teller said:

> It's an individual job. You have nobody over your head. You're completely autonomous. You deal only with your terminal. Not even the chief teller can intervene in your work. You know the margins of your responsibilities – they're all set within the computer.

This is a very important aspect of work organization transformed by the computer: the control of the labour process is now system-integrated. It enables workers to avoid other, more subjective, means of control over their performance. Women have more difficulty than men in resisting pressure by (male) managers in face-to-face confrontation.

It is understandable that a computer-integration of control seems a gain for women in a situation where the worker has been subjected to less rational, and highly personified, control through seniority (experience and age) and patriarchal relations. Besides, the job, being repetitive and of a service character, and offering no opportunities for overtime and career advancement, is unattractive to men. All these things confirm it as 'female' in the gendered division of labour in the bank.

Gender in the trade union: politics of the ostrich

The gendering of the new jobs created by the application of on-line/real-time technology in the bank was neither discussed nor questioned by the union. It showed serious interest in the consequences of the advanced technology and the organizational changes involved only when the specialized 'male' jobs in computing – those of console operators, programmers and analysts – were threatened with degradation (Federation of Bank Employees' Organizations 1990).

Computerization, after all, undeniably disturbed the established internal labour market, so precious to the union, in a number of ways. First, as we have seen, certain new jobs and specialisms were created, unrelated to traditional banking, such as keyboarding, console operation and program-analyst. Second, some traditional banking specialisms were abolished and more general integrated jobs created – such as that of teller. Third, the grade hierarchy was restructured due to a drastic reduction in middle level posts. Finally, and most importantly, the preconditions emerged for a new type of labour relations based on *flexibility* – for instance in working time, work contract, payment and social security.

The union's reaction to these changes however was spasmodic, and mainly a response to personnel unrest which reached a peak in strikes at the EDP centre in 1988. The issue here was the bank's intention to buy ready-made application packages, seen as threatening to those (mainly men) in the highly specialized computer-related jobs. The union did, in the face of this, draft a detailed proposal for a special 'collective agreement on technological modernization' (Federation of Bank Employees' Organizations, 1988) which attempted a global approach to the problem, but it never reached the negotiating table.

Those changes in work content signifying a deterioration in working conditions in 'female' jobs never preoccupied the union. The causes of inaction lie in the 'male' character of the union, in terms both of its sex composition and its manner of setting priorities. Women, though 37 per cent of union membership, are largely absent from its leadership. In 1988 there were only two women on the 25-member union board, and they were only there because they represented members in a totally 'female' job, that of cleaners. It was not until 1990 that women from the main banking staff joined the board.

As far as priorities are concerned, the union is primarily motivated to reinforce the internal labour market, a traditional strategy in support of the 'skilled family breadwinner'. Besides, the union leaders' discourse showed them to be less concerned with the everyday problems of bank employees than with party politics and matters of political concern on the national stage. This alienated many workers – especially women – some of whom ceased to be actively involved in the union. Thus preoccupied, the union neglected demands for the improvement of working conditions and a more equitable distribution between the sexes of the gains and losses from new technology. Dissatisfaction with worsening conditions in the 'female' area of data entry, for instance, could only gain expression when men entered the job and secured the union's involvement.

In summary, then, the gendered division of labour in the bank, perpetuated and deepened in the process of its information technology revolution, cannot be laid at the door of management alone. It was facilitated by a male-dominated union that questioned neither the content nor the conditions of the new jobs.

The credit card: selling the new way to pay

We turn here from the production to the consumption of bank services. Bank loans have always been extremely difficult to obtain in Greece and used to be almost exclusively available to public sector employees whose tenured jobs and stable monthly income were credible guarantees for banks and consumer loan funds. Consumer borrowing, especially by low and middle income groups, was instead facilitated by various non-banking institutions.

In the 1960s a common source of household credit was buying on instalment. A small trader, usually male, would knock on the door offering goods for purchase by instalment. The door would more often than not be opened by a housewife whose husband was out at work. The aim of the trader was to prise out some of the small financial resources available to the housewife. What attracted her was the opportunity of acquiring something she wanted quickly for a small down-payment. And, by deft management of her housekeeping allowance from his weekly wage, to do so 'without the husband knowing'. This transaction had no written guarantee on either side. It was a bona fide agreement involving a simple signature and the trader's personal assessment of the client's credibility, based on her husband's job and the appearance of her home.

Electrical retailers also offered their appliances on an instalment plan. In this case the arrangements were more formal and the guarantee more secure, since the agreement had to be signed by the head of household, usually a man. Such agreements were officially recognized and could, when national credit policy permitted, be used as security by the dealer to obtain a bank loan. In this way banks had a limited and indirect role in consumer credit, though for the most part, like household activity itself, it was effected outside the official economy.

In the 1970s and 1980s with the steady increase in both women's employment and service industries, the number of salary earners in low and middle income groups also grew. In conjunction with other developments in the Greek economy, this resulted in important changes in the type and forms of consumption. First, there was a growth in the supply of consumer goods, leading in turn to increased consumption, whether measured in quantities of goods purchased or volume of expenditure. Second, distribution became more concentrated in large outlets such as department stores, supermarkets and hypermarkets. Third, households' financial liquidity fell.

All these things prompted the appearance of the first credit cards. They were not accepted by households straightaway, nor did they receive the immediate support of the banks. Not until the late 1980s did their use take off. From that moment however the number of cards in use increased by 25 per cent per annum and purchases per holder by 20 per cent. Even today however the use of credit cards remains extremely low in Greece compared with the other European countries. As late as 1991 only 10 per cent of consumer purchases were handled through credit cards.

In 1992, there were 16 different credit cards in circulation. Most are issued by banks; a few, such as the Diners' card, are independent. Different cards serve different income bands. For high income groups most cards have a 'gold' option, affording practically unlimited credit, and for those with dollar accounts there is of course American Express. Middle income groups are served mainly by international cards such as Visa, Eurocard, Mastercard and Diners. These are popular with businessmen in small and medium-size firms and with professionals. One of their attractions is enabling travellers abroad to obtain more foreign exchange despite official restrictions.

Low income groups are served by the Greek cards, such as 'Ethnokarta' (the card of the National Bank of Greece) and 'Emporokarta'. These indigenous cards share more than half the credit card market: Ethnokarta with 40 per cent, Emporokarta with 23 per cent. They are the choice of salary earners who want a card mainly to facilitate an extension to all consumer goods of the credit available on purchase of consumer durables. They are also popular in the family as extending credit for household consumption. Payment by instalment is particularly attractive to households suffering from the price inflation and earnings stagnation characterizing the Greek economy in recent years. Credit cards defer the unpleasant consequences of declining purchasing power and cushion the standard of living, thus relieving the social tensions produced by economic crisis.

Despite the use of credit cards the instalment trader has not disappeared. The pattern of selling has changed however. In addition to door-to-door touting, the instalment trader seeks out his (female) customers at their workplace, and his household wares have been superseded by clothing, jewellery, books and ornaments.

The Ethnokarta

In 1971 the NBG created an affiliate company, National Management and Organization (NMO) to organize and administer lending to private individuals and to develop payment systems and credit card facilities. The company was at first limited to the supply of consumer loans and developed only slowly. It first issued Ethnokarta in the 1970s. In the first decade the number of card holders grew from zero to 60,000. In the second, however, growth accelerated so that by 1992 there were 450,000 cards in circulation. In the late 1980s NMO also issued two international cards in restricted numbers: Mastercard with 40,000 holders and Eurocard with 8,000.

Ethnokarta's growth reflects in part householders' responses to restrictions placed on their liquidity by government austerity policies, which particularly curbed public sector wages. It was also however the result of active promotion. The National Bank stopped underwriting NMO, 'setting it free' in the increasingly cut-throat credit card market. NMO was obliged to seek new customers for Ethnokarta using modern marketing strategies. One has been its magazine *Ethnoshopping*, designed to compete with Ethnokarta's successful rivals Diners (*Signature Exclusive*) and Visa (*CitiVISA*).

Gendered messages to gendered users

The marketing of credit cards and their related services, which involves the shaping of consumers and consumption patterns, relies on such magazines. They were interesting to us for the way their text and images construct a gendered user. The magazines are periodicals, made up mainly of advertising and are mailed free of charge to card holders. They aim to persuade readers of the necessity of certain consumer goods which can easily be acquired with their credit card. Certain traits are implicitly attributed to card holders and potential users, including their intuited interests, lifestyles and personal needs. The users portrayed fall schematically into two groups, identifiable by choice of topic.

First, there are the middle income holders of international cards who demand quality and speed of service and who pay at the moment of the card's use (rather than settling their debt at month end). These are mostly business people, higher company personnel and professionals. Such users are seen in the main as being men. Diners for instance publish a supplement entitled *Businessman*. These publications addressed to men contain 'serious' articles on economic and scientific developments, and news from the stock market and business world. They clearly envisage a reader with a high standard of living, whose personal interest derives from his job.

Advertisements feature travel, business gifts, expensive hobbies and clothes. Special offers refer not only to price reductions but also to services such as time-saving by telephone or postal ordering. Offers by credit companies themselves mainly comprise gifts for 'good' customers, that is those who have increased the level of their transactions or recruited their friends.

Second, there are lower income Greek credit card holders who expect little from their cards beyond the facility of deferred payments. In the marketing magazines addressed to them they are represented as, in the main, salaried earners of both sexes with 'ordinary' interests. Such publications contain little but advertising, the small amount of written text relating directly to advertised goods. Examples might be an article on ozone-layer depletion in the context of ads for sunglasses and suntan lotions, or a travel piece amidst travel agency ads.

Most advertisements in this second group of magazines concern products and services consumed in the household or by the family: clothes for men, women and children; family holidays; domestic equipment; household ornaments. Special offers in this context are mainly money savers through price reductions or better credit terms. In *Ethnoshopping* in 1992, all companies and stores were offering three to six months' credit from the day of purchase. Such offers responded to intensifying economic crisis, falling turnover of retail stores and the shrinking of household incomes among this group.

Plastic money: gendered payment practices

The Ethnokarta users we interviewed were seven married couples in which one or both partners worked at the National Bank of Greece. They had varied feelings about the card's utility. In the case of two couples in which the wife was a full-time housewife, we found both partners were positive. Both considered the main incentive for acquiring an Ethnokarta to be its use as a tool offering 'security and facilities in the face of unforeseen needs', but not as a means of spending more than permitted by the household's monthly income.

In the five households where women were in paid work in the NBG, however, there were differences between the sexes. Women considered the card a means of satisfying consumer needs. 'I thought I could buy the whole world and pay in instalments' said one salaried woman. Men expressed more negative feelings about the card. One said, 'It's not a good bargain, it has high subscription fees and high interest rates.' And another said, 'You pay the instalment and you're left with less cash from your salary.' Several men attributed their decision to subscribe to the card somewhat obscurely to 'changes in their family situation' and being unable to buy for cash on the nail all the things their families might need.

As to the two housewives we interviewed, the decision had been made for them by their husband, alert to the possibility of checking expenditure on the monthly statement. By contrast, in the case of the five employed women, the decision to acquire the card was made by them alone, on strictly personal grounds related to the satisfaction of their needs and escape from their husbands' financial control. One woman said, 'I wanted things I couldn't afford till then, because I didn't have an income.' Another said, 'During the first months of my marriage we put our money in together, and I had to report everything I wanted to buy. I was used to moving freely, and suddenly someone was trying to put me on a leash.'

The type of consumer goods women and men reported buying was in line with the above answers. Men used the card infrequently but regularly – for example to kit out with clothes at the beginning of a season, or to buy presents at Christmas or Easter – and when an unforeseen need arose, such as a car repair. Housewives for their part bought clothing for themselves and the children; seasonal goods like school items; and of course presents. Salaried women more frequently reported using the card for personal items (clothes, cosmetics, jewellery) or items for house and children over which the husband, if asked, was likely to disagree. Few women of either group used the card at the supermarket.

The salaried women appeared to stop spending only when their credit limit was exhausted and when difficulty in paying the instalments was first encountered. Neither women nor men checked the way their interest was calculated in relation to debit and credit balances. They scanned their statements superficially and for rather different reasons. Men and housewives checked the balance because, for peace of mind, they had to maintain a small and relatively stable level of annual expenditure within budgeted constraints. Salaried women looked at the statement not to check the calculation of charges but to see whether they would be in difficulty over paying the instalments. Their expenditure often hit the upper credit limit and exceeded their budget, causing them anxiety and distress. Often, they said, they would try to restrain themselves or devise tricks to reduce the instalments. They might make a distinction whereby family expenses were paid out of cash, while personal overconsumption drew on the credit card. Or, in an extremity, they might buy everything on the card and subsequently use their cash to pay the monthly interest.

Even the more prudent among the men we interviewed maintained that the card was 'a great temptation', to which women succumbed more easily. Women admitted this too. Housewives did so less readily – 'I'm not extravagant, but if I like something I'll buy it.' Salaried wives concurred however: 'when I have it with me, I always get carried away', 'anything that doesn't require cash is tempting'. Some salaried women represented extreme cases in which the card was used uncontrollably, with destructive consequences. One of these reported:

> With the card I got a lot of the things I wanted, but didn't enjoy them. I get anxious, I feel insecure, I'm afraid in case my husband finds out the level of my debt. Yeah, he'll divorce me. I don't care. But he'll take the children because he'll prove to the court that I'm unable to manage money. I'm afraid I may die and my debts will burden my children. I'm afraid that as soon as I put everything in order, I'll collapse. I'm afraid every lunchtime when I go home that I'll find a summons at my doorstep, and they'll take me to prison.

Money management in the household: a gender power game

In the four couples in which neither spouse held a socially prestigious position, and neither were interested in their careers, the household's money management seemed to be a prime field for the exercise of power in the relationship. Each of the partners tried to dominate the other, each to delimit the other's area of control, responsibility and autonomy. These attempts ranged from simple negotiation to outright rupture.

In these households, men did not trust women to have sole charge of money management, notwithstanding the fact that the household is that realm of the 'private sphere' universally held to be women's responsibility. The less power a man had in the public sphere, traditionally male, the more importance we found he ascribed to the power of decision over household finances. Perhaps he derived therefrom some compensatory status and reassurance.

If men were bidding for more power, however, women were bidding for greater autonomy. The five employed women with their own income did not want to concede financial management to men. The resulting strife, the inability to find an agreed equilibrium, sometimes led to the setting up of two 'money boxes'. Most commonly, such couples would pay individually for their personal expenditure, but share agreed common expenses: rent, electricity, phone, food, car, expenditure on children and expensive consumer durables. However, expenses of this kind that the husband might consider unnecessary – gifts, ornaments, things for the children – often, in the event, came out of the women's budget. 'He checks the expenditure and if he doesn't think a thing's necessary, he doesn't share', said one woman in interview. Some men cultivated this approach: 'He's a miser, especially about his own needs. He won't go and buy something he needs, but always waits until I buy it for him and I end up getting it on my card.'

What women seemed to want out of this arrangement was to safeguard an exclusively personal space, free from male control. Money constituted the most easily established area for such autonomy, an area in which their contribution, underwritten by their own monthly pay cheque, could not be questioned, an area in which they could be fully confident of the legitimacy of their demand.

Housewives, however, differed. They did not have sufficient power to contend for autonomy. The common money box was controlled, directly or indirectly, by the man, sometimes by issuing money in small sums as needed. 'He doesn't check on me' said one such housewife. But she added 'I simply tell him I bought such and such, and explain why.'

The credit card: safety valve or vehicle of deviance?

Men tended to be prudent in their use of the credit card, not easily carried away. This gave them the upper hand, morally speaking, in attempting to reimpose the masculine authority threatened by their partner's participation in the household's money management. Men felt displeased and worried when they observed that through their use of the card, women gained more control over money, and money controlled women more. It seemed that men would have preferred to maintain control, albeit more discreetly than their fathers, over both wife and money. To do so would remove a source of many family conflicts. In addition, some men considered all women liable to financial excess. 'I believe women get carried away more by the cards' we heard repeatedly. We sensed a male fear of the mythic woman, imperilled by her natural drives, bringing catastrophe in her wake. It kept men alert, ready to intervene, gently or drastically, should their wife commit the crime of overconsumption. One man told us, 'I urge her to burn it. She works overtime to pay for it. So it's no good.' And another said, 'in the beginning she got carried away, and I told her, you either stop it or . . .!'

For employed women, spending on credit seemed to function as a painless release from pressures at work and stresses at home. Shopping could salve disappointments. There was something to show for it too: 'you look at yourself in the mirror in your new fashionable clothes, and your self-esteem grows', a woman said. Although real material needs were met through the credit card, these women seemed rather to get their satisfaction from using it to cultivate an illusion of freedom and self-sufficiency. One might expect the cards to serve mainly for the purchase of expensive consumer durables, for which it is hard to find cash on a limited monthly income. It seemed, however, that the women spent to discharge the tensions generated in family life and to build their self-respect. Such a psychological hunger could not be sated once and for all. It had to be fed repeatedly. This was why their spending was mostly directed to non-durables, things to adorn self, and the home – which is of course another space for female self-affirmation.

Some women seemed to feel they 'stole' the autonomy the card gave them, rather than earned it. They lied to their husbands about the amount of their debt or what they had bought, then wondered at their own behaviour. One said, 'Sometimes it crosses my mind, that if someone watched the type of my transactions, or the frequency or amount, they'd laugh and say, "Look what she's buying!"'

The temporary palliative for daily misery was obtained at a high price – anxious dread of the monthly statement. 'When I spend too much, I may avoid telling him, not because I'm scared but because I feel bad. For instance, when I have no money and I buy dress materials worth a hundred thousand drachmas,' a woman said.

Because the use of credit cards is relational within the marriage, in a partnership in which the woman feels dissatisfied it can stir up disturbing depths. Some women's spending it seems is manic, continuing even when they know they cannot meet the payments. It is a self-destructive phenomenon, comparable to compulsive eating, at its most intense when a woman's self-respect is lowest and she is least able to communicate. Consumer goods become a substitute for emotional fulfilment, trapping women in a vicious circle: spending solves one problem but creates another.

Money and technology as power: control of women

This chapter has described the transformation of bank jobs, the marketing of credit cards, and personal payment practices, in order to provide material for analysing the way the new money technology contributes to the shaping of gender relations, both in the workplace and at home. What it has shown in particular is how the gender relations so created and recreated are relations of *power*, involving control or attempts to control, women. We can draw from the analysis certain pointers.

In the bank, women entered the period of technological transformation in a disadvantaged position and they ended it in new jobs in which their struggle to fit the work to the needs and constraints of their lives, and in new (equally gendered) structures of control, which combined to hold them in a continuing subordination. The women tellers, for instance, were now subject to computer-integrated control. But their gender positioning rendered them more ready than men to submit to this: it seemed an improvement on the direct control of (mainly male) supervisors and managers whose legitimacy lay in experience, age or patriarchal authority.

To turn to the home life of bank employees, we have seen how plastic money reorganized consumption patterns in the family and the partners' payment practices. The control of the men of the family over their wives, particularly when those wives had an independent income and their own credit card, was threatened and we saw their attempts to reimpose it.

Women's bid for autonomy, however, had been only partly successful – and had in any case been at the cost of a new source of anxiety and stress. Some of the control the husband had exerted over them was now transferred to the bank's credit management system – governed by another set of men. Women it seems felt this to be a step for the better. Like the tellers, they were more willing to accept this impersonal, invisible and objective control (in this case over their consumption) than the highly personified, visible and present control on the part of their husbands, and the daily conflict it generated.

Thus, the use of plastic money created a new field of struggle within the couple in pursuit of satisfaction, power and rights. Male control of women was not reduced in these processes – it simply came to be exercised through different men. In addition, its form shifted from prevention to repression. For one facet of the control lost by husbands their wives seemed to have interiorized, in the form of the wagging finger of self-admonishment.

The study has shown how women and men have a very different relation to technology. Technology had long been a male concern, and men have used their control of it as a medium of social supremacy over other men, and over women. New money technology challenged the control of some men, too, however. It shook it in the workplace, *vis-à-vis* the employer; and it shook it in the home, *vis-à-vis* their wives, who now deferred instead to the bank as creditor.

Money is a source of power. In market economies, power uses money as a medium of transfer and transmission. Money circulates from women to men, from companies to households, from employers to employees and back again, vested at each step with a modicum of power. The expansion of white-collar employment, the growth of commercialized services and the increase in consumer goods, have all boosted the significance of money. They have simultaneously subordinated both sexes to the individuals (mainly men) and organizations (mainly banks) who exercise power through control of the circulation of money.

Technology too, as we have seen, is a medium of power. Through the new technology applied to the reorganization of labour processes and payment practices, women and men have become yet further entrenched in gender inequality. Because of already existing gender difference, it confronted them with opportunities and constraints, in the face of which they performed differently, expressed different needs, satisfied different wants and realized different options. Women and men conceived, designed, applied and used the technology in different ways, and the ways changed along with the change in gender relations.

In the new money technology of the banking system the two media of power are powerfully interrelated. In this study we have used these changes in money technology to dramatize gender relations. In the enactment we have seen just how damaging to women – and in a different way to men – are the power relations gender involves. They have painful expression in a structured organization like the bank. They take an even more hurtful form in the highly intimate space of marriage.

References

Federation of Bank Employees' Organizations (1988) *Trapezitiki*, Monthly Journal, Issue No. 504.

Federation of Bank Employees' Organizations (1990) *19th Congress* (in Greek). Athens.

Hellenic Banks' Association (1987) *Report of the Commission for the Reform and Modernization of the Banking System* (in Greek). Athens.

National Bank of Greece (1956–90) *Annual Report of the Board of Directors*. Athens.

Sakellis, Yannis (1984) *Internal Labour Markets: The Case of the Greek Banking System* (in Greek). Doctoral thesis, Panteios School of Political Sciences, Athens.

Stratigaki, Maria (1992) *Technological Modernization and Gender Division of Labour in the Banking Sector: The Case of the National Bank of Greece* (in Greek). Doctoral thesis, University of Thessaloniki.

Zavvos, Georgios (1989) *Banking Policy in the Face of 1992* (in Greek). Athens: Hellenic Banks' Association.

4

Women users in the design process of a food robot: Innovation in a French domestic appliance company

DANIELLE CHABAUD-RYCHTER

The French contribution to this cross-national project is a sociological study of the trajectory followed by a kitchen appliance, from its genesis as a product idea formulated by an engineer or marketing executive, to its transformation, by use, into an instrument of domestic labour. The appliance is an electric food processor, with the basic functions of grating, mincing and chopping food. Depending on the model, it will also knead dough, make mayonnaise, beat egg whites, mix soup or squeeze citrus fruits. It may come combined with a blender. Because of its versatility this type of appliance is often tagged 'food robot'.

I set up a research project[1] with the overall intention of following the processes of design, production, distribution and use of a new line of processors. The research is, at the time of writing, still in progress and only the innovation phase is discussed here. The aim is eventually to be able to show how the form and meaning of the technical object are negotiated all along its trajectory by the different social actors participating in its progression from conception to usage. The choice of a household appliance makes it possible, by following the transfer of the object from the productive to the domestic sphere, to study how the process of construction of the object is inscribed in social organizations, relationships and stategies of different natures (Chabaud-Rychter et al. 1985; Chabaud-Rychter 1992).

My study is being conducted in a French company that produces and markets small household appliances. The company comprises several industrial plants, each specializing in the production of certain appliances, and a central structure which includes the commercial and marketing departments. The field work, which aims at 'following the actors' (Latour 1989; Boltanski 1990) in the course of their activities and interactions, combines several methods: direct observation, analysis of sequences of verbal and non-verbal exchanges during meetings, analysis of objects (prototypes), study of documents (from the corpus of the marketing studies on food processors, to the working documents of the personnel concerned), and unstructured and semi-structured interviews.

The process of innovation, the phase discussed in this paper, involves an ongoing negotiation of the form of the product under development, linking together a composite set of elements stemming from different domains, logics and coherences: the needs and practices of consumers, the market and competition, productive investments and cost price, technical options, design, etc. But this linkage is far from evident. Indeed, the actors in the negotiation process have heterogeneous activities, which give rise to equally heterogeneous experiences and conceptualizations. Each field has its experts: marketing, research and development (R&D) engineers and technicians, quality control technicians, designers, managers, etc. I have thus been studying the modes of cooperation practised by these actors, the procedures and instruments they use to pool their different fields of work and skills, the controversies and the construction of successive agreements underlying the progressive transformation of the object. The terms designer, innovator, and design group, have been used here to designate the collective actor constituted by this common work of the individual actors.

In the firm, only a minute number of women work on the designing of new appliances.[2] Yet women are the users of these products. This raises two questions. First, there is the question of the designer–user relationship: What is the nature of this relationship? In what cases is it one of power? Does it have specific forms when it is between women and men? Second, there is the question of the prescribing of activities by artefacts, machines: What are the limits of this prescription? What is its specificity in the sphere of domestic work? The first question is dealt with here; the second must wait for future publication.

The relationship between designer and user can be seen as a dialogue:

> Machines carry the word of those who have invented, developed, perfected and produced them. They carry it with them, written in the hardware (this button has this function, these operations are impossible . . .); they carry it in the form of the more or less esoteric or ambiguous directions for use that accompany them, they carry it by imposing the use of certain standardized connections to existing equipment . . . As we can see, the machine is a spokesperson, no more or less precise, no more or less faithful than the others. It represents much more than itself alone. Like all spokespeople . . . it can be renegotiated, challenged, and sent back to its mandators.
>
> (Callon 1989: 18)

The main response of the user to the designer's word (the object) is use – in its numerous forms. By her or his way of using the object, the user submits to the prescriptions inscribed in it, or reinterprets, circumvents or transforms them; in this way, she or he replies to the designer. But the temporal structure of the dialogue between designer and user favours the former. It is the designer who takes the initiative, who has the first word, to which the user, at a later stage, reacts. It may be noted that for the designer's word to reach the user, the latter need only buy the object; the user's use-response, however, does not reach the designer directly. The machine cannot be spokesperson for the user – unless it has broken down and been sent back to the after-sales service of the company.

Getting the users to speak during the design process is essential for the company. No firm can afford to produce objects that will be refused by those for whom they were intended. The object needs to be sold, and the firm must thus make allies of potential buyers and users and transform them into real buyers and users. The production of an object thus entails an ongoing negotiation with the users that begins at the stage of conception and continues through to the after-sales service.

For there to be negotiation, however, there must be a party to negotiate with. Various 'technologies of representation' (Knorr-Cetina 1981) are thus employed to bring into the company, as it were, the population of women which the actors of the design process will then attempt to transform into users of the developing object. But they are very particular users: they are users who are relevant for the firm, that is, who are defined and constructed on the basis of characteristics selected for a dual purpose: to provide information on buying practices and uses of the machine (or similar machines) in order to answer the questions posed by the designers, and to draw out the elements that they can use, or bend through rhetorical or material arguments. The construction of women users thus grows out of a two-fold stategy that aims both at learning about them and at shaping them.

This chapter will discuss some of the different ways in which the actors in the design group bring women users to the innovation process: by constructing knowledge about them, by identifying with them, and by casting them as subjects of usability trials.

Marketing and the 'scientific' construction of women users

The marketing department is, within the design group, the expert that masters the overall knowledge of the market and of the practices and needs of women consumers. It analyses trends, makes recommendations, and writes up product profiles that it then transmits to the management of the company and of the manufacturing plant, and to the R&D departments. In its capacity as expert, the marketing department grounds its construction of women food processor users on data generated in formalized procedures. These include statistical studies from various sources as well as the department's own studies. On the basis of this material produced by codified survey and data processing methods, Marketing provides the design process with what can be called the 'scientific' construction of women users.

This construction brings into play several approaches to users. The first is implemented through the analysis of the market, one of the permanent activities of the marketing department. A major tool used in this analysis comprises the surveys sold by market research agencies which monitor the sales of panels of distributors, product by product. These surveys are constantly updated and provide information on the size of the food processor market, the products that are selling well and their prices. In this statistical approach, it is not consumers or users who are being examined, but acts of purchase stripped of all other characteristics. Supply, by contrast, is detailed by brand, reference product, price and place of sale. This information, combined with an analysis of their products and advertising campaigns, is used to study competitors' activities and strategies, and make it possible, through an analysis of variations in sales volumes according to such factors as advertising, price, brand, product features and novelty, to define patterns in buying behaviours.

The study of existing products and how they are selling constitutes one of the essential elements used for the development of the firm's innovation strategies; that is, for determining whether it will position itself in the market through original products, or through the updating of its existing food processor lines by modifications in design or the introduction of new combinations of functions. The market analysis shows which competitor products are selling well (let us say processors combined with a blender) and the firm can then decide to enter the same market segment with a product that fulfils the same functions but has an added advantage (such as a larger capacity or a new security device). It also helps locate the 'empty spaces', such as types of products that have not yet appeared in certain marketplaces and that can be expected to sell.

If the company's current strategy is to diversify the range of products, a more detailed knowledge of the marketplace is required in order to identify target populations and needs. In this case the market is no longer analysed as an aggregation of acts of purchase. Instead the focus shifts to studying consumer characteristics. For the definition of target populations and needs, use is made of general (and statistical) knowledge of sociodemographic trends and practices. Thus, in the product profile of a multifunctional mini food processor, the trends to smaller households, the destructuring of meals and the professional activity of women (as a consequence of which they spend less time preparing meals), are all taken into account. Use is also made of knowledge acquired through repeated marketing studies: they know from these, for instance, that women want small machines that are easy to clean. Finally, specific studies are conducted to explore needs: there are those carried out in different countries to determine food preparation practices, while others will focus on women users of food processors to find out which functions they use and for what.

We are thus now beyond the generalities of the market, and it is here, in this analysis of consumer characteristics, that women enter the picture, as consumers and users of food processors, and it is they who become the focus of Marketing's research on needs. Specific though the studies may be, however, it is the characteristics that are common to the largest number of women possible that are being sought out: the aim is not to respond to individual needs, but to define market segments.

Once the process of innovation has been launched, further marketing studies punctuate its course. These may be concept studies, in which a group of women, representative of the target population, discuss a product idea. An example might be the combining in one product of functions currently performed by very different appliances. There may also be studies designed to test the aesthetics of the product by setting out a maquette among other machines for choice tests. Then there are the usability trials conducted at the different stages of production, from the first operational prototype to the first machines off the production line, the tests to compare the performance of the machine with competitor products, and finally, consumer satisfaction surveys conducted with women who have owned the machine for a certain time. The results of these various tests are taken into account in the construction of the appliance, and also serve to develop the graphics and documentation that accompany it (instructions for use, recipe booklets and packaging) as well as the sales arguments.

The marketing studies are generally purpose-made and very flexible. They most frequently seek to answer one or two specific questions that arise during the process of conception, production and distribution of a product. Even recurrent studies, like the consumer satisfaction surveys, conducted several months after the sale of a product, are not standardized, but focus on precise or critical aspects of the object.

Thus an entire armoury of formalized methods for collecting and processing data is deployed to capture the practices and opinions of women users, in order to find the answer to whatever question the company might pose. The knowledge of users generated by the studies is kaleidoscopic and essentially functional. However, it is also cumulative in that it becomes part of the experience of the marketing executives, as an integrated knowledge that is reactivated in situations in which their expertise is called upon.

Marketing's diffusion of its user construction

Marketing's role within the innovator group is to see that its knowledge about users and the marketplace is incorporated into the design of the product. Part of its work is thus to communicate this knowledge to the engineers and technicians. The launching of a new project, especially when at Marketing's initiative,[3] is a high point in this process. The main vehicle for passing on this knowledge is the text of the product profile and its verbal presentation to the design group at the meeting following its circulation. The knowledge is not transmitted in the form in which it was produced: market surveys are not directly passed on to the engineers and technicians. Rather, what is transmitted is the knowledge that is being used to dispose or deploy women users in such a way as to construct upon them a project of action which, by means of a product, will bring them to perform certain activities.

Thus, in the product profile of a compact food processor, the women users, or more broadly, the consumers, were considered in a succession of different states: target population, beneficiary, operator and owner.[4] Each state allowed Marketing to describe specific associations of consumer needs and services that the appliance should render. For instance, the state of *beneficiary* was expressed by two categories of needs: 'eating pleasures', and 'the culture (eating dishes which correspond to the traditions of the country)', which were accompanied by two lists of dishes that the machine should be designed to prepare. The state of *operator* was expressed by ergonomic needs, with a list of the related qualities of the machine (compact, easy to use, etc.), and productivity needs, which were accompanied by a description of its functions (beating, emulsifying, etc.) and the level of performance desired. The state of *owner* was associated with status-related needs to which the features expressing the modernity of the object should reply, and to economic needs that the price and life expectancy of the machine should satisfy.

In the product profile, then, the attributes of the object are configured, explained and justified on the basis of a knowledge of the market and consumers. The deployment of the various consumer states serves to guarantee that none of the properties demanded by the marketing department is gratuitous. The very general and synthetical nature of these states highlights, once more, the fact that what we are dealing with here is the construction of the contours of a market for a product. That is to say, of a large population which is of interest for the properties (such as needs) it holds in common.

In its verbal commentary on the product profile, Marketing's formulation of its knowledge about users and the market differs from that used in the written text. While the discourse has, in part, the same function as the product profile, that is, to explain and justify the attributes of the product and its range in terms of suitability and timeliness in the marketplace and services rendered to consumers, its form is that of everyday language and rhetorical procedures. Thus, the project of a mini food processor was backed up by a description of how inconvenient the present-size processors were for the user. The opposition between the uses of the two types of appliance was repeated several times in a descriptive mode, and often couched in terms full of imagery.

> You realize that . . . in fact, the only advantage of today's food processor, compared to what this line could be, is its power, that is the fact that you can make large quantities of food. So let's limit

ourselves to quantities for two or three people . . . and try to get to the stage that when you want to grate carrots it's not the whole big business it is with the food processor, so that we get down to something that would be a lot like what seems to me to be the simplest act in small kitchen appliances, like mixing soup. That is, you have a hand blender, you mix your food, you take it out, rinse it, wash it, and it's all done, whereas with the food processor you end up with several cubic feet of washing up.

(Marketing executive speaking to the Head of Research)

This extract reveals another recurrent rhetorical procedure, the comparison between the projected object and existing products that are familiar to all those attending the meeting. These two modalities of comparing uses – by opposition and by seeking out references – enable Marketing better to outline and explain the project by placing it on familiar ground.

Other features differentiate the verbal commentary from the written text of the profile. For instance, the consumer was not split up into a succession of different states as described above, but was regarded as a unity. This was partly because the mode of presentation of the written profile was an innovation of the marketing department and not yet part of the common culture of the design group. It was also, it seems, because such formalization was not compatible with the mode of the verbal commentary which tends, on the contrary, to set Marketing's analysis of uses and users within the realm of common sense.

The recourse to everyday language and its rhetorical forms appears as essential to the cooperation between the various actors of the design team whose functions and fields of expertise are, after all, different. Cooperation requires that each actor vulgarize her or his discourse for the others. Thus, in the group meetings, the engineers and technicians have to use the least scientific and technical terminology possible to present the state of progress of their work and the technical solutions they have found for the appliances to fulfil the functions required of them at a given cost.[5] Similarly, Marketing transmits the results of its analyses and studies but does not present the technical processing of the data.

The effects of this vulgarization are not symmetrical, however. Unlike the engineers and technicians, the marketing executives are confronted with the fact that the experiences of consumers of food (which has been chopped, sliced, etc.), of users of domestic appliances, and of observers of women users, are experiences shared by all and used by each in the construction of his representations of consumers and users. Marketing's field of expertise is thus in part, unlike that of the engineers, accessible to all. It is the object of common sense as well as of a formalized knowledge. Thus, part of the common culture of the innovator group is expressed as a series of clichés relating the stable characteristics of what women users 'ask' of a food processor: that it not be noisy, that it not take up too much space and that it be easy to store, easy to set up and to use, and easy to clean. All these demands fall within the realm of common sense, and are part of everyday experience, but they are regularly verified, validated and reconstructed by the marketing studies.

From identifying with the user, to relegating her to the background

The engineers, technicians, marketing men and designers all have recourse to their personal experience to construct representations of women users and the uses of food processors. They use their own experience as consumers of grated carrots, minced meat and soups to establish what women users expect – or should expect – from a food processor. They observe their wives and other women they know preparing food with and without food processors, and transform these concrete, individual observations into typical (Schutz 1987) characteristics of women users as a class. In their professional work, they handle food processors and their prototypes, simulate their use, and test their ergonomics. Their gestures in these situations and the impressions that they gain during these manipulations are also used in their construction of users. It is this last type of experience that I now want to analyse.

The food processors are, of course, subjected to a succession of trials and manipulations in the test and quality-control laboratories. In addition to these, the various protagonists of the design process handle, together, the prototypes and products during their meetings. The objects are examined and tested down to their finest detail. For example, a knob is tested for its movement, its prehension, the strength needed to turn it, the catches at its various positions, how it is set into the casing (must it be flush with the surface or protrude; fully or partially?), as well as the markings on it and the casing to indicate the positions of operation (stop, speed I, speed II, pulse). All the senses are brought into play: the aim is to feel and to experience, with their own hands, the surfaces and volumes, the efforts entailed and to listen to the noises. They also taste: the whole meeting goes off to the laboratory kitchen for usability trials. These group manipulations serve an essential function for the design group, that of constructing a shared experience of the object in gestation, on the basis of which the various protagonists will be able to reach agreement on its diverse aspects, down to the very tiniest detail, in order to make the decisions that will further the progress of the evolving object.[6]

What takes place during this handling of the machine from the point of view of the relationship between the designer and the users? The members of the innovator group are in the process of conceiving and designing an object and its usage. Conceiving usage does not mean prescribing it completely. Open uses can be conceived. In the constellation of actions constituting use, some will obey a univocal mode of operation prescribed by the object, whereas others will be freer. For instance, the safety device built into the food processor will impose a determined sequence of gestures since the bowl must be positioned and the lid locked in place before the machine can be started. On the other hand, the speed for, say, chopping cabbage, though there will be a recommended value, will ultimately be open to choice.

What the designers are looking for is to construct use – that is a more or less open series of actions to be performed by women users, which must also be efficient, comfortable and pleasant. In order to achieve this, and to get the object to communicate it to the user, they mimic, experience, test use. In short, the designers perform, themselves, the gestures involved in use; that is, they have recourse to their own bodies and to their own judgements of how well the object is adapted to its use. In doing this, each actor in the design process identifies with the woman user. He puts himself in her place (or does he put her in his place?) so that he can conceive for her, as it were, the reasonings and the gestures that she will have to perform in order to use the machine.

However, this identification of the designer with the woman user can only be effective for the process of conception if it is not total. It must remain constantly connected to the technical thought processes and activities of the invention and transformation of the object. One episode nicely illustrates the necessary limits of identification. During the tests performed by the quality-control laboratories on the finalized prototype of a processor, it was found that when the maximum amount of dough was kneaded, the motor gave the impression of 'labouring' at the end of the operation, even though the function had been fulfilled. Following these tests, the problem was discussed at a meeting in which the design group was to decide on the launching of production.

The impression of the motor 'labouring' was a matter of common experience: 'I think that everyone is an expert in this matter, you don't have to be an extraordinary expert to see whether something is labouring. Everybody is an expert on that', one of the quality-control technicians said. But no one knew how to translate this impression into parameters and measures, that is, into a technical problem. Moreover, for various reasons, including the price, there was no possibility of putting in a more powerful motor, which would have solved the problem. Consequently, the only option was to act on the parameters of the impression itself. The members of the design group attempted to analyse the factors contributing to the impression that the motor was labouring: was it the (auditory) difference perceived between the noise made by the motor at the beginning and the end of the operation, or was it the (visual) difference perceived between the speed at which the kneading accessory rotated? The analysis remained introspective, and what the designers could say about the impression of a labouring motor always made reference to their subjectivity and not to an outside, organized system of reference. Since the problem could not be formulated in technical terms, the analysis could not be pursued by a search for technical solutions. The professional 'testers' found themselves, here, in the same relationship to the object as the users, that of the subjective perception of a defect which they were unable to objectivize. The (forced) identification with the user constituted, in this case, an impasse for the designer.

Another episode that occurred at one of the meetings serves to illustrate a process of partial identification of the designer with the user. Under discussion was a project for a food processor and its safety system. The design included a vertical rod, running down the side of the bowl under the shaft of the handle, which would be pushed down when the lid was locked on and so press on a switch inside the casing. This contact would allow the machine to be started by the speed selector knob. The problem was that the selector knob could be left at the 'on' position, and the motor stopped by unlocking the lid, and then started again by simply fastening the lid back into place. The designers clearly felt that this contradicted the message communicated to the user by the control knob, and were uncomfortable with this potential short cut in the prescribed sequence of gestures. Thus, the discussion turned to finding a device that would oblige the user to turn the speed selector back to stop. At some point, the suggestion was made to weld a plate to the speed selector so as to prevent the vertical rod in the bowl from lifting if the knob had not been turned back to zero. It is this suggestion that is being discussed in the following extract.

> *Speaker 1* (Development Engineer): We can't add in an independent rod system because there's always the risk that it would get stuck and that's where the real safety risk lies. But, since we are, as you say, on the speed selector, that's where it would work. Because there, either the product [the bowl with the blade] can't be put on, because the knob is stuck, or it can't be stopped, but in either case, there's no risk to the user. There's no defect that isn't visual.
>
> *Speaker 2* (Marketing): Oh yes – OK.
>
> *Speaker 1*: We'll take a look into that.
>
> *Speaker 3* (Plant Manager): When the inside rod is up, then, that means that the bowl isn't there, and so it mustn't be possible to turn the knob. And, inversely, when the rod is down, there . . .
>
> *Speaker 4* (Head of Industrialization): The rod will have to have a notch.
>
> *Speaker 2* (to speaker 3): Yes, you mustn't be able to take it off unless the knob is at zero.
>
> *Speaker 3*: The rod is down, I start the thing, it runs, fine. I stop it, open the bowl, open the lid, and the rod comes up. And if the rod comes up the knob must also go back.
>
> *Speaker 1*: Oh yes, yes, that must be connected.

The progression of the discussion is interesting from the point of view of the identification with the user. Speaker 1 used the indeterminate passive voice, and referred to the user in an equally indeterminate way, not including himself in the category. Speaker 3, who was trying to imagine the mechanism, repeated this mode of expression in which the user was not determined, and not named. Speaker 2 then used 'you', personally involving Speaker 3. Who took this up and used 'I': this time he was the user and this helped him to imagine the mechanism. However, this was only a partial identification: although putting himself in the user's place, Speaker 3 remained himself, a member of the innovator group, for what he was describing was the combination of the action of the user with the mechanism. However, real users do not have access to the inside of the machine: the casing of the marketed appliance is closed with a particular kind of screw for which screwdrivers are not commercially available.[7]

The identification with the woman user is essentially ambiguous. On the one hand, it cannot be dissociated from the technical activity of conception, or it becomes an impasse. And on the other, the designers' use of their own bodies (their gestures, sensations, judgements) in the position of user to work on the object–woman user relationship tends to transform this into an object–designer relationship. This is clearly visible at the times when the connection between mastery of the craft and creativity is particularly efficient, the times during the design process when the product is being invented 'for the pleasure of it'. At these moments, when the actors handle and operate the prototypes, one could say they are doing it for themselves. The user disappears, and all goes on within the relationship of the designer to the object. Practically all the engineers and technicians interviewed used the word 'baby' to designate the object during its design phase. They also spoke of 'gestation' and the 'baby that's coming along nicely'. What is felt when manipulating the prototypes is thus also how the baby, their own creation, is coming along. And in this intimate relationship between the designer and his product there is no place left for the user.[8]

The usability trials and the 'otherness' of the woman user

One would think that the usability trials, where the object–user relationship is central, would constitute the privileged means to gaining knowledge about the behaviour of women users in the activity that most directly concerns the designer. The main focus of these trials is to see whether the appliance fully performs the functions for which it has been designed, according to the stipulations provided, first, in the product profile, and later in the schedule of specifications, concerning the quantities of food to be processed, the duration of operation, and the quality of the results. These trials use real food and real recipes (such as cake mixtures). The functional tests involve both evaluating the results (the state of the processed food) and the performance (the behaviour of the object and the user).

I followed the usability trials, conducted with prototypes of the same food processor, in three different laboratories. These were the R&D test laboratory, which works on the technical definition of the various components of the appliance; the quality-control laboratory of the manufacturing plant, which steps in when a finalized prototype is available for the test procedure that will identify any problems that must be solved before it passes to production; and the quality-control laboratory of the head office that also has a programme of pre-production tests.

The interest shown by these laboratories in the three aspects of the usability trials I have mentioned – the results, the behaviour of the object and the behaviour of the user – was variable. The test laboratory technicians repeated the functional tests until the machine parts on which they were working had been perfected. What was important for them were the results and the behaviour of the machine and each of its components during the performing of the functions. As for the behaviour of the user, they considered this to be more the sphere of the plant quality-control laboratory that conducts the 'client' tests. The two quality-control laboratories were more explicitly interested in the user, and their approach to the functional tests includes examining such matters as the setting up of the machine, the ease of the manipulations and whether the recipes are understandable. Here, particular attention was paid to the visible behaviour of the machine, that is, to what is perceptible to the user.

The usability trials have a dual function: they are used for the material designing of the food processor and must be translatable into technical language; and they are used to develop the adequacy of the object–user relation, and must thus provide information about the behaviour of 'real' users of the food processor.[9] This duality was illustrated in the practices of the laboratories. In the test laboratory, the results were measured whenever possible. For example, grated vegetable strands were examined under a microscope to see if the blade made clean or jagged cuts, and the diameter of the filaments was measured; soups were filtered through finer and finer sieves and the residues weighed. In contrast, the mincing of meat is not measurable; while there certainly are criteria for evaluation (the meat particles must be of the same calibre and neither too big nor in a mush), these still leave a wide freedom of judgement. In this case, the test technician would ask his laboratory colleagues (who had all worked on food processors) to evaluate the results. He appealed to their experience and competence to back up, reinforce, or possibly question his own judgement. The same approach was followed in the plant quality-control laboratory where, in addition, the tester had the machine circulate so that colleagues with a particular competence on specific points, such as safety or noise, might try it out and give their opinion. In the head office laboratory, the full test programme was carried out by one person each time, but all the other laboratory workers would also be given the appliance to test one or two of its functions. Thus, in the laboratory, when it is not possible to have recourse to actual measurements, human expertise is called upon in order to guarantee the reliability of the tests and their results.

When the purpose of usability trials is obtaining information on user behaviours a different approach is used. Instead of colleagues with the same level of competence it is novices who are chosen as subjects. For reasons of secrecy, it is considered undesirable to have the prototypes circulate outside the firm. Subjects sufficiently innocent to be able to play the role of real users are sought out in the workshops, offices, or even the laboratories. The role of the head office quality-control laboratory is particularly interesting in this respect. Its task is to test the appliances in the way women would use them in their kitchens. And, indeed, only women work in this laboratory. This is how the head of the department described their qualification for this task and the work they do:

It's the same people who rotate; they're here in the test lab for a month, and the rest of the time they're at inspection,[10] they check the products. So they're people who aren't always working on the same product, they haven't really formed the habits that someone who would be working for 10 years on pressure cookers would have. That allows us to get a different viewpoint on the product . . .

I give them the product and the instructions for use and they do what they would do if they'd just bought the product: they use it. They make their first comments before operating it: they handle it, open it, look to see what all the knobs and buttons are for, and they look at the instructions to see if they correspond; well, we don't always have the instructions when we're in pre-production . . .

They use it just like a housewife would. Up till now, they've been working alone, each one taking her turn with the product, and making her comments; but then we realized that when they were in a group, there were a lot more comments: there's one who says something, and that sets the other one's mind working differently. I think that now we're going to work like that, and we'll have something much more complete . . .

And once they've made all their remarks, and they've used it, we give it to someone who'll do the standardized tests; she'll measure the temperature, the speed, the effort it takes to turn the knob (that can happen) . . . If there's a breakdown, she'll try to figure out where the problem is, why that happened.

The laboratory, one might say, constructs the qualification of its workers as 'real users' by organizing their rotation and preventing them from getting used to one or another type of product, thus preserving their housewifely innocence. But at the same time, these women will, in the future, be asked to play this role in a group in order to stimulate their attention and their critical viewpoint: this will make their approach to the object more efficient, but will it not weaken their qualification as real users? The ambiguity of their position appears all the more clearly in the last part of the interview quoted, because one of them (and potentially each one) will have to carry out a test programme comprising technical measurements and diagnoses of the dysfunctioning of the machine, and thus switch from ordinary, practical use to experimental use with technical aims. There is clearly anxiety as to their qualification as real users, and in the same interview, my respondent pointed out that when the tests organized by Marketing with women from the general public bring back similar remarks to theirs:

It reassures everybody, because they can easily say to us as well: you've already worked on electric fryers and pressure-cookers, so you've been a bit conditioned by your work; and in fact, we don't always have the same behaviour as someone who buys a product she's never seen and doesn't know, that's true.

At the plant quality-control laboratory, the pre-production test programme includes a user trial. This is performed by five people (or more if necessary) who are asked to follow the instructions and recipe booklet to use two functions of the appliance. All their remarks on the ease of use, mounting and dismounting of the accessories, ease of cleaning, noise, clarity of instructions and other factors are written down. However, although very similar to that conducted in the head office quality control, this test is not performed by laboratory staff (mostly male). Instead, employees (mostly women) are called in from production, specifically from a department producing something other than the food processor line. The R&D test laboratory also occasionally organizes usability trials with production and office workers, mostly, it would seem, when quality control does not have the time to do these.

The innocence of the users is guaranteed by their position as outsiders to the laboratories. The laboratory staff organizing the tests have a quasi-ethnographic approach: the persons put in the position of woman user are observed attentively; everything they do and say is noted down to be presented later in a report. This ethnography, as any other, underscores the otherness of the observed population at the same time as contributing to its construction.

The gender of users

I have attempted here to analyse some examples of the different modes of representation of women users encountered during the process of innovation – the representations constructed as knowledge by Marketing through the use of formalized procedures; those embodied by the members of the innovator group when they identify with the women users; and those elaborated in the definition of 'real users' and their staging as subjects for observation in usability trials. These all bring into play the variable relationships the designer establishes with the women users, in which the gender of the latter is taken into consideration according to different modalities.

In its studies of the market, Marketing constructs the generality of women users by means of procedures of homogenization and aggregation. Women users are of interest for the characteristics that are common to a large number of them and which serve to define them as a possible market for this or that kind of food processor. Gender here has the status of one of a number of variables to be taken into account in the construction of the market.

In the second case, the process of identification with women users, partial though it may be, is based on the interchangeability of the (male) designer with the (female) user in the act of using the food processor and the perception of its attributes, by virtue of the fact that both belong to a common culture, in which the proliferation of technical objects is part of everyday life, and where the form of rationality implemented in their use is shared by all, women and men alike. This interchangeability is based, ultimately, on the reciprocity of perspectives in the everyday social world, by virtue of which each implicitly credits the others with a capacity for the practical apprehension of objects similar to her or his own (Schutz 1987). Gender is non-relevant here, the process of identification having as background the common social humanity of women and men, and not gender difference.

In the 'user' trials organized by the firm's laboratories or the marketing department, it is not a matter of interchangeability between designer and woman user, but, on the contrary, of the designer placing the user in a relationship of otherness. The gender of the users is an important component of this relationship. In the quest for 'real users', it is not only their quality as outsiders – to the laboratories, to the production of food processors, or to the company – that is desired as the guarantee of their innocence,[11] but also their specific quality as housewives confronted daily with food preparation and the instruments thereof. In other words, it is their gender as defined in the sexual division of labour that contributes to making them real users, and to positioning them as other in relation to the designer.

Notes

1 This research, entitled 'The social trajectory of a technical object: from its innovation in the household appliance industry to its use in the home', is funded by the Interdisciplinary Programme for Research on Technology, Work and Ways of Life (Programme Interdisciplinaire de Recherche sur la Technologie, le Travail et les Modes de Vie – PIRTTEM) of the French National Centre for Scientific Research (CNRS) and the French Ministry of Research and Technology.

  Given my undertaking to preserve the anonymity of the company where I conducted my research, as well as that of its employees, I cannot thank them here by name. I would however like to extend my thanks to all of them collectively for allowing me, the sociologist, into their midst to 'watch them working', in an attempt to understand the processes involved in the birthing of new products. Without their infinite patience, their cooperation and the many hours they spent with me, this research would never have seen the light of day.

  I would like to express my indebtedness to our international group. The warm, affectionate relationships we established and the pleasure derived from our meetings greatly contributed to the freedom and fruitfulness of our intellectual exchanges. My thanks to Ruza Fürst-Dilić for having set up the group and for all the work she put into keeping the project going from year to year despite the many personal and institutional difficulties generated by the geopolitical transformations in Eastern Europe and finally the war in former Yugoslavia. My thanks finally to Cynthia Cockburn for having facilitated and stimulated our group work with such warmth, energy and clarity of thought.

2 The women participating in the design process have one of two functions: either they test prototypes and products in the laboratories, or they are office workers – in financial management or doing secretarial work.

The R&D test laboratory is staffed by about ten men and, on occasion, one woman who is called upon to perform functional trials and revise the instructions for use and recipe booklets.

The plant quality-control laboratory employs four men and one woman. The head office quality-control laboratory is staffed exclusively by women (see section 'The usability trials and the "otherness" of the woman user').

The secretarial work in all the departments involved in the design process is, as can be expected, done by women. It is also women who, in Product Management, work on costing all the elements entering into the cost price of the appliance under development, using data supplied by the project manager.

The Plant Manager, Marketing executives, R&D engineers and technicians, and the designers (who are contracted from outside agencies) are all men.

3 While developing product ideas for the plant that manufactures the food processors is one of the functions of Marketing, this department does not always have the initiative for new products. Ideas and innovations also originate with the plant management and heads of the research and development departments. In such cases Marketing's role is to see that the products are adapted to users and uses.

4 We find here a reasoned deployment of some of the different user states that Dominique Boullier, Madeleine Akrich and colleagues (1989) have described, with an analysis of their poorly controlled proliferation, in other innovation processes.

5 The young technicians and engineers who have recently joined the company have difficulty in complying with this requirement, and either get involved in scientific demonstrations or long presentations of the results of their technical trials, or are not sufficiently explicit when they switch to everyday language.

6 I base this on a remark made by Laurent Thévenot at the seminar 'Objects in Action' ('Les objets dans l'action', Paris, 15 December 1992) on the 'group handling' of a baby buggy by technicians of a British standards laboratory and the (French) manufacturer, as a way of constructing a common perception and interpretation of the object, and a common past.

7 Steve Woolgar (1990) shows how the manufacturers of personal computers establish a boundary between themselves (the company) and the users, metaphorically represented by the case of the computer. The mere opening up (trangression) of the case, which means the user must break a seal, cancels the guarantee: the inside of the computer is the inside of the company, and users don't fiddle with parts of the company.

8 It was a comment made by Cynthia Cockburn on an earlier version of this text that drew my attention to these moments when the designers are not in the least interested in the women users.

9 See Steve Woolgar (1990) for an analysis of the search for 'real users' in the choice of subjects of the usability trials for personal computers.

10 This is the department that spot-inspects the finished products coming off the assembly line. These products do not include food processors, manufactured at another plant.

11 Although (for lack of anything better?) this can suffice: men are not excluded from the laboratories' usability trials.

References

Boltanski, Luc (1990) *L'Amour et la Justice comme Compétences* [*Love and Justice as Competence*]. Paris: Métailié.

Boullier, Dominique, Akrich, Madeleine, Le Goaziou, Véronique and Legrand, Marc (1989) *Genèse des Modes d'Emploi: la Mise en Scène de l'Utilisateur Final* [*The Genesis of Instructions for Use: The Staging of the End User*]. Cesson-Sévigné: Euristic Media.

Chabaud-Rychter, Danielle (1992) La famille comme acteur social [The family as social actor], *Cahiers du GEDISST*, no. 4, Paris: Impr. IRESCO.

Chabaud-Rychter, Danielle, Fougeyrollas-Schwebel, Dominique and Sonthonnax, Françoise (1985) *Espace et Temps du Travail Domestique* [*The Space and Time of Domestic Work*]. Paris: Méridiens-Klincksieck.

Callon, Michel (1989) Introduction, in Callon, M. (ed.) *La Science et ses Réseaux* [*Science and its Networks*]. Paris: La Découverte, Conseil de l'Europe and UNESCO.

Knorr-Cetina, Karen (1981) Introduction: The micro-sociological challenge of macro-sociology: toward a reconstruction of social theory and methodology, in Knorr-Cetina, K. and Cicourel, A. (eds) *Advances in Social Theory and Methodology: Toward an Integration of Micro and Macro Sociologies*. Boston, London and Henley: Routledge and Kegan Paul.

Latour, Bruno (1989) *La Science en Action* [*Science in Action*]. Paris: La Découverte.

Schutz, Alfred (1987) *Le Chercheur et le Quotidien* [*The Researcher and Everyday Life*]. Paris: Méridiens-Klincksieck.

Woolgar, Steve (1990) Configuring the user: the case of usability trials. Paper for the Discourse Analysis Workshop, University of Lancaster, 25–26 September.

5

Technological flexibility: Bringing gender into technology (or was it the other way round?)

ANNE-JORUNN BERG

Why gender and technology – again?

It took me a long time to get (what I thought was) a grip on what technology is. During the 1980s Scandinavian social studies of technology went through phases where different definitions of the concept 'technology' were heatedly debated and in turn rejected (Berg and Rasmussen 1983; Lie *et al.* 1988). Each new definition seemed to lack something. The solution for some of us – so far – has been to understand technology as *process*, a social *process* involving relations and negotiations where the tangible 'thing' or artefact can be analysed as a non-human actor in line with the human actors. Having for the moment resolved this, I returned to my main problem – understanding the integration of technology and gender – only to discover that I no longer knew what *gender* was. Frustrating, to put it mildly! The solution – so far – is of course to understand gender, too, as process.

The point where technology and gender meet as social constructs or integrated processes is something I have pondered on for some time. Unfortunately, writers in the flourishing field of 'new' social studies of technology have not been much concerned to develop a gender perspective. This does not necessarily mean however that it is an impossible thing to do inside the framework of 'constructivism' – albeit with certain provisos. Judy Wajcman (1991) is one of the few who has seriously tried to do it, and I happily agree with her when she argues:

> It is impossible to divorce the gender relations which are expressed in, and shape technologies from, the wider social structures that create and maintain them. (p. 25)

And I also think Wajcman makes a very important point when she continues:

> In developing a theory of the gendered character of technology, we are inevitably in danger of either adopting an essentialist position that sees technology as inherently patriarchal, or losing sight of the structure of gender relations through an overemphasis on the historical variability of the categories of 'women' and 'technology'. (p. 25)

This is the dilemma today. Gender is not simply one phenomenon that might or might not be added to a more 'general' theory of technology. It is rather that the sociology of technology is in need of a better understanding of the *relationship* between gender and the development of technology. In this chapter I will briefly present some of my thoughts on the meaning of technology in terms of gender, in connection with my research on the experimental introduction in Norway of Minitel, a teletext minicomputer associated with the telephone.

Towards an optimistic feminist sociology of technology

When I say 'feminist' rather than 'gender studies' or 'women's studies' of technology, this is because the term feminism includes a perspective of political change. Of course, feminists look at technology in many different ways. But when we (feminists) criticize technology, broadly speaking we do so with a focus on the possibilities for change in gender relations – or the ending of male dominance in and over technology (Cockburn 1983).

Feminists have certainly understood that technology can have effects for social relations. Failing to find many changes for the better, however, we have had a tendency to assume that it is for the worse. Feminist studies have been imbued with pessimism, partly arising from a deterministic view of technology, partly from our tendency to study impacts (Berg 1991). Technology has been regarded as a finished product, non-negotiable, and all that was left for us to study were the harmful social impacts of the new technology on women or gender relations.[1]

An important political insight from the constructivist studies of technology is an understanding of the way *human beings shape technology*. Feminism can use this insight to generate political strategies for change – one of the main contributions of a feminist sociology of technology.

The new social studies of technology are strongly critical of technological determinism. They do not however simply replace the pessimistic view of technological change with an optimistic account. Rather, their most important insight is that optimistic and pessimistic views of technology may *equally* be deterministic (Berg 1991). This is important for feminists to bear in mind. The constructivists' critique of determinism emphasizes human agency and creativity in relation to technology. These things have been lacking in many feminist studies of technology, as well as in mainstream technology studies prior to or outside the constructivist approach. It is not that impact studies are irrelevant – on the contrary, they have given us insight into important aspects of technology. By focusing on the shaping of technology, however, our scope is expanded. Space is opened up in particular for studies of how *gender relations* may play a role in the making of technologies.

Once technology is seen as a process instead of an already-made 'thing', the *user* of technology is no longer its passive recipient but can come into view as an important actor in its shaping. Intentions baked into technology may restrict the flexibility of a given artefact, but they cannot altogether determine its use or meaning. Intentions can enable or inhibit actions or the range of possible actions. We might speak of enabling or inhibiting structures. But the user negotiates these structures in different ways through human agency and creativity, and the outcome can be a subversion of intentions. In this chapter I am particularly concerned with such possibilities for the flexible interpretation of a technology.

Conceiving of the user as an agent in the construction of technology is specially important with regard to gender. Women, by tradition, are more often users or consumers of technology, while men are its designers (Berg 1989). A focus on users, therefore, at least introduces the possibility of making women visible in studies of technological development.

In the early/mid-1980s Norwegian feminists were asking: is technology good or bad for women? This is a difficult question to answer, and revealed our rather determinist cast of thought in that period. One answer however – a rather advanced one for the time – was 'that depends on the kind of technology we study' (Lie *et al.* 1988). What was new about this was that it offered an incentive to look at *diversity*.

In this chapter, with diversity as my focus, I will draw on some of the new writing in the sociology of technology to organize my reflections around the case study of the Norwegian Minitel project.[2] I will look at *variation* in the ways of using technology, and thus at technology's flexibility. I believe this will map a route out of our predominant pessimism.

Minitel in Norway

Minitel is a videotext system. Associated with the ordinary domestic telephone, it is a small specialized computer terminal with a built-in modem. It gives the telephone subscriber access to a range of information services such as news, timetables, banking information, ticket reservation and home shopping facilities. Physically, Minitel as used in Norway is a small grey box with a black and white VDU and fold-away keyboard.

A French innovation, Minitel is only one of many teletext and teledata systems for personal use in the home. It is however famous as the only success-story in this field. In embarking on a pilot project for the introduction of domestic teledata technology to Norway, therefore, the Norwegian Telecom (Teledirektoratet) adopted the ideas behind this successful example.

Before making Minitel generally available, Telecom set out to test and learn more about the technology in use by placing Minitel in the homes of a sample of volunteer users. In a letter sent to every household in Lillehammer, Telecom offered a free Minitel. People were invited to apply for it, and either received one immediately or were put on a waiting list. Telecom financed our research in 1990–91 monitoring Minitel in use. The Norwegian Research Council (NAVF) funded the subsequent gender research reported here. The project took us into 25 households supplied with Minitel.[3]

Telecom's initiative is an instance of a 'technology-push' innovation: there was no prior demand for such a technology in Norwegian households (Berg and Håpnes 1991). Telecom saw our research as providing them with feedback about this pilot experience of the Minitel technology they had launched. They of course are interested in the possibilities of widespread diffusion of Minitel and a rapid growth in telephone use – they can only make profits when phone lines are busy (Berg and Håpnes 1992). For our part however we were interested to see the varied things people were doing with Minitel. We focused on the flexibility that might exist in the technology in use.

Our approach is based on a particular concept of the role of the user in shaping technology. A limited view would be that information fed back from users might influence designers in producing new models or services. By contrast, we suggest that in a fully social understanding of technology an artefact only acquires its meaning in *use*. The creative input of users to the shaping of technology can be studied, therefore, in the whole culture of use.

Flexible gender

For a feminist sociology of technology, learning more about gender and technology in the home is of crucial interest. Gender was central when I planned the research project, but when writing the first report on the fieldwork we ran into an unexpected problem. When analysing gender in the interviews, we seemed to find no stable patterns depending on the sex of the user – nothing one could call a gendered pattern of use. Users developed their own individual approach to the Minitel, it seemed, annoyingly unaware of traditional sociological categories. This became quite a challenge. Was something wrong with my theoretical understanding both of technology and of gender? To make a long story short, I turned for help to the constructivists. Their concept of flexibility in relation to technology had taught me a great deal. Would it likewise help in understanding gender? When working with the interviews I had noticed something interesting: there seemed to be a gendered pattern of negotiations in connection with Minitel inside each household, but the *content* of these negotiations varied from one household to another. So in a way it did make sense to analyse gender as flexible also.

In this chapter I will try, in a pragmatic way, to show how gender can indeed be flexible in connection with flexible technology – although 'gender flexibility' is not a term I am entirely happy with. I will demonstrate these two forms of flexibility or diversity by focusing on how users, through their negotiations, may be actors in the shaping of Minitel in terms of gender. Technological diffusion takes place through emergent patterns of use and meaning. Different patterns of use become visible when we shift from a traditional producer's point of view to a broader user-oriented point of view, from an emphasis on utilitarian values to one on the cultural integration of technology. I suggest that the latter approach may be one way of helping us escape the gender blindness that is characteristic of much of the sociology of technology and contributes to our pessimism.

The active user

Technological diffusion is conventionally analysed as an economic process. In this light, the distinction that appears pertinent and is the focus of too many diffusion studies is that between the quick 'adopters' and the reluctant or protesting slow 'adopters' of the technology. This may be one important aspect of technological diffusion, but is not a sufficient framework for a full understanding of it. To place emphasis on the nature of use rather than the pace of adoption is in itself to make a criticism of mere economic diffusion theory. Users are more than 'adopters' – like designers and producers they help in constructing or shaping technology.

Some interesting theoretical and empirical attempts to understand the diffusion and implementation of domestic or consumer technology have been made during the last decade. Three of these in particular have informed our study.

Ruth Schwartz Cowan convincingly argues the case for understanding the diffusion of technology through a focus on *the consumer* (Cowan 1987). With the user or the consumer as her starting point, she applies actor-network theory (Callon 1987; Law 1987) to the diffusion of domestic technology, illustrating her points with a reanalysis of empirical data on the diffusion of cast-iron stoves in North American homes in the nineteenth century. Contrary to Callon and Law, Cowan tries to place the consumer in the centre of the network and to see the network from the inside. She stresses 'the place and time at which the consumer makes choices between competing technologies', calling this the *consumption junction* (Cowan 1987: 263). The consumption junction is important as the interface where diffusion actually takes place, the moment at which actual users enter the picture as actors. Actor-network analyses will be different, she argues, if the user instead of the producer is chosen as starting point.

In our study of Minitel in households we start in this way with the user. By being 'near-sighted', investigating actual users and patterns of use, we do indeed get a different picture of the technology and its implementation process from that given by a more traditional approach starting with the producers. Cowan also points out that the consumption junction is the location where technology begins to reorganize social life. She points to the necessity of opening up analyses in such a way that 'unintended consequences' may be taken seriously as an important characteristic of technological diffusion (Cowan 1987: 279).

Although Cowan does not amplify the way technology can transform social life, her approach points towards the relevance of studying domestic technology in a more culture-oriented perspective. In the introduction to this chapter I argued that a feminist analysis of technology is often oriented to *change* in gender relations. Paying attention to the consumption junction and the possibility of technology reorganizing social life, enables us to include a consideration of gender relations – not merely gender representations.

A second and interesting research approach to technology, consumers and the home, is that of a group of researchers at Brunel University in England (Silverstone *et al.* 1992). From their culturally-oriented perspective these authors see the implementation of technology in the home as having four elements or phases: appropriation, objectification, incorporation and conversion. We found these concepts useful in the Minitel study.

The *appropriation* phase is the moment of acquisition of the technology, the act of ownership, the arrival of the new commodity in the home. This may involve buying the new technology or, as in the case of Minitel, deciding to say 'yes' to the offer of a free commodity.

Objectification refers to the way the household or its individual members express their own values, tastes or style through their 'display' of the new technology. In the Minitel project we asked the users where the Minitel was located in their home and how they felt about and reflected on its appearance – thus acknowledging that the utilitarian value of an object is not its only significance, that aesthetics also counts for something.

The *incorporation* phase concerns use and invites us to follow how the technology is integrated in the routines of everyday life. In our interviews we asked informants to describe their 'incorporation' of the new artefact by telling us about its use during the previous week and month.

Finally, the *conversion* phase connects the household once more to the outside world. It concerns the way the household members try to adjust the technology to their own values, their view of how society at large is or ought to be. These wider values are 'translated' into the new technology and influence its use. In our project we tried to grasp this 'conversion' process through questions about the respondents' views on domestic technology generally and whether and how Minitel fitted into this picture.

The four elements or phases of the Brunel study, as I understand them, are different aspects of the cultural integration process. Integration of technology in the domestic sphere can be seen as a process of *negotiation*. In our own study this concern with negotiation has enabled us to see *gender* as negotiated, in relation to technology.

A third source of inspiration has been research on technological flexibility. The common belief about technology is that we encounter it as a producer's immutable commodity. And indeed the designer has assumed a certain use. In reality, although technologies are developed with certain user behaviours in mind, these are not entirely predetermined. Users can 'negotiate' the artefact in such a way that new patterns of use and new areas of application evolve.

The designers' visions of future use and meanings engraved in the artefact can be, in Madeleine Akrich's terms, a 'script' or a 'scenario' (Akrich 1992: 208). The users are obliged to relate to the scenario in one way or the other, but they can select their strategies in relation to it.

By the time of our second interviews with Minitel users they were familiar with the new technology and could evaluate its role in their home. It became clear that Minitel's diffusion was not only that of an already-made artefact with predetermined patterns of use. On the contrary, we could see new areas of application being established and new meanings emerging. Minitel, like information technology as a whole, is a highly flexible technology, compatible with several patterns of use. As is the way with many artefacts, it must be seen as *in process*, as technology-in-the-making.

Women's appropriation of the technology

At the time of writing, our research on Minitel has reached the stage where the interviewing is over, together with the initial writing up of most of the empirical findings (Berg and Håpnes 1991, 1992). We have learned just how complex is the relationship between gender and technology in everyday life. Being alert to flexibility forced us to expect the unexpected, and to be creative in recognizing creativity.

Below I illustrate some of the theoretical points made above. First, drawing on our interviews, I will give some examples of the variation we found in the reasoning of women Minitel users in the process of 'appropriating' this new technology.

The most common pattern, we found, is that one person in the household, either woman or man, is interested and seeks the agreement of the other. The partner's resistance varies, but very few reported conflict or disagreement. Rakel Ostby describes a characteristic family discussion:

> We didn't talk much about it. My husband was more eager than I was, but we both agreed that this was a good offer. We both thought it would be fun if we were drawn into getting such a terminal. To the extent we discussed it, my husband gave me an idea of what the letter said. What Minitel was about . . . We didn't have much information to go on.[4]

In Rakel's family the husband was more interested in the Minitel than she was, but there was no disagreement or discussion about it. In some households both the man and the woman applied. Kari Breseth, for instance, said:

> First I got the information through my bank. I applied at once, but didn't get one. Then I applied once more . . . I thought: I do feel like having this. It was only a matter of applying. There was no discussion in the family. I decided it there and then. I didn't know that Tor had applied. I'd no idea. I heard that later.

So Tor and Kari were equally interested and each had made the decision without discussing it with the other. Minitel was a free offer and evoked their curiosity. The introductory letter by Telecom made it sound fun and gave straightforward information that made it appear reassuringly uncomplicated. Signe Svarva describes her reaction to the letter offering a free terminal:

> We didn't discuss it, I informed him. [Laughs] He doesn't understand much about it. That's the way it is, you hang back a bit when you're unfamiliar with computers. He's got a job where he doesn't use a computer, so he doesn't know much about it. Not many people have jobs like that any more.

Signe is being humorous in the way she describes 'discussing' Minitel with her partner, but her story is interesting for being very far from the traditional feminine approach to computers. She does not mention gender, but attributes lack of understanding of computing to lack of experience. Siv Aune tells a somewhat similar story:

> It's exciting to test something new. And I thought it would save me a few trips to town. Apart from that, I didn't have any expectations in the beginning . . . Otherwise it's open eyes and an open mind. I suppose it was a mixture of curiosity and need. I told the kids what it can be used for, but nothing beyond that. They're interested in computers and things like that.

Her husband joined us in the middle of the interview, but said little. It was obvious that Siv controlled the use of the terminal. He said something about Minitel being expensive, a comment she overheard. Siv was a very friendly person and talked a lot about technology and her children. Later in the interview she commented dismissively to her husband 'You – around keyboards!' He laughed, obviously embarrassed.

Signe and Siv both displayed an interest in Minitel as a new and possibly exciting technology, and in different ways they asserted their control of it. Inga Hansen however had a different story to tell:

> It's of no interest to me. I always think I don't understand. I leave it to Egil. It's his domain. If I was interested or wanted to learn, he'd be very pleased. He enjoys teaching me things . . . He felt like trying

it, interested. He can do what he wants to if he enjoys it. It costs next to nothing. If it'd been expensive we'd have discussed it.

Later in the interview Inga said that she would have liked to be a little more interested in computers. She talked about her partner in an admiring tone as a 'local Gyro Gearloose' (a Norwegian character, inventor of strange technical solutions) and in their relationship one way of expressing her love for him would have been to show more interest in computers. By appreciating computing, she would also tell him that she cared for him. But she said she found computing both difficult and boring, and therefore left it to him.

The women's attitudes and experiences varied from household to household. Of course, a small sample of 25 households cannot tell us what is 'normal' in the appropriation phase, but my point is to show that women have not one but several approaches. Men also differ from each other. Both women and men span a range of attitudes, from what has come to be known as 'techno-fear' to downright enthusiasm. It seems technology may have very varied meanings for gender identity. I had anticipated gender-specific attitudes about Minitel. My data instead showed me how both technology and gender have flexible meanings, depending on the users' interaction with the artefact. They are processes, not fixed or stable categories. 'Near-sighted' detailed studies like this are valuable in that they can put us on the trail of change – both in the meaning of technology and gender, and in the interaction or relationship between the two.

Female creativity and traditional roles

As I have said before, in this Minitel project I was looking for a *relational* approach to gender and technology in everyday life. Two small instances from our study illustrate this: the negotiations we found in the households around the style and location of the terminal; and those around the use of the electronic telephone directory. I do not pretend to conclude anything about the Minitel as such from these two small illustrations. My intention is rather to use them to show how creativity can be a central element in the gendered shaping of technology.

Design and location: does it go with the decor?

A concern with the cultural integration of new technology in everyday life moves us beyond purely utilitarian or practical matters. Aesthetics and meanings come into play. We raised these kinds of question with the Minitel users. The terminal, this small grey box with its black and white VDU and foldaway keyboard – what aesthetic do people feel it expresses? What does it signal to the users and how is it seen to fit with their domestic environment? We asked where they had located the terminal in their home and why. We asked their opinion of its design and styling. We were surprised how easy we found it to discuss these questions in the interviews. The topic generated valuable and ambiguous information.

Most people had thought about the possible location of their Minitel in terms of a balance of function and style. Function, because it cannot be placed just anywhere: a telephone socket is needed for connection to the Telecom network. We found a great deal of variation in the degree of visibility Minitel had in the home. It was variously placed in the sitting-room, the kitchen, the hall, the study, or in a 'computer corner' under the stairs. It was interesting, however, to note that on our second visit we learned of more surprising places, such as the woodshed, the storeroom or under the sofa: by now some informants had stopped using the Minitel.

Location is discussed in relation with Minitel's looks. Kari Breseth carried on a conversation with herself about this:

> It's been put in the kitchen. Actually it isn't all that lovely. But it has to be close to the phone. It's not the kind of thing you want to show off or brag about. Telex, telefax, telephone – those are fascinating tools and they can stand to be put out on view. It's plain enough for the kitchen. It doesn't blend with the suite of furniture in the living room. Definitely not on the desk. We've gone for pinewood and bluish colours.[5] To fit in, the VDU ought to have come in that material or colour. Perhaps it could have been designed with a roll-top. But it's small and neat, that's fine.
>
> It's the same with the phone, too. It doesn't fit in. I like some of the more special models, the one with a peasant style of painting or rustic art [*rosemalt*], I think. That was fun. I'm a bit vain, I suppose. It's important that it goes with your interior or furnishing scheme. That's the way it is with our new music system, too. [Kari and Tor had recently bought a piece of music equipment that could be relayed to different rooms, operated by remote control. It was of 'Bang Olufsen' brand, which is expensive, has a 'hi-tech' image and is regarded in Norwegian culture as particularly advanced.] Bang Olufsen design doesn't blend in easily with the scheme of furnishing here. I wanted the equipment kept out of sight. Tor wanted to display it on the wall, but I said 'no!' [None the less, the Bang Olufsen equipment was centrally displayed in the living room.] We've got everything from the same brand now.

Kari is clearly very concerned with style, appearance, furnishing and the question of having 'matching' technology. Tor Breseth, Kari's husband, does not have as much to say as his wife about the VDU's style and location. When asked about the design of the Minitel he talks about style and practical aspects at one and the same time:

> Now, the VDU isn't exactly lovely. It is more like a box. Doesn't look very exciting. Perhaps it should be equipped with a colour screen. We've put it in the kitchen because of the cats, but it isn't an

ornament either. It's just as well that it's not so visible. But I think it's more important that the services and data bases are practical and user-friendly, than how it looks. Like I said before, the functions of an ordinary telephone ought to be built into the machine.

Tor and Kari are both concerned with the appearance of the Minitel, its style, location and display. The difference is that Kari is very conscious about its appearance in the same aesthetic sense that she cares about her furniture. She wants it to be tasteful, to blend in with the style she sees her home as representing. She wants objects, not only the Minitel, to show up to their advantage, but she and Tor do not always agree on this, or rather on how it should be done. For him, it is more important that the technical content is displayed.

Appearance, then, does mean something for these people who have Minitel in their homes, and that applies to both women and men. It is not the case that appearance is something that only women care about, as the stereotype has it. But appearance carries different meanings for women and men. The introduction of Minitel in the household presents people with a new opportunity to negotiate style. In this negotiation men tend to talk about function and women about taste. But how they stress it, the content they give 'taste' and 'function', varies from household to household. The main feature of the gender difference is that women are concerned with aesthetics and want the technology to blend into the totality of style in the home, while men are more concerned about the signalling of technical content. Men talk more about function, and they want the Minitel to *appear* functional.

This description of the objectification of the Minitel shows a different aspect of the technology from that seen in other research that suggests women are mainly concerned with the usefulness of a technology. Technology and gender are more ambiguous than that implies. Our findings on men, however (they want their technology to display its technical content) are concordant with other research that has found men relishing technology for its own sake: 'technology as masculine jewellery'. Yet what we found in both cases is that appearance has different *meanings* for women and men, and it is these they negotiate in connection with Minitel. Gender difference exists, but its forms are flexible.

The electronic telephone directory: curiosity killed the cat

One of the services supplied with the Norwegian Minitel, as with the French Minitel, is the electronic telephone book called the 'El-catalogue'. As an alternative to using the paper telephone book or telephoning 'directory enquiries', a subscriber with Minitel can connect to the directory, write the name of the person whose number is required, and this will appear on the screen.

There are however alternative ways of using the El-catalogue. Instead of writing the name and finding the correct number to call, it is possible to write a number and find the name of the subscriber(s) to that number. In this way one can get certain information about subscribers, their names, their addresses and how many people subscribe to the same line. It is also possible to key in any address and find out who lives there and their phone number.

The first time we became aware of these possibilities in the use of Minitel was during our first interview with Heidi and Stig. Heidi was 16 and her younger brother 13. They shared a computer at home and now they were keen to use the new Minitel technology. They had been fighting a great deal over the computer, and when we asked them about their familiarity with information technology in general they continued the argument. Stig started by saying that he used the computer for almost any kind of games, which he often played with friends. Heidi said:

> You and your childish games – stupid games! There's no point in games, none! [But you told us before that you used to play games as well?] Well, that was a skate board game. Driving through ramparts and things – the point was to get as high a score as possible. But I don't do it any more. I hardly ever use the computer any more. [You told us you use the Minitel though?] Yes, I use it mostly for fun. Like when someone is selling something through the newspaper. I notice the telephone number and can find out who it is. [She laughs] So what I use is the telephone book. I have looked at other data bases too. And the electronic notice board. Some crazy things there! . . . Minitel's more useful, not as childish as a computer.

Here Heidi is mentioning a new way of using the electronic phone directory, the El-catalogue, and we shall return to this. But first look more closely at what she is saying about gender and computers in general. She continues to talk about the 'stupid computer':

> I won't choose any subject that has to do with computers in high school. Science is boring, I like maths though. Yes, I really love maths. It's OK. [pause] Boys, they play with computers, but girls really use them for some purpose.

She is very concerned about the way boys use the computer, and flatly refuses to be associated with this kind of use. She goes on to talk about the boys:

> You should have seen when we had a party for our classmates here. Boys partying! They occupied the computer all the time. Some of them even decided to walk over to our neighbours to borrow their machine. That's pretty unsocial. Hff! Of course it is not all of them, some are a bit special. But they aren't many!

Heidi wants Minitel to be her technology. She therefore defines Minitel as a machine that is more suitable for girls (herself) than for boys (her brother). Furthermore she ridicules the way boys in general use computers. In terms of gender, she says that girls are clever and think about what is useful. Minitel is useful, therefore Minitel is suitable for her as a girl. She defines the computer Stig has in his room as a childish toy – a rather surprising contrast to the hi-tech, male image conventionally associated with computers, but it fits with the research which shows men 'playing' with the cleverness of the technology and women using it for practical tasks. Heidi's own definition of her use of Minitel as practical, in contrast to Stig's use, is important for her. The main point here is that it is not necessarily what they actually do with the computer so much as this way of conceiving gender and IT that is important for Heidi in her definition of Minitel as a suitable technology for girls. Both Heidi and Stig use the home computer, and specially Minitel, for their homework, looking up words in the electronic dictionary and gathering information for essay writing.

When we re-interviewed Heidi seven months later she told us that she had continued using the El-catalogue to obtain information:

> I look up to find out who's hiding behind a phone number I've seen in the newspaper. And I've used the El-catalogue to find out where my classmates live. I've started in a new class with new people, and I can find their addresses with the Minitel. It's kind of fun. Some times I do this with other people too – find their addresses.

Heidi's mother, Sissel, had no intention of using the Minitel the first time we interviewed the Godås family. When we came back for the second interview, however, she told us rather proudly that she had started using it. She began by helping the children with their homework and:

> In addition I've checked out phone numbers. Simply out of curiosity! [Jens, her husband, and Sissel both laugh] It goes like this: when I see a phone number in the paper, some ad for selling a house for example, then I can look it up and find out who's selling.

When Jens and Sissel laugh at Sissel's curiosity, they both signal that they know that some forms of curiosity – 'nosiness' – are not really socially acceptable. She knows it is 'wrong', but she does not care. She has shown her neighbours how to use the El-catalogue for this purpose too. Sissel has found a new way to keep herself (and her friends and family) informed about local goings on. Jens does not criticize her or tease her about her curiosity. Obviously they do not make a strict distinction between talking about social events, trying to find exact information and looking it up in the El-catalogue. She makes it clear that she realizes it is not socially quite acceptable to be curious about people in her immediate neighbourhood, but as long as she admits her curiosity she finds it acceptable to use the Minitel to satisfy it.

We found the same 'negotiation' about curiosity and the El-catalogue occurring in other families too. With one exception, we found that it was women who talked in a positive manner about this kind of use of the Minitel. This is not surprising. Women are the ones who traditionally have the role of 'information-worker' in the family and local community.

However, being curious about local matters is a dubious moral quality. It is not far removed from the feminine stereotype of 'gossip'. And indeed, when we were interviewing the Hagnes family, and Kjersti told us about the El-catalogue, her husband, Hans, felt very uncomfortable:

> *Kjersti*: What I find interesting or amusing is to use the electronic phone book. You can find out addresses with it. You can allow yourself to be a bit curious.
>
> *Hans*: If you're that type of personality, curious, yes. But the El-catalogue has very limited possibilities if you're not the curious kind.

Hans says this in a very moralistic tone. To be curious is obviously nothing to be proud of in this connection. He defines curiosity in strictly negative terms. Kjersti does not want to pursue this line of thought and changes the direction of the conversation. A bit later she says aloud to herself: 'But the El-catalogue is good if you need to find some addresses, for letters or Christmas cards.'

To say one uses the El-catalogue for 'getting a job done', as in finding the address of someone you need to write to, is obviously acceptable, while its use for gathering more informal information is of dubious legitimacy and is something that has to be negotiated inside the household – and possibly outside too. Studies of the history of the telephone reveal something similar. Women's 'gossip' on the telephone has been condemned, not regarded as a creative way of using a new technology (Martin 1991; Wajcman 1991). Minitel technology, then, can be seen to change in the process of use. It changes from being a practical tool for socially acceptable 'rational' information gathering, to being the object of moral debate, of the negotiation of acceptable behaviour. This 'acceptable behaviour' can be seen to have gendered implications.

The Minitel is flexible enough for users to find applications outside the 'rational' area of use. When women, as the main 'care-takers' of social relations in the community, use it to garner personal information about neighbours, the sexual division of labour is preserved, *but* at the same time it is also exposed to view. In connection with Minitel it is placed on the agenda anew for renegotiation. The actors negotiate a dual valence in the notion of 'curiosity' and in doing so are simultaneously renegotiating the traditional meaning of gender. It is an interesting example of gender (female creativity) and technology (Minitel) being negotiated, each by means of the other, in everyday life.

Gender, technological flexibility and political pessimism

In conclusion, then, we found understanding gender and technology as interwoven processes to be difficult but fruitful. The shift from a producer's point of view to a user-oriented approach widened our possibilities for seeing technology as an actor in social (gender) processes and an element

in social (gender) relations.[6] We saw Minitel, a new and unfinished technology, whose patterns of use are still emergent, negotiated simultaneously with gender. Gender relations exist, but take on varied forms. Gender
has meaning, but its meanings are negotiated. The categories masculine
and feminine are in relationship but are not stable. When the meaning of
gender is being negotiated, Minitel can play a role in that negotiation
process. Style and socially acceptable use – *cultural dimensions* lacking
in traditional diffusion theory – are examples of what can be discussed in
such a context.

Women encountered in the study had found ways of asserting control
and using the Minitel in connection with their own traditional work,
such as information gathering about social events in the neighbourhood
and decorating the home. Such preoccupations are often labelled nega-
tively – 'vanity', 'gossip' – especially by men. Women admit that, in the
case of information gathering, it is their 'curiosity' that prompts this kind
of use. Yet curiosity can be related to creativity. Interior decorating, too,
is a creative activity. And creativity is a personal quality that is usually
highly valued, especially in connection with information technology.

In what way do our findings give rise to optimism? Because, seen this
way, the diffusion of technology is manifestly capable of influence by
creative women users. I do not argue that women always *are* creative in
relation to technology. My point is to show that they *can be*. By substituting an emphasis on cultural integration of technologies for one on
utilitarian values, and by substituting a view of technology as in process
for one in which it is seen as non-negotiable, we can overcome both the
gender blindness that vitiates so much of the sociology of technology and
the pessimism that pervades feminist technology studies.

Our findings are also positive in that they move our theories forward.
As Judy Wajcman says in the preface to her book:

> The argument that women's relationship to technology is a contra-
> dictory one, combined with the realization that technology is itself
> a social construct, opens up fresh possibilities for feminist scholar-
> ship and action. (Wajcman 1991: x)

Feminists in the social sciences are currently interested to learn more
about process, relation and negotiation. Constructivists in technology
studies are interested in just these things. The conclusion is obvious: we
need more studies of gender and technology to increase our knowledge of
how these processes, relations and negotiations knit together.

Notes

1 For an excellent review of the literature on gender and technology from a feminist point of view, see Judy Wajcman (1991).
2 A grant from the Norwegian Research Council (NAVF) has made it possible for
  me to do this work.

3 The research was carried out in 1990–92 at the Institute for Social Research in Industry (SINTEF-IFIM), Trondheim, by Tove Håpnes and myself. We interviewed household members in the 25 households at two different stages, first a few weeks after their Minitel was installed, and again after 7–10 months of use. Tove and I shared the ups and downs of field research. This chapter owes much to many discussions with her, but I take full responsibility for any shortcomings in the finished text.

4 It is difficult to translate interviews that are in the shape of informal conversations. The double meaning of many words and the local idiom is lost in translation. A further problem is that colloquial Norwegian tends to sound abrupt in direct English translation. The quotations should be read with this in mind.

5 The Norwegian word is *syreluta*. Norwegians will recognize the style, but it is impossible to find an equivalent in English.

6 This does not mean that what are traditionally labelled 'innovation processes' are gender neutral. That gender is relational implies also that gender relations are at work among male developers in the construction of artefacts (Berg 1991).

References

Akrich, Madeleine (1992) The de-scription of technical objects, in Bijker, W.E. and Law, J. (eds) *Shaping Technology/Building Society: Studies in Sociotechnical Change*. Cambridge, MA: MIT Press.

Berg, Anne-Jorunn (1989) Informasjonsteknologi i hjemmet – den nye hjemmefronten [IT in the home – old or new forms of resistance], in Sørensen, K. and Espeli, T. (eds) *Ny Teknologi – en Utfordring for Samfunnsforskning [New Technology – A Challenge to Social Science]*. Oslo: NAVF-NTNF-NORAS.

Berg, Anne-Jorunn (1991) *The Smart House as a Gendered Socio-Technical Construction*. Working paper. Trondheim: IFIM.

Berg, Anne-Jorunn and Håpnes, Tove (1991) *Nysgjerrige brukere. Beslutningsprosesser og førsteinntrykk i forbindelse med Minitel i husstander [Curious Users. Decision-making and First Impressions in Households with Minitel]*. Trondheim: IFIM.

Berg, Anne-Jorunn and Håpnes, Tove (1992) *Den Tapte Nysgjerrigheten – Om Tvilende Minitelbrukere [Curiosity Lost. On Doubting Users]*. Trondheim: IFIM.

Berg, Anne-Jorunn and Rasmussen, Bente (1983) *Jakten på det Kjønnsspesifikke Teknologibegrep [On the Look-out for the Gender Sensitive Concept of Technology]*. Oslo: NAVFs Sekretariat for Kvinneforskning.

Callon, Michel (1987) Society in the making: the study of technology as a tool for sociological analysis, in Bijker, W.E. Hughes, T. P. and Pinch, T. (eds) *The Social Construction of Technological Systems*. Cambridge, MA: MIT Press.

Cockburn, Cynthia (1983) *Brothers: Male Dominance and Technological Change*. London: Pluto Press.

Cowan, Ruth Schwartz (1987) The consumption junction: a proposal for research strategies in the sociology of technology, in Bijker, W.E., Hughes, T.P. and Pinch, T. (eds) *The Social Construction of Technological Systems*. Cambridge, MA: MIT Press.

Law, John (1987) Technology and heterogenous engineering: the case of Portuguese expansion, in Bijker, W.E., Hughes, T.P. and Pinch, T. (eds) *The Social Construction of Technological Systems*. Cambridge, MA: MIT Press.

Lie, Merete, Berg, Anne-Jorunn, Kaul, Hjørdis *et al.* (1988) *I menns bilde: Kvinner-teknologi-arbeid [In the Image of Men: Women – Technology – Work]*. Trondheim: Tapir.

Martin, Michele (1991) *'Hello Central?': Gender, Technology and Culture in the Formation of Telephone Systems*. Montreal and Kingston: McGill-Queen's University Press.

Silverstone, Roger, Hirsch, Eric and Morley, David (1992) Information and communication technologies and the moral economy of the household, in Silverstone, R. and Hirsch, E. (eds) *Consuming Technologies: Media and Information in Domestic Spheres*. London and New York: Routledge.

Wajcman, Judy (1991) *Feminism Confronts Technology*. Cambridge: Polity Press.

6

Hopes and disappointments of technological change: A case study in Russian hosiery production

VITALINA KOVAL

The research reported in this chapter was carried out in 1990–91 during a period of revolutionary change in the territories of the former Soviet Union. In Russia and the other former Soviet republics the transition to a free market economy was giving rise to profound economic crisis and hardship for the population. *Perestroika* had brought a welcome political freedom but with it a catastrophic decline in living standards due to rocketing prices and lack of essential commodities. Above all, there was widespread anxiety and uncertainty about what the future would bring.

The Russian contribution to this book, therefore, has to be seen as of its time. *Perestroika* had produced a new freedom for researchers such as ourselves to carry out genuine sociological enquiry.[1] At the same time, the people we interviewed were often understandably sceptical and reluctant to answer questions.

In the Soviet literature we had no lack of studies of the impact of new technology on the development of society. From the 1960s onwards the economic, political and social correlates of technological change in the Soviet Union had been an important research theme. Science and technology were understood in our analysis as prime movers of contemporary developments. Entirely lacking from such studies however had been any concern with the impact of technological change on gender relations. How might gender relations influence technological development, and how might technological change bear on gender relations? Such questions had been explored neither at the macro nor the micro level. Nothing had been published.[2] I was thus stepping into unexplored terrain.

Even as we approached the subject, however, some facts sprang to view. The ability of women and men as groups to develop or adapt new technology to their own interests as a sex were clearly unequal, due to their historically different position in society and in the labour force. The claim of official Soviet state ideology was that the 'woman question' had essentially been solved, that any continuing inequality was merely residual. The reality was different. In the Soviet Union and the countries that succeeded it attitudes continued to reflect the old patriarchal traditions and women continued to be considered second-rate people.

It is undeniable that women are numerically and economically important: there are 16 million more women than men, 92 per cent of women of working age are economically active, and as a result women are 48 per cent of the labour force (Goscomstat 1991). They are not however rewarded with matching responsibility or influence. Key posts are occupied by men: among national economic decision-makers women are only 7 per cent, and they are only 5 per cent of elected deputies in the Russian Parliament.

Certain features of the Russian economy, inherited from the Soviet system, demonstrated at the very outset of our research a gender structure that was likely to cause new technology to have a different impact on women and men. The process of industrialization beginning in the late 1920s drew women in large numbers into the paid labour force.[3] National economic policy placed priority on the development of heavy branches of industry, including engineering, employing mainly male labour. It has been characteristic of the Russian economy that women have predominated in the 'light' branches of industry such as food and textiles, public and social services. It has to be added however that those women who have worked in the 'male' sector of heavy industry have often done the dirtiest, heaviest and most unhealthy.

Second, whatever the branch they worked in, women did not participate equally in decision-making. Until recent times all enterprises had belonged to the state and the command-bureaucratic authoritative administration, from which women were largely absent, decided autonomously what new technology would be introduced and where. In this system, priority had been given to 'male' branches – particularly weapons manufacture, in which all the latest technological achievements and all the most qualified personnel were concentrated.

At this macro level therefore it was possible to see at the outset a direct connection between technological development and gender relations. Those industries in which most women work had been starved of technological investment by the state and indeed were by now in deep crisis; technology was consequently having different overall effects on women and men in the labour force; and military production had long had priority over manufacture of the consumer goods that could have improved everyday life.

The context in which the research began, then, was one in which we could talk not just of discrimination against women in technological choices but discrimination against whole 'female' sectors and aspects of the economy. From 60 per cent to 90 per cent of the labour force of industries such as the food industry, of trading, of culture and of social services such as medicine and education, was women. The immediate replacement of obsolete and worn-out equipment with new technology was urgently needed. More than 40 per cent of work in these sectors was being done *manually* by women in labour-intensive, monotonous operations. Wages were among the lowest in the country. Yet the *nomenclatura*, higher management, members of state planning committees and ministry personnel (almost all male) were in no hurry to press for investment so long as these state-owned enterprises could continue to exploit women's cheap labour.

Thousands of women were working in intolerable conditions, while men, it seemed, were creating new technology for themselves and using it in their own interests. Krasny Proletary, a well-known heavy engineering plant in Moscow, may stand as an example. Some years previously a new production shop supplied with electronic equipment was set up at this plant. Recruitment of highly-qualified workers for the new department was announced: *only men*, from 25 to 35 years of age with higher or specialized secondary education were to be considered. No women were taken on except as cleaners. Open discrimination of this kind, while not legal in Russia, continues to occur. The research in the present chapter seeks to move from the level of anecdote, such as this, to a detailed study of such social processes.

It is not only macro factors that produce gendered effects and influence technological change. In the report that follows I pay attention also to the human dimension. The relations between management and the collective of workers, between the head of a brigade and the rank and file, the relative numbers of male and female workers, their relative satisfaction with labour conditions, the attitude of male workers to female colleagues and managers, such micro factors create a workplace atmosphere that must also be understood if we are to perceive the gender significance of new technology.

New production technology in the hosiery industry

For our case study of technological innovation we carried out research in an enterprise producing one of those consumer goods so badly needed by women: panty hose (tights) for themselves and their children, socks for the family. We were afforded access to the Tushinskaya hosiery factory, an old Moscow branch of this sector of light, 'female' industry. Panty hose now constituted just over half its output, 70 per cent for children, 30 per cent for women. There were 1750 employees at the time of a study, 80 per cent of them women – it was a characteristic 'female' sector.

This was still a state enterprise, not yet privatized. As a half-measure, however, the administration were technically now renting the plant and building from the state. The collective of workers controlled such matters as distribution of bonuses and investment in the social fund. The Tushinskaya hosiery plant had been modernized four years previously by the replacement of its old knitting machinery with automatic, computer-controlled production equipment – the main focus of our interest in it.

The research had three phases. First, a questionnaire (69 questions) was distributed to 250 workers, the entire labour force of one particular shop that was operating the new technology. Two hundred usable replies were received, 180 from women, 20 from men. Questions sought information on the social relations of the factory in general. Second, a selection of 77 employees was made from the original 250. They were 43 women and 34 men who had been working in the factory before, as well as since, the technological innovation. All answered the second questionnaire which aimed to explore their feelings about the consequence of new technology for their lives and in particular for gender relations. Third, the opinions of decision-makers were felt to be particularly significant, so ten people (five men, five women) in mid-level managerial posts were approached by questionnaire, but were also interviewed in depth. In all cases the information sought included questions about the subject's home life and consumption, from which, together with the information about production, we have attempted to develop a rounded picture of the gender relations of technological change.

The findings of this case study are to be reported in full in Russian, and, for lack of space, may only be summarized here. The following details seem particularly relevant.

First, the educational level of the employees at Tushinskaya was found to be high. Among the general sample, no less than 83 per cent had achieved 10 years of secondary education, some with compensatory or additional vocational, specialized or higher education; only 17 per cent had incomplete secondary education without further vocational, specialized or higher education. Among the second sample, those who had experienced technological change, the educational standard was even higher. Of these, who were mainly in the age band 35–50 years and who were trusted, long-serving employees, only 6 per cent of men and 2 per cent of women had failed to complete secondary education.

There was, besides, a striking gender difference in educational standard. Forty per cent of women in the general sample, against only 26.5 per cent of men, had higher education. In the Tushinskaya factory women, as well as being the great majority of employees, did also have a substantial presence in supervisory and management posts. The overall director of the factory was a woman, as were two out of three deputy directors. Three of the five shop forepersons were female, together with a majority of brigade leaders. (An exception was the knitting shops where most of these supervisory posts were filled by men.) It appears however that this presence of women in supervision and management does not, significant as it is, reflect the leadership role women *feel* their education merits. Only 70 per cent of women, against 88 per cent of men, felt their job matched their educational achievements. As we shall see, this feeling arose partly from women's inability to benefit from the new opportunities deriving from technological change. It is a finding that reflects a widespread awareness among women of an undervaluation of women endemic in Russian society, a failure to use and reward their considerable abilities.

New technology had, it seemed, been a mixed blessing at Tushinskaya. Drawing on the questionnaire to those who had lived through technological change at the factory, we found that most people's experience was broadly positive (67 per cent rated it so). One important factor in workers' current satisfaction with the enterprise, it should be noted at the outset, may have been that soon after the technological innovation, at the time of reform of the price mechanism, the enterprise social fund increased and the administration began spending more on subsidy of facilities such as canteen, day nursery, rest home, sauna and sports complex. In connection with the introduction of new technology itself, in addition, most reported that labour conditions had improved. Wages for both sexes had risen.

Women were even more positive than men (76 per cent as against 59 per cent). They reported a number of gains from new technology. They felt it had afforded them greater responsibility and called for greater skill (61 per cent of women, 45 per cent of men). More than half these women workers had been retrained, acquired a new occupation or advanced their qualifications in the course of the technological innovation. In the case of men it was less than half (due however to the fact that more men than women had had appropriate qualifications beforehand.)

Against this however must be set a number of factors. Two-thirds of all respondents, women and men alike, felt new technology had increased stress and adversely affected their health – though it was difficult, we felt, to be sure this effect was one of new technology rather than a general decline in nutritional standards in Russia, a deterioration in the environment and increases in stress in the society generally in this period. The wage increases due to new technology had been largely eaten up by inflation, and 70 per cent of women and 65 per cent of men felt anxiety about their financial situation. The inequalities in pay between women and men (women earning 70 per cent of the male wage on average) had not diminished. While new technology, for instance, had led to an increase in pay for both the female and male managers we interviewed, and the gender difference at this level was only 5–10 per cent. None the less it was men who had gained most.

More importantly, there had been no relaxation of the technological sexual division of labour. In fact, sex segregation had been exacerbated by the change. In the days of old technology, women and men engineers had done similar jobs in the plant. In the new technological regime, men got the controlling jobs and it was particularly young male graduates who entered the leading positions generated by the electronic and computer revolution. Fifty-three per cent of forepersons and assistant forepersons were men and men were particularly the ones in charge of the new electronic equipment. Among the five male managers we interviewed, all were in engineer/technologist posts and three had been appointed to management for the first time in their lives after the introduction of new technology.

Of the five women managers, by contrast, only one was fully technical while of the others three were engineer/economists and one was the enterprise accountant. In general the roles women in the factory had entered in connection with the new technologies were subordinate roles: those of programmer, operator or perforator. Even when they received special training – as was the case with a batch of 50 young women – it was only for routine work of this kind.

Some older employees nearing pension age were made redundant, particularly those whose knowledge was considered obsolete – and these were mostly women. Many other women chose to move from production into more social or service roles. Women were thus consolidated in departments and jobs involving distribution, finance and administration. Women however were the majority of economists, accountants and brigade leaders. Overall, women felt a technological dependence on men, who were so frequently their technical superiors, the ones familiar with electronic techniques and control systems.

It is not surprising that men among the respondents were more likely to feel their new jobs interesting and worthy of their capabilities (87 per cent as against 56 per cent of women). Eighty-five per cent of men, against 53 per cent of women, felt new technology had given them the possibility of being involved in decision-making in the workplace. More than twice as many men as women reported 'regular participation' in decision-making at brigade level, but the degree to which workers feel they 'participate regularly' in decision-making falls off rapidly when one moves up from brigade to department and thence to enterprise level. The gender difference in these responses also declined with increasing level.

What are the social explanations for the intensification of the technical sexual division of labour? Some light is thrown on this by answers to questions revealing attitudes of women and men to the opposite sex and to their own sex – particularly in relation to technology and management. We asked our respondents for instance whether they believed work with the new technology to be 'of more interest' to men or women. We wanted to know how people related gender with technology – whether it seemed an equally attractive and creative option for either sex. We were surprised to find 59 per cent of men replying that work with new technology was of equal 'interest' to both sexes, whereas only 35 per cent of women answered this way.

It appears from this that it is less the attitudes of male colleagues' than women's own attitudes that distance women from technology. The administration, who make appointments and promotions, but also and perhaps more importantly, women themselves, tend to underestimate women's capabilities and capacities for technological work, despite women's higher educational level. Related to this, we felt, was our finding that among the 10 managers interviewed the women tended to be satisfied with their position and did not seek further promotion, while the men seemed alert to possibilities of improving their careers and reaching decision-making positions – more of which, indeed, had opened to them with new technology.

Further evidence that immediate workplace relations are not major factors in oppressing and deterring women comes from the fact that four out of five respondents felt relations in the plant to be good. Of the second sample, those whose experience spanned the period of technological innovation, the majority of both sexes (86 per cent female, 94 per cent male) were satisfied with the human relations before the change and felt that new technology had not been detrimental in this respect. Only one person of each sex felt that relationships had deteriorated in the change-over. Fourteen per cent of women and 12 per cent of men felt they had improved, while around half (49 per cent female, 56 per cent male) had observed no change. One complaint however (endorsed by 44 per cent of both sexes) was that favouritism existed in the factory and that heads of brigades and departments in particular used their position to advance the careers and rewards of favoured workers.

About one-third of both sexes in the larger sample considered equality to pertain between women and men in the factory. There seemed however to be a discrepancy between what women thought men's reaction to women to be, and the way men reported themselves to feel about women. Thus 21 per cent of female respondents believed men's attitude towards them in the factory to be 'friendly', while only around 9 per cent of men said that was the case. Male workers' responses may perhaps be the more trustworthy on this matter – a fact borne out by the rather smaller proportion of men than of women who had 'no preference' as to which sex they worked with (53 per cent against 67 per cent). In the general sample of workers (of whom two-thirds had women as their immediate superiors) 53 per cent of men as against 30 per cent of women felt men made the better managers. Such partisanship was strongest among our ten managers – all five men favoured male managers while all the women contested this. This apparent male preference for men as colleagues and bosses was countered, however, by the fact that the majority of workers of both sexes felt that females worked more productively than males, and that women (who were the majority of trade union representatives in this factory) defended workers' interests best.

In conclusion of this part of our case study, drawing on this and other material we unfortunately have no space to report here, we may say that women in many respects play an important role in the Tushinskaya panty hose factory: they are a majority in number, they are the better educated sex, they have higher professional skills and they occupy quite a few leading and middle management positions. They are more active than men in social and political life. They do much to create such friendly human relations as exist in the plant. *Yet their role in using and controlling new technology is significantly less important than that of men.* While new technology is welcomed by women, men have gained far more than women from its introduction.

The responses to our questionnaires suggest that if women proclaimed themselves more satisfied than men with the effects of technological change it was only because they had experienced such marked disadvantage *prior* to the change. The small gains they had made were pleasing in comparison when women remembered the past, but women's position relative to men's in fact remains one of inferiority, with disadvantage now taking a more markedly technological turn.

Why? How can we account for such a fact, particularly given that women held key management roles in this factory? First, we need to put women's leadership here in Russian perspective. Women managers and even directors of light industry are not uncommon. This is not unrelated to the fact that the female sector is held to be less important than the male, and the pay and status of its managers is considerably lower. To be director of a factory such as this is not such a powerful position as it may sound to a Western reader. It is essentially to be a functionary with little initiative, answerable to state bureaucrats. More significant is the *technological leadership* within the sector, to which, it becomes apparent, very few women accede. This is, we suggest, as a result of patriarchal attitudes shared by both sexes. In our study, it was not only men, but also women who believed men to have an affinity with new technology. Although 58 per cent of engineers in Russia are women, the majority are in, and prefer, administrative posts. The gender identity of men is widely associated by both sexes with technology. The feeling is often expressed that a link between women and technology is 'unnatural'. Women's natural affinity is with administration, service work, home, kitchen. Thus, among our managers (women and men alike), though some were agnostic concerning the masculinity of new technology, none saw new technology as being of *more* 'interest' to women than to men, and most of course saw it as a masculine concern. Even some women managers thought it 'natural' that men had been given the leading posts in connection with the new technology at Tushinskaya. It is attitudes of this kind that are tying women, in connection with new technology, to monotonous, tiring and unrewarding jobs, while men get the creative opportunities.

Under-investment in housing and household technology

Unlike most of the studies in this book, our research in Russia dealt with new technology in the production process, not of a piece of domestic equipment (for example, microwave oven, vacuum cleaner), but of a commodity consumed by women and children in everyday life: panty hose. None the less we hypothesize that the effects of technological investment in society bear on women and men differently not only in the workplace, but also in the home and in consumption. Panty hose as product, and the process of hosiery production, make as good a starting point as any other to examine this. We therefore used our opportunity of questioning women and men in their role as workers to explore also their experience of the state's investment, or as it has usually happened, failure to invest, in domestic life and consumption.

Housing and the equipment used for unpaid work within the home may be seen as technology, technology applied to unpaid domestic work as the new electronic and computer equipment of the Tushinskaya factory is applied to the paid work of production. Given women's greater responsibility for and commitment to housework and the sustenance of domestic life, investment by the state in these technologies may be seen as of particular benefit to women, and failure to invest as penalizing and undervaluing women. There was always an acute shortage of housing in the Soviet Union – and the housing crisis in Moscow today is its continued expression. Only the state, local authorities and state enterprises had the power to build new apartment blocks and distribute them among the population. The answers we received from Tushinskaya employees and managers clearly demonstrated that the home is a second field in which Soviet society had signally failed to invest technology in and for women.

More than half of our respondents were married and had children, and they, in the main, were those that had separate dwellings, albeit with less than adequate floor area. According to collective agreement, the enterprise assists its employees in solving their housing problems, subsidizing them to the extent of 40 per cent of the price of a cooperative flat. In 1991, at a cost to the enterprise of 200,000 roubles, 52 workers at Tushinskaya had been enabled to buy new apartments in this way. All of the 10 managers we interviewed were living in separate family apartments, through this or other means.

It was the remainder however (around half those questioned) who expressed themselves seriously dissatisfied with their housing conditions. Overcrowding is the normal condition in Moscow flats, and 11 per cent of our sample were living with relatives and another 12 per cent in 'communal' flats in which they had a room and shared cooking and washing facilities with other families.

Of particular interest however are the 35 per cent of respondents living in hostel accommodation, the majority of whom were young women. Hostel living is the product of the system of labour force recruitment in Moscow. To overcome the shortage of young labour, Moscow enterprises are permitted to recruit a restricted number from villages in the rural hinterland. For the individual this is the only way to obtain a right to reside in Moscow. The enterprise must provide these *limitchiks* as they are called with accommodation, usually in hostels. After five years of unbroken employment for the one employer a *limitchik* obtains the much-prized right to Moscow registration and in ten years the right to seek permanent accommodation, usually at first in a communal flat. They join the ranks of hundreds of thousands of native Muscovites waiting for their own apartment.

The Tushinskaya enterprise owned hostel accommodation for 100 women and/or family units. Our data confirmed that 29 per cent of respondents had been working at the enterprise less than five years, and these in the main were the hostel dwellers. Young women *limitchiks*, apart from their miserable living conditions and restricted private lives, are dependent on their superiors at every level. They are tied to the one enterprise for ten years. In case of dismissal they lose not only job but housing and Moscow resident's rights. Not surprisingly many are resigned and unconfident.

If the Soviet state failed to invest in housing, and the market is as yet far from being able to address the shortage, what about domestic equipment? The labour-saving and quality-enhancing domestic machinery that Western households take for granted had always been in short supply in the Soviet Union, often of low quality and obtainable only through the employing organization after months or years of waiting. Responses to our survey showed that the technologies the majority of households have managed to obtain are: refrigerators, televisions, vacuum cleaners, washing machines, food mixers and sewing machines. Still rare are cars, videos, microwaves and other kitchen gadgets, although not surprisingly some of the small sample of managers owned such luxuries.

As at the workplace, there emerged a gender difference in relation to household technology. Because so many of these women were living in hostels, or otherwise in low-grade accommodation, in comparison with men in the sample, more of whom were permanent Moscow residents or living with parents, more men than women answered positively that they had particular artefacts in their home. For example, 97 per cent of men had a refrigerator against 91 per cent of women; 85 per cent had a vacuum cleaner against 77 per cent of women; 85 per cent had a washing machine against 77 per cent of women; and 97 per cent had television sets against 86 per cent of women. More than twice as many men than women had use of a car (32 per cent against 14 per cent). Only in the case of sewing machines and food mixers did more women than men say they owned them.

Two other gender differences in relation to domestic technology echo the gender relations of technology in paid employment. First, even if men have access to the technology it is mainly women who operate it. Thus 70 per cent of women and 71 per cent of men said that these pieces of equipment were as a rule used by the woman of the house. Second, when the equipment needs repairing women are more likely than men to apply to the service bureau, men are more likely to undertake simple repairs to the equipment themselves.

The argument we propose here, that failure to invest in housing and household technology is failure to invest in women, depends upon the fact that women spend most time in the house and are the ones who do most housework. The patriarchal relations of the family still pertain in Russia: it is expected of women to perform most of the housework and child-rearing. A national survey showed women to work between 40 and 48 hours in the home per week, against men's 10 to 12 hours. The lack of services, poor housing and inadequate technology make women's double shift particularly intolerable in Russia. Their oppression at home circles round to damage their chances at work. Women have far less likelihood of acquiring professional qualifications or additional skills training such as would give them access to new technology at work. A national study of 51,000 workers' and farmers' families carried out in 1989 showed that women employed in industry had on average no more than 11 minutes per working day to devote to study or skill enhancement.

We asked our Tushinskaya informants to tell us about the division of labour in their homes. Although the results were not sufficiently reliable to warrant statistical expression, we formed the clear impression that, as reported by both sexes, men were participating in work in the home to a greater extent than before, and more than the national experience suggested. We tentatively concluded that men were driven by the extreme pressures bearing on women today to help them more than in the past. Many women are obliged, because of escalating prices, to seek second jobs. The public services available to the family have declined with a consequent dramatic increase in the demands of housework. In particular, the liberalization of prices has increased the cost of day nurseries to prohibitive levels. Many have closed. Despite the fact that the Tushinskaya administration and trade union subsidize the factory day nursery from the social fund, only just over one in five of the children of these respondents was attending the nursery. It is increasingly common for children to be left in the care of grandparents. As a result of the increasing pressure of the double burden, four out five women in our study reported feeling deprived of leisure time. (It must be added that almost as many men feel this too.)

A second impression we gained is that, if the hours committed to household activities by men and women are less unequal than they were, or than they are elsewhere, the *kind of work* done by the two sexes continues to differ. Again, we did not in our questionnaires sufficiently differentiate the various domestic tasks to be certain of this. However it was clear that women are more active in caring for children (70 per cent of female respondents and 82 per cent of male respondents answered that this was so. And since, as we saw, around 70 per cent of both sexes reported that it is women who use the domestic equipment – it seems that women continue to be the ones to cook and clean.

Finally, one activity that may be increasingly demanding the attention of men during their free time is *gardening*. Recently, the Moscow city authority gave many Moscow families small plots of land to enable them to supply themselves with food to combat the hardship of the winter months. (It is widely reported that today, due to the divergence between wages and prices, 35 per cent of families in Russia have fallen below the poverty line.) More than 70 per cent of the Tushinskaya sample were involved in this time-consuming weekend labour, raising crops for the benefit of their families.

It seems safe to conclude that women remain the ones who spend most time in the home, who do the routine household chores and who look after the young and the needy. If men's greater participation in 'household tasks', broadly defined, is a function of the crisis currently affecting women's capability to perform everything as before, we should perhaps be pessimistic about the permanence of the change. When circumstances normalize, unless the patriarchal relations of the family are transformed in the meantime, men's tendency to share more in the work may well move into reverse.

Problems of distribution and consumption

The breakup of the Soviet Union and the conversion of Russia from a centrally-planned economy to a market economy, which is transforming the relations of production, is also having a dramatic effect on the distribution of consumer goods. Distribution in the Soviet Union used to be highly centralized, under the oversight of the State Planning Committee. Production enterprises, which were state monopolies, produced according to official plan. The task of management was merely to fulfil, or overfulfil, the production plan received from above. Retailing of goods from factory to consumer was no concern of the production enterprise. Distribution, and the setting of prices, were functions of quite other official structures.

It frequently occurred that the state production monopolies produced inappropriate and poor quality goods that people had no wish to buy – yet there existed no mechanism, no feedback from the consumer, to staunch the flow of inappropriate production. Since there was no competition, there was no advertising. Stocks of unsold products simply accumulated and the state continued to subsidize the production monopolies' losses, for which nobody could be held responsible. It is estimated that in the early 1980s the value of accumulated unsold stock in the Soviet Union amounted to 30 billion roubles.

It will be apparent that the system described above, with its lack of competition, provided no incentive to authorities or managers to introduce new production technologies, which in other circumstances might have been seen as a means of improving product quality. As a result, the manufacturing sector producing consumer goods of all kinds was technologically backward in the Soviet Union.

Since it is women who are primarily responsible in Russia for the maintenance of home and family, including shopping for food, clothing and other commodities, the hardships caused by the failure to modernize the sector producing consumer goods, and by a chaotic system of distribution, have fallen disproportionately on them.

Perestroika involved the introduction of self-financing and self-accounting among production enterprises. Today enterprises like the Tushinskaya hosiery factory have the right, and the responsibility, to decide what kind of products to manufacture and to what quality and quantity. They may also determine the wholesale selling price of at least some of their goods. An effective link between production and consumption, an expression of consumer demand, is slowly beginning to be established.

We have seen that the Tushinskaya factory now operates with slightly more independence, leasing its premises from the state, but taking more responsibility than before for production decisions. Under the provisions of the new economic reforms, such enterprises as Tushinskaya are required to sell a fixed proportion of their product to state shops at stable, agreed prices. Tushinskaya, for instance, has an agreement with 400 state shops. Any additional output however may be sold on the open market at any price. The shops through which this 'free' component of output can be sold have been recently privatized, and they, like the factory, may now set their own prices – up to a maximum of 25 per cent above the fixed price of state shops.

With these processes of change there has occurred a dramatic increase in the price of consumer goods. The official state price for a pair of cotton tights for women in 1990 was 2.5 roubles. In 1991 they cost 24 roubles. At the time of writing, the price is 98 roubles. The price of nylon tights has risen equivalently. Such increases are due to inflation in the cost of raw materials and wages, and the price liberalization of 1 January 1992. Even now, however, the price of Tushinskaya panty hose in the private shops is lower than the price of similar products imported from abroad, which fetch 140 to 180 roubles a pair. The introduction of new production technology four years ago, besides, improved quality. Consequently the consumer favours this factory's products and demand is greater than supply.

What does all this mean for the woman worker at Tushinskaya? We saw that new technology had had a good effect on her working life, while at the same time men had gained more and so increased their relative advantage over women. As a consumer, this woman has also undoubtedly gained from the improved production and availability of panty hose, which she may buy direct from the enterprise at discount prices to a certain monthly value. But the course of the improvement has scarcely been smooth and the gains are in danger of being nullified by inflation.

In the former Soviet society, women felt they had little encouragement or opportunity to enjoy their bodies, to buy attractive clothes, to express themselves through personal choice in adornment and fashion. Always overworked, unsupported by the technologies that were available in Western countries to ease drudgery in the paid workplace and in the home, Soviet women had few personal comforts. All-in-one stretch tights are one such comfort that Western women have long taken for granted. They permit women to remain warm and look good without the discomfort of suspender belts, girdles and corsets. They also ease women's lives in providing warm, practical and easily washed leg-wear for their children.

The new production facility at their factory, a much-needed new investment in technology in this 'female' sector, potentially enriched women's lives as consumers by making such improved hosiery products available to them. The reality however is more complicated. The old economic system of the Soviet Union always involved the factory in the process of distribution to its own workers. The worker could sometimes obtain, through her or his workplace and after a long wait, such a commodity as a television, costly or unobtainable in the state shops. In 1990 the workers at Tushinskaya were receiving special coupons that enabled them to buy at discount prices the panty hose produced by their enterprise. Some of these they might sell on, at a profit, in local street markets, so increasing their personal income. However, at the time of liberalization of prices at the beginning of 1992, this practice was ended.

At the time of writing, some consumer benefit does continue to accrue to a worker, but in a different form. An interim measure in economic reform permitted factories to enter into barter arrangements with each other to exchange products for their employees. Panty hose might, for instance, be exchanged for other kinds of clothing to be distributed to Tushinskaya workers. Since liberalization, however, barter agreements are only permitted with farming collectives and the advantage of being a hosiery worker is only realized in access to food products, which are sold in special weekend fairs organized for the employees.

The main impediment, however, to women experiencing gain from the investment in panty hose production is the continuing problem of availability in relation to price. Both before and after liberalization, confusion has reigned. In some cases, where price has been the problem, consumers have stopped buying and stocks have accumulated in the factories. In other cases, where shortages have threatened, consumers have bought excessively and stockpiled goods in their homes. In general, because the rate of inflation in the price of food and consumer goods has been many times the rate of increase in wages, people are finding it difficult to buy what they need and many young girls and women even now prefer to wear jeans or slacks to cover their legs instead of tights. The comfort and pleasure women deserve still elude them.

Before concluding this case study from Russia, there is one further moment in the cycle of technology relations of which the gender relations merit a footnote. We have seen something of technology relations in production and in domestic life. New technology is also slowly influencing the process of distribution, both as retail technique and as commodity. Very gradually, electronic tills and stock control methods are being introduced into the bigger shops. We may speculate that it is men who will be controlling these systems, as we have seen is the case in production. Second, with privatization, thousands of private shops, both small and large are opening throughout Russia today, selling everything from food and clothing to cars and other technological artefacts. Informal observation shows the sales personnel to be noticeably sex-stereotyped. In the former shops and departments the sales personnel tend to be young women. It is young men, however, many with higher education, who are the salesmen of the newly-available, and highly profitable, technological products.

Gendered choices, gendered effects

In conclusion, the social impact of technological change and, conversely, of the failure to invest in new technology, can be seen to be a markedly gendered phenomenon in Russia. Patriarchal attitudes, as both cause and effect, can be seen at both macro and micro levels.

At the macro level of Russian society as a whole, as we saw, women have been largely absent from high-level decision-making positions in the state planning departments that have determined levels of investment in technology, and the kind of technologies, for both industrial production and individual consumption, that society requires. These decision-makers for many decades operated in a context of Cold War that dictated high investment in the military and heavy industry, while light industry in which more women work was relatively starved of status, skills and technology.

At a national level, new technology has brought both advantages and disadvantages to women in the workforce. Its introduction into 'male' branches of industry for instance has seen a doubling of the number of women in engineering, including the electronics industry and the manufacture of automated machinery. In the manufacture of radio and precision instruments, for example, women are now around two-thirds of the workforce. However the great majority of them are in routine assembly work seen as calling for 'women's qualities' of accuracy and attention. This is work that is unpopular with men.

In the economy generally the introduction of computers and other electronic equipment has led to the appearance of new professions such as those of operator, perforator and programmer. Women are more than half the total in these occupations, but fill mainly auxiliary positions. Women are impeded in taking advantage of new technology by the fact that their educational qualifications are less frequently based in science and technology than those of men, more frequently in the humanities. Even women with appropriately specialized qualifications, however, are not able to use them to the full. Their terms of employment are worse than those of men and their progress into management is slow. This study is not alone in finding that, despite equal educational achievements, the employment gap between women and men has been widening.

Turning from production to consumption, *housing*, so important to women, has never been provided in adequate quantity or quality, and the state bureaucrats (mainly men) have failed to develop industries that could produce household labour-saving technologies. Perhaps most damaging of all for women, this system failed to develop effective mechanisms of *distribution*. The *nomenclatura* managed to satisfy their own needs, but ordinary families could provision themselves with food, clothing and commodities only by means of punishing effort. It is difficult to avoid concluding that men have created technologies and used them mainly in their own interests.

It is not surprising if our study at the micro level finds that the experiences of workers and managers in the Tushinskaya hosiery factory confirm trends observable in the country as a whole. We saw the undoubted benefits new production technology had brought to the plant and its people. Despite increased pressure of work and some reported deterioration in health, there was general satisfaction with the outcome: fewer harmful manual tasks, more interest and responsibility in the work, new job opportunities, higher wages. Increased revenue had enabled the provision of more amenities by the enterprise social fund. These gains were reported by women as well as men. *Yet the changes associated with new technology had not narrowed and in some cases had widened the gap between women and men.* The gender wage differential remained unchanged. The sexual division of labour, with men in skilled and responsible posts in new technology and women in subordinate, less skilled and routine occupations, had *increased* with new technology. We found possibilities for career advancement were only feebly and ineffectually used by women. The professional standing of the two sexes overall had diverged further. Women, particularly older women whom it was felt were unlikely to adapt to the computer and electronics, were besides experiencing more technological redundancy – exemplifying a trend observable in Russia as a whole.

The effects of Tushinskaya's technological innovation do not stop here of course. We saw that increased labour productivity and an improved product had enabled the factory to become competitive in price and quality with foreign manufacturers of panty hose. Tights, a commodity long desired by women, were now widely available on the market. The Tushinskaya development is in many ways a model of what women might wish for from any industrial capital investment policy. It could be a model for the diversion of production capacity from military to civilian – even domestic – products.

However, the full gains will not be experienced by women unless technological change is accompanied by a purposeful policy to end patriarchal attitudes and the disadvantage of women these entail. We summarize the following points for inclusion in a future technology policy in women's interests.

1 Priority should be given to technological investment in industries in which most women work and those which produce commodities most needed for the support of everyday life.
2 Every opportunity offered by new technology should be used to revise production norms and to free women from the unhealthy work so many do today.
3 Technology should be designed on ergonomic principles, taking account not only of men's but also of women's particular abilities and needs.
4 Special training and retraining provision should be provided to prepare women for new technological job opportunities, both practical and managerial.

5 The opportunity of technological change should be used to restructure jobs in such a way as to make non-standard hours available to those who need them, making it more possible for a worker to combine domestic responsibility with paid work without harm to health and without loss of job security.
6 New legal measures should be considered to guarantee an end to discrimination against women, for example, in recruitment, redundancy and retraining.
7 Research should be carried out to aid the development of a technology strategy for women, for example, on factors determining women's occupational choice and on the correlation between women's qualifications and career achievements.
8 Women should be equally involved with men in decision-making concerning new technology, in trade unions, enterprise management and state bodies.

Notes

1 The empirical research at Tushinskaya factory was carried out by Vitalina Koval and Tatjana Usunova.
2 There did however exist some research reports by Russian authors on women and automation, women's working conditions and women's professional qualifications. Among the authors are Drs L. Rzanitsina, Z. Hotkina, N. Pozdnjakova, L. Sadovnichia, N. Zacharova and Prof. Dr. N. Schischkan.
3 The number of women in the national labour force grew from around 14 million in 1940 to 68 million in 1989. Women also gained by the parallel growth in educational and professional qualification: by the end of the 1980s they were 61 per cent of those with higher or specialized secondary education.

On the other hand women cluster in certain feminized professions. Figures from the late 1980s show them to be 67 per cent of doctors, 87 per cent of economists, 89 per cent of bookkeepers and 91 per cent of librarians and bibliographers. Women are also 58 per cent of engineers – though this figure is somewhat misleading, since they tend to fill more administrative and fewer technical positions in engineering.

Even in management women have done well: 26 per cent are now to be found in the general category of manager. They are by no means absent among directors and departmental heads in manufacturing enterprises or of scientific production associations. Yet only 7 per cent of true 'decision-making' posts are held by women.

References

The following books and papers were consulted in writing the chapter. Where the item is published in Moscow the original title is in Russian and an English translation by this author is shown.

Family and Family Policy (1991) Moscow: Academy of Sciences of the USSR.

Francis, A. and Grootings, Peter (eds) (1989) *New Technologies and Work: Capitalist and Socialist Perspectives*. London and New York: Routledge.

Goscomstat USSR (1988–91) *Women in the USSR*, statistical materials. Moscow: Finance and Statistics Publishing House.

Grusdeva, Elena and Chertichina, Eleonora (1983) *Soviet Women at Work and at Home*. Moscow.

Job, Family and Home in the Life of Soviet Women (1990) Moscow: 'Juridicheskaya Literatura' Publishing House.

Krevnevitch, Valentina (1987) *Automation and Satisfaction with Work*. Moscow: 'Misl' Publishing House.

Problems of Work Security and Health of Women Today and Ways Towards Their Solution, Thesis of the Reports at the All Union Practical Scientific Conference, Ivanovo, 30 October–2 November 1988.

Schineleva, Ludmila (1990) *Women and Society*. Moscow.

Women in Society: Reality, Problems, Prognoses (1991) Moscow: 'Nauka' Publishing House.

Women in the Modern World (1989) Moscow: 'Nauka' Publishing House.

7

Bodies, machines and male power

M. CARME ALEMANY GOMEZ

In this study from Barcelona we follow the trajectory of one technical artefact: the clothes washing machine.[1] The washing machine, it goes without saying, is not a new invention. The features today's models display have been evolving for over 40 years. We shall see the considerations that have gone into its design in the past, and the reasons behind a recent remodelling. We look at how it is manufactured and by whom, and discuss its design implications in use in the home.

The artefact's trajectory is analysed as a *social* process, one in which both gender and class relations can be seen to be constructed and activated. In following its course we can see something of the interrelation between productive work in the factory and reproductive work in the home, as part of gender and class relations.

This approach, expecting to see gender and class relations in the life story of a machine, is one of three theories with which we approached the study. Second, we draw on a tradition of thought that is by now strongly established in social studies of science and technology (Callon and Latour 1988; Callon 1989; Latour 1989). We suppose that technology and society are not two interconnected domains, which none the less overlap, but that they are superimposed on each other (Woolgar 1991). Technology, in this view, is not seen as 'having social aspects', but as being social in its very constitution. It follows from this that in our study we do not understand technology as constructed outside gender and class relations. Rather we see technology, gender and class relations being a process in which all are a part, and all are simultaneously constructed.

Third, we see gender relations as a set of power relationships that not only involve the construction of values, behaviours and attitudes, but also constitute a process of bodily submission, as evidenced in postures, gestures and movements (Foucault 1979). Following the approach used in a different context by Michel Foucault, we extend it to the way in which gender and class relations are established by different social actors, placing particular emphasis on techniques and tactics of dominance.

The Spanish domestic appliance sector

In 1990, the most recent year for which figures are available, the 'white goods' industry in Spain had a turnover of 150,000 million pesetas and employed approximately 12,000 people. It was characterized by a heavy concentration of production and the dominant presence of large transnational groups. The sector's current form is the result of intense changes over the past decade, both in the sector itself and in Spain's industrial fabric as a whole, due partly to severe economic recession and partly to the processes culminating in Spain's entry to the European Economic Community (EEC) in 1986.

The Spanish white goods sector had grown fast throughout the 1960s and the first half of the 1970s, as a result of changes in both supply and demand. On the supply side, early in this period a technological transformation, led by Italian industry, began the sector's trend to mass production that eventually resulted in a significant reduction in prices (Owen 1983; Bianchi and Forlai 1988). By the end of the 1970s, white goods, especially refrigerators and washing machines, were no longer luxury items for a restricted market.

On the demand side, Spain saw a considerable demographic growth, rising incomes and rapid urbanization, and a development towards the consumer patterns of the more developed societies. These factors all favoured the purchase of domestic appliances by Spanish households. The tariff protection that operated in this period helped Spanish industry in particular to benefit from this growing market.

Since the manufacture of white goods calls only for relatively simple technology, the development tended to take place through medium-size enterprises. Spanish capital was clearly dominant in the process, even though the period did also see the expansion into the Spanish market of some transnationals – the American company Westinghouse and the Italian companies Ignis and Zanussi – with their own technology and brand-names.

A preferential treatment agreement signed by Spain and the EEC in 1970, anticipating Spain's accession to the Common Market, enabled Spanish white goods, among other industrial products, to enter the EEC countries under favourable conditions. Exports to non-EEC areas, particularly Portugal and North Africa, were also growing.

However, this period of economic expansion, or 'soft growth', in the sector was curtailed at the end of the 1970s, due partly to economic crisis, but also partly to certain inherent problems besetting the domestic appliance sector. The recession came at a time when the first-purchase market was showing signs of saturation in the most important ranges, such as kitchen stoves, refrigerators, heaters – and washing machines. It was besides very clear that Spain's imminent entry into the EEC would mean the end of protection for the industry in its home market. It would be thrown into open competition with the European white goods industry at a time of considerable excess capacity.

All these factors impelled the white goods industry in Spain into far-reaching changes that were to persist well into the 1980s. The government's Industrial Reconversion Plan for the sector set about eliminating surplus capacity, adjusting supply to demand and effecting labour reductions. Its main instruments were a consolidation of production and a series of fiscal, financial and labour measures. Its implementation did indeed effect a drastic reduction in the number of firms. By 1988 four-fifths of production was concentrated in three large groups, two of which were transnationals, with a loss of almost half the sector's jobs.

Technological innovation in washing machine production

Turning now to washing machines in particular – we will see that the design of a new prototype to replace existing models was shaped more by these macroeconomic factors than by any intention to produce a machine that would ease the burden of domestic washing. What we found to be motivating the manufacturer was that the new model would make possible the introduction of a quite different manufacturing process that promised a substantial rise in productivity. How many customers, when purchasing a 'technologically-improved' washing machine, understand that the improvements have been not to the machine's functioning but to the production line?

In Spain, 60 per cent of washing machine production is by two transnational groups, in both of which the central design and innovation unit is located at group headquarters. As a result, there is no research into new washing machine design in Spain itself. Technological innovation in domestic washing machine design is in any case limited. It is a technical appliance whose form has evolved over the decades to a point at which few improvements are now anticipated by its manufacturers. Engineers in the sector say that, to them, 'innovation' now means mainly the progressive incorporation into models for the lower end of the market of technological features already in use in quality or high-performance machines.

The company in which the fieldwork was carried out produces washing machines, under a well-established brand name, for the middle-to-bottom end of the market. Its factory, where we interviewed personnel, is situated in a large industrial area in the province of Barcelona. The firm was badly affected by the crisis in the sector, as a result of which it joined the

Industrial Reconversion Plan in 1986. Despite absorbing workers from another company, under the Plan the firm's overall workforce was reduced, by almost half, to 400 employees.

The aid received under the Plan did not bring about any modernization of the plant, nor the re-launch of the company. On the contrary, its only consequence was this shedding of labour and a virtual salary freeze for three years. The employees embarked on a long struggle to retain their jobs, and indeed this company has one of the highest levels of union activism.

In 1989, three years after the restructuring, the company was taken over, along with some others in the sector, by a large foreign group. Its new owners gave priority to increasing profitability by the following means. First, the entire management team was overhauled in a bid to put an end to the management policies of the 1980s. The manufacture of the various washing machine models was redistributed throughout the companies of the group in Spain and abroad, to enable longer production runs. Small-scale investments were made at various points in the production process with the aim of increasing manufacturing capacity and productivity. In particular, certain specific tasks that had been a source of conflict with the unions were now automated. Most important, however, was the introduction of the newly-designed washing machine mentioned above, so as to transform production methods and double output by 1993, without any increase in labour.

It will be evident, then, that it was not developments in the *washing process* but in the *manufacturing process* that were the main motive force behind this technological innovation. The quality of the machine as experienced by the user might be improved in the process but this would not have been its designers' prime concern.

The design process: limited input for women

It is striking that the network of actors we found taking part in both commercial and technical decision-making about washing machine development was male to a man, while women only appeared as users. Technological design and development were the responsibility of a specialist department of the firm: Product Engineering. The only woman here was the secretary.

We learned from the engineer in charge that small-scale improvements to a model might arise from the initiative of any one of several social actors, including the 'organization and methods' department, the production department, the marketing department and the department responsible for after-sales service. In the case of full-scale remodelling however the initiative would originate with Marketing. This department, working from market studies, from research carried out on their own products and from experience gathered through the commercial network, would draw up a detailed commercial specification for the new model, a blueprint or brief for Product Engineering, who would subsequently translate it into a design.

The interests of Marketing and Product Engineering do not necessarily coincide. The former is concerned primarily with the commercial success of the appliance. They must assure its popularity with the consumer, whose needs and motivations they must take into account. Product Engineering on the other hand introduces an additional objective: that of ensuring the new model is producible cheaply enough to be both competitive and profitable.

Women are explicitly considered only in the former perspective. Marketing make use of market surveys focused principally on women users. They also have women in mind in creating a public image for the washing machine and deciding an advertising strategy. Product Engineering, by contrast, with the excuse of working solely to technical objectives, seeks to ignore the fact that the principal users of the machine will be women. The engineer heading this department made this clear. 'In the conception and design of the washing machine, engineering does not take into consideration the person who's going to use the appliance', he said. The concern of the department, he admitted, stopped with manufacturing. 'This is a factory and we sell washing machines to our commercial representatives, and in some way it is at this point that there's a slight breakdown in communication with the outside world.'

Management clearly prefer communication with the user to be limited to the commercial departments. None the less, like it or not, Product Engineering does in reality need to know the reactions and responses of users in a more direct form. Product Engineering, we found, arguing the deficiency of Marketing's research reports, had invented its own strategies.

In the first place, the engineers invoked something they called the 'washing machine culture', informal knowledge accumulated over many years. In addition to beliefs about washing machine use generated within this culture, the image of the user was further shaped in the Test Laboratory where the technicians tried to 'imagine the errors that might be made during use'. This involved constructing a series of scenarios depicting women's 'clumsiness' and 'technical ignorance' that justified the incorporation into the machine of devices that, in the technicians' perception, would prevent it from malfunctioning however inept its use.

Images of the users so constructed are of course highly coloured by gender relations. The devices the *male* designer incorporates in the machine do not always lead to an improvement in the machine as actually put to work by *female* users. For example, in the prototype we studied at design stage, the drum was positioned higher in relation to the door than in the model it superseded. This had been done for a strictly techno-economic reason: reduction of assembly time and hence of production cost. The effect was that in use the water level in the machine would be higher than the bottom of the door. This in turn necessitated a safety catch (in fact incorporated in most modern washing machines), in case, as the engineers put it, 'the woman were absent mindedly to open the door during the washing cycle', or 'a child were to open the machine'. Women and children were often associated in the engineers' thinking in a way that clearly reduced women's capabilities to those of a child. Product Engineering entirely failed to imagine, or perhaps having imagined chose to ignore, the clear disadvantage to the user of being unable to add extra items of clothing to the wash after the start of the cycle.

A further strategy of Product Engineering to get access to user knowledge is to build a limited number of prototypes of the new model and distribute them among members of the company's senior staff for their 'wives' to test in use and give their opinion. Such interaction between the firm and 'the domestic sphere' is of course highly unusual, home life normally being rigorously distanced from working life. Its artificial importation in this way is explainable only as an effect of the sexual division of housework: company engineers (male) have no personal experience on which to judge the effectiveness of their designs. They justify using company wives by saying they are distant enough from the design process to be objective critics but close enough to the firm to be trusted to keep its secrets.

Finally, a prototype is also tested in the Test Laboratory, which communicates its findings back to Product Engineering. The laboratory is, not incidentally, staffed by women. Like the mobilization of company wives, this is a mechanism to introduce the user, in a strictly retrospective way, into a late stage of appliance design fully controlled by men.

Test Laboratory staff are not in a position to effect any fundamental change to design. Their concern is limited to the finer details of the machine in use, such as noise levels and the duration of washing cycles. They devote a good deal of attention to the design of controls, their size and ease of use, testing them against the strength of the hands of female employees, and they study difficulties encountered in loading clothes, assessing the optimum door size and fastening. By the time the prototype reaches the Test Laboratory, the basic conception of the machine is fixed, and it reflects men's interests rather than women's. Since the women laboratory technicians do not have sufficient technical training to query the technical aspects of the various devices incorporated, men's technical control of the appliance is not challenged.

Consider for instance the fundamental choice between top and front loading machines. Top loading is more convenient for the user, who avoids having to stoop or kneel, and can open the lid at whim at any point in the wash cycle. Yet, very few manufacturers in Spain today make top loading machines. They require more assembly time and are for that reason unpopular with production engineers. Instead, the firms' commercial departments use every means to promote their preferred front loading models, which as a result have become the norm in the Spanish market. At the same time, interior designers and manufacturers of kitchen fittings have been inflexible in designing washing machines into the kitchen, prioritizing worktop space and hence the front loader. This too has inhibited the demand for the top loading machine.

Housework is the 'female domain' *par excellence*. These are the tasks considered to be the 'natural' role of women. Yet what we see here, and what other research shows (Chabaud-Rychter 1987), is that *men model and control women's domestic work through the electrical appliances they design*. Furthermore, this control that men exercise extends even to women's *bodies*. The design of a washing machine not only specifies in general how clothes will be washed. It predetermines the washing practices a woman must adopt down to the very movements she must make, over and over again, as she uses the machine.

This control over women's bodies through technical design, even though it is not stated explicitly at any time, is detectable in the way the design engineers dwell on those gender differences that can be interpreted as physical inferiority in the female – weaker hands for example. One can surmise too that the choice of the front loading solution in preference to top loading is a gendered choice. The stooped position, the bending motion required to put clothes in the front loader would be rejected out of hand were men the anticipated users: to be manly is to be upright. Bending and kneeling is an acceptable concomitant of the design only because the user is that already subordinated creature, a woman, and the designer is not. Had things been otherwise perhaps more energy would have been put into seeking 'appropriate technical solutions' to avoid subjecting the user to this daily obeisance to the machine. We shall see some similarly gendered ergonomic processes occurring in the case of factory jobs.

Production: myths of strength and skill

What we saw happening above, in 'design for use', was totally gendered thinking in engineering. It is thinking in which in reality there is always a gender model, yet in which gender is never fully admitted in such a way as to be incorporated openly into professional knowledge and design skill. It has this semi-conscious, shadowy existence because to bring it fully to view would involve the engineers in admitting their own masculinity and partiality. For they are partial in two senses – biased and incomplete. An exactly parallel process visible in 'design for manufacture' supports this interpretation.

Asked who they thought was going to do the various production jobs they were planning, the chief engineer said 'when you design, you are automatically and logically thinking how the appliance can be made'. It was this *how* he admitted as his concern, not a specific *who*. In this way the design and development appear to be asexual, or at least a process in which gender relations are peripheral. In practice, however, since the engineer is male and he does not bear a woman in mind, the process has reference to a male norm.

This is important, since the technological choices in the design of the appliance have, and are intended to have, direct implications for production, and hence for the work of the producers. Following the washing machine from design to production it became clear to us that those implications involved the reproduction of gender difference and inequality.

The engineers we spoke with, working in the design and manufacture of washing machines, were agreed that there were no longer any physical barriers to prevent women participating fully in the manufacturing process – with the unimportant exception of a few particular tasks that would in any case soon be redundant. Yet we found women to be only around 15 per cent of the workforce in this industrial sector and an even smaller minority (10 per cent) in the company in which our study was made.

An analysis of the distribution of tasks in the washing machine manufacturing process showed, as other gender studies of technology have shown (Cockburn 1985), that the technology factor in a job operates to exclude women. In some tasks, given differences in average male and female size and musculature, this is literally the case. Certain controls are designed to suit the size and strength of a male hand. The height of certain machines, such as sheet metal presses, is too great for the average woman's stature. The resulting jobs are considered by women and men alike as being more suitable for the latter. Women however are clear that this is due to the design of the tool or machine, not to the type of work, which they say is not essentially difficult.

It is not that tools and machines are designed or selected for the production line without conscious thought. On the contrary, size, cost and functioning are hotly debated within the development team. The neglect of gender, the failure to take professionally into consideration as one relevant design factor the ways in which women and men differ is, ironically, *gendered*. It has to be read as a specific and significant omission, an expression of gender power relations in the workplace.

As Foucault suggests, however, power is not simple repression but 'a complex network of strategies' (Foucault 1979: 108). It achieves its very effect from the way we all, in one way or another, participate in it: even the oppressed gain something. Power operates in gender relations in such a way that women's oppression is sometimes expressed as, even experienced as, something positive. One male worker for instance declared 'it's not right that a woman should work on the metal presses, because if a man loses a finger, that's one thing. But a woman! . . .' The exclusion of women from certain operations in the workplace may thus be legitimized as kindness – protecting them and their femininity from harm.

Weakness and strength

Physical strength is an important factor in job design. Advances in technology, such as conveyor belts, handling equipment, automation and robotics, have gradually reduced the number of jobs calling for a great deal of physical strength. The jobs so transformed, incidentally, have often been the ones that were a source of labour conflict. In the manufacture of washing machines, however, certain jobs are still classified as 'heavy'. Press maintenance work, which calls for occasional removal of the extruders from the presses, was one such. The handling of the washing machine drum in the manufacturing process was another. Both these jobs were performed by men, who earned a special wage supplement entailed by law in the case of tasks involving the application of a force of more than 5 kg. In cases where the physical force required exceeded the legal limit of 25 kg, men had invoked the law and refused to do the work. Drum handling was, through such action, eventually lightened by introduction of mechanical aids.

It is important however to distinguish between the *absolute level* of strength required and the *frequency or continuity* with which effort has to be sustained. It is significant that the law only governs the former and has nothing to say about the continuous repetition of smaller amounts of exertion, as involved in many women's jobs. In washing machine manufacture we found some sections staffed exclusively by women – for example, bundling and attaching electrical cables for the programmers. These are jobs which seem 'light', since they do not call for exertion of a 5 kg force at any one moment. Yet the movements involved impose repetitive strain on the hands, elbows, shoulders and back.

In these sections the typical health hazard is not the one-off sprain of a muscle or ligament, but a chronic condition caused by the rhythm of production that may in some cases be irreversible. For instance, a significant number of women in the cable section have had to have surgery for carpal tunnel syndrome due to repetitive strain injury to the wrists. The arduous nature of the work characteristically performed by women in the factory was not recognized by management however. They were unable to claim any wage supplement because their tasks was not heavy work as defined in law.

Some 'light' repetitive jobs, for instance certain subassembly activities, as it happened involved both sexes. In these cases we found the behaviour of women and men in relation to the health hazard entirely different. Women had no hesitation in complaining of physical strain induced by their work. To do so in no way affronted their gender identity. The men, however, were inhibited by their sense of themselves as men. Men cannot, without diminishing their own virility, admit to fatigue when the job is 'light' and calls for no visible level of physical strength.

In the mixed sections it was therefore the women's complaints that sometimes brought about an improvement in working conditions for both sexes. For instance, men, despite frequent cuts and other minor injuries, had refused to wear protective gloves on the production line. When women were introduced to the line, free from the constraints of masculine self-identity, they adopted the protective wear, which in due course became common practice for men too. This obviated one job at the end of the production line: wiping off the blood stains on the white enamel. It had been a woman's job, no doubt because it was felt to need a feminine hand to raise the product to the houseproud standard demanded by the market.

Finally, there are certain men's jobs in which automation is eliminating the demand for physical strength. Seen in this light, technological innovation benefits 'the worker', but in practice the gains accrue mainly to men. Despite the fact that women could now do them, such jobs in the washing machine factory had seldom been opened up to women. The forklift truck had been introduced to take the strain out of 'manhandling' heavy goods. Women however continued to be excluded from goods handling long after the objective justification had gone.

Because the forklift truck symbolizes strength, the job of driving it is masculine like the manual job it replaced. Implements, tools and machinery expand human potential to lift weights and manipulate materials. They could in theory empower women by enabling them to transcend their current physical limits. Given prevailing gender relations and gender symbolism however they serve instead to enhance male power.

Masculinity is associated not only with physical strength but also with physical mobility. We found women doing jobs that *required* less mobility than the jobs men did. For instance, the machines they operated called for less physical movement than men's machines. They were also in the main doing the kind of jobs that *permit* less mobility. We found women moved about less than men from one section, or one part of the factory, to another. Their exclusion from forklift driving was a case in point. Sections staffed only by women were often located in marginal areas of the factory from which the women rarely emerged. Male sections occupied more central areas, so men's presence was more visible and significant. Women performed more stable tasks that did not involve rotation nor permit of contact with many people. For example, there is one activity that offers just this kind of interaction. If a worker needs to leave an assembly line like this one for even a moment to visit the WC, she or he must call for a 'pee relief'. Although there were women who were well qualified, having performed every job on the line, we found not one filling this role.

Finally, women's work is often performed sitting down or in a bending position, postures that we have already seen are considered suitable or natural for women, but not for men. Men refuse such tasks whenever possible, opting where they can for an upright position. It may be more tiring, but at least it is not effeminate. This was brought home to us in interview by a young male operator. He mused on the women at their benches in the electrical cable section. 'It looks as if they're *sewing*', he said. He showed what he meant by bowing over the bench, in an ugly gesture that spoke even more clearly than his words. 'Having to work in a bending position like that isn't what you'd call *virile*'.

We are used to analysing 'women's jobs' in terms of the attitudes and aptitudes they call for. If we look, however, as we have done here, more closely at bodies and physique, we can see clearly just how men use technology to secure domination over and control of women.

Ignorance and knowledge

We found the association of masculinity with technology in the factory to be profound and widespread. Men were given priority over women in the retraining schemes made necessary by the new manufacturing process. Men were taught about the technical features and functioning of the equipment, while women's training was limited to simple instruction in operations. Again, machine maintenance technicians in the factory were exclusively men, even though some had no specific training in the area. It was inconceivable that a woman with equally little training be offered such a job.

Women were assumed to be technologically ignorant. When a woman did take on a job that had formerly been done by a man, there was a general scepticism as to her ability to do it. She was obliged to prove her value to the group if she were to be recognized and accepted as an equal. Similarly, when women suggested modifications to tools or pointed to problems with the work methods imposed by the foreman, they were seldom taken seriously. Only when their suggestions were seen to work was their ability acknowledged. Getting their ideas implemented, however, involved such prolonged insistence that women were of course labelled 'obstinate'.

The exclusion of women from technical knowledge and technical work, as research in other countries has found (Kergoat 1978), blocked their possibilities of promotion. Women were stuck in the lower category jobs, while men climbed out of them. None of the positions of authority in the plant was held by a woman, even in all-female sections. Yet most of the male supervisors and foremen, as women well knew, were no more than workers promoted up from the production line or other manufacturing jobs. 'It's not as if they have qualifications. We know them . . .'

Such supervisory jobs enable those who do them to accumulate technological knowledge. As men get these opportunities, and women do not, the gap between the sexes widens. Nor is women's exclusion from requisite knowledge unique to production. In the administrative departments too we found women had few possibilities for promotion. Women in both situations know full well what is happening. They seldom complain, however, because they consider promotion or professional advancement beyond their reach.

The difficulties encountered by women in getting their jobs reclassified or in getting promotion out of them were absent from the union's negotiating agenda. The union was simply ignoring women's problems. As one woman put it, 'They look after "working conditions", not women's issues.' We found very few women participating in union activities. Women agreed that if there were women on the committee, women's issues would be more likely to be put forward. Often however domestic responsibilities were a barrier to women organizing and making their own demands. One woman explained, 'I'm very limited. I've got my children and my job . . .', whereas 'if the men have a meeting, they think "I'll see the children later", and they leave them with their grandmother or someone.' Inequalities at home and work reinforced each other.

Implications of the new model machine

As already mentioned, our research period coincided with the design stage of a new model of washing machine. Product Engineering's objective in this was 'to double production and improve quality with an investment of about 1,000 million pesetas ($10.3 million or £5 million), without increasing the number of employees'. The new model would introduce new materials and a different production process, including simplification of certain assembly sequences. In turn, these innovations would call into existence a new mode of work organization, most importantly the virtual elimination of existing assembly lines, each with their 30 work stations and quality control at the end.

Instead the machine was to be constructed in a series of 'islands', in which each individual would carry out several work sequences and be responsible for quality control and self-rectifying of mistakes. The production job would thus become more varied and responsible. The assembly line as such would be virtually defunct, reduced to six unskilled functions at the end of the new island processes.

The 'new technical solutions', as the engineers called them, were expected to reduce production time by 60 per cent and greatly improve product quality. By eliminating the conflict-prone jobs they would eradicate nearly all the sources of worker unrest that had been troubling the factory. They would also make less onerous some other jobs that, though not a source of strife, did have a record of low productivity and high absenteeism for reasons of ill health. Since these improvements would benefit the workers, we may perhaps acknowledge them as being, in part, won by class struggle.

The management clearly recognized that the new methods were going to call for a somewhat different quality in the worker. The engineers were talking about a new 'manpower culture' and envisaged a need for conversion training and re-skilling. In principle the restructuring in the factory could have been used as the occasion for a new personnel policy, geared to reducing the sexual division of labour and lifting women out of the low job categories to which they were confined. There were no signs of this happening. Indeed, listening to the engineers in Product Engineering and Organization and Methods, we felt the innovations were likely to reinforce existing gender relations.

When, in our interviews, the discussion was on a general level, they used generic terms such as *gente* (people), *personal* (personnel) and *personas* (people of both sexes). However, whenever the conversation turned to specific jobs calling for degrees or other qualifications, they automatically slipped into using masculine nouns and pronouns. For example, one engineer explained the island system as follows:

> It would be a job where the *person* [*la persona*, i.e. man or woman] would be more fulfilled. It wouldn't any longer be just tacking on your little piece and then the next *man* [*el siguiente*, masculine gender] fixes his on and passes it on to the one after . . .

The masculine form used here is a deliberate masculinizing of the statement, since its usage in fact breaks the rules of Spanish grammar. *La persona*, though a feminine noun, refers equally to woman and man. The correct correlative would be the sex-neutral *la siguiente*.

This was by no means an isolated slip. We heard, 'The *person* will have responsibility. But if a part is defective, it's not *his* problem [*no es problema de el*]. *He* just has to reject it.' And again,

In the assembly line, one *woman* [*una*] put on the water connection, another [*otra*] fixed on the electricity connection, and each was one job. But in the new system, the one *fellow* [*este senor*] will put on several things, the water connection, the electricity supply, the condenser and so on.

Despite the management's hope that the changes could be effected without increasing staff, it appeared that a small amount of recruitment would be unavoidable. Who would get the chances? One engineer foresaw 'every attempt will be made to retrain the people [*la gente*, women and men] who already work here'. Gripped by this pervasive inertia, however, he added 'although we'll need some new *operarios* [grammatically, *working men*].' And he went on, 'We are planning more complete jobs so that the *operario* will be more satisfied with *his* work.'

Some would be good jobs calling for technological qualifications. The engineering departments foresaw taking on staff 'who could be *delineantes* [draughts*men*] or *tecnicos* [male technicians], a *man* who also knows how to calculate'. They were talking about employing a *maestro industrial* (graduate engineer) or an *ingeniero tecnico* (technical engineer). Alternative feminine forms for these terms do exist in Spanish, but clearly did not spring to mind. The engineers did not have the same difficulty in finding feminine terms, however, when the discussion turned to the need for additional office staff.

The engineers had given no thought to the possibility of adapting the new jobs to the physical capabilities of women, for instance by specifying appropriately sized tools and parts. The modifications considered had any and every reason except involving women more equally in technical production. Certain men's jobs, we knew, were going to be 'lightened'. When we asked one engineer specifically whether these would in future be unisex jobs, he prevaricated. 'Yes, there's no reason why not, since there's no great strength needed – nor – no, there's no reason why not. Of course it depends on how many workers we have and the new ones we'll have to take on. I don't know. But in principal...', and so on, and so forth.

Jobs are thus conceptualized, evaluated and structured by those who have power over them, in line with masculine values. Women are left with residual tasks that are not 'proper jobs' for men. An engineer in Product Engineering made it clear enough: 'Women are far more effective than men for repetitive, routine tasks.' Another in Organization and Methods echoed him: 'Women are ideal for assembling wiring... they are more careful and delicate, much more skilful manually.' They were in total harmony in agreeing that 'it's better for women to be in the jobs where a certain delicacy is needed, because they're more refined and careful than men'.

In all these subtle and not-so-subtle expressions of gendered thinking we see how men's power is perpetuated and expanded in the process of technological innovation, how always justifications are ready to hand for excluding women from all but the jobs men do not want.

The washing machine in use

As with other researchers in this European project we particularly wanted to make the conceptual connections: workplace/home, production/consumption, design/use. We therefore went on to interview seven washing machine owning couples, the better to understand the social relations of washing machine use. They were heterosexual couples, married and unmarried, between 25 and 50 years of age, representing low, middle and upper-middle income brackets. In each instance the woman had paid work outside the home. Two of the couples were in fact employed by the washing machine manufacturer. Each individual was interviewed separately, some being seen at work, some at home.

Of course the numbers here are small and even our in-depth interviews cannot permit of generalization. None the less, we found some interesting examples of how a household technology-in-use is shaped by the gender dynamics of the heterosexual relationship.

Ownership of a washing machine depends partly on the duration and stability of a marriage or partnership. Students and young unmarried couples not long living together seldom have a washing machine. We therefore found ourselves interviewing couples who had been together some years, and who had jointly chosen and purchased their machine.

Among the men of these seven couples we noted a clear age difference in attitudes to housework. In the oldest couple interviewed (45 and 50 years), the man had never approached the washing machine to put in a load, nor yet to take one out. Nevertheless, he was quite familiar with its operation since he and his wife were employed by the manufacturer. He, besides, had a second occupation repairing appliances.

His wife, it transpired, was in any case unwilling to abandon control of the laundry, justifying herself by saying she understood better the care of her husband's clothes and the household linen. In any case, as she said, 'with two jobs, my husband is never at home'. This woman, it must be noted, perhaps by virtue of her involvement in washing machine manufacture, was fully capable of repairing and adjusting her washing machine.

The elder of the two daughters in this family, though she did not participate in any family laundry chores, often used the washing machine for her blue jeans for which she had her own routine: wash in cold water and spin dry at top velocity. She would also occasionally throw in dirty underwear, unearthed when cleaning her room.

The youngest couple in the study had an approach not dissimilar to that of this young woman. Their laundry was not done systematically, but coincided more or less with room cleaning. Should one or other have need of a specific article of clean clothing, that person would take steps to wash it. The man would do his own shirts on an emergency basis, and look after the washing of his jeans without devoting any special care to them. His partner, by contrast, used the washing machine thoughtfully having evolved a sorting system for the wash. While her companion often spontaneously threw in a half-load, she was the one who took responsibility for the greater part of the household laundry.

Justifying his practice, this man explained that his partner did a good deal of careful hand-washing and he did not want to risk damaging her delicate things by mixing them in with his own. She, for her part, said his rough approach to washing would not do for her silk blouses. 'He doesn't have to take care of his clothing the way I do.'

In some homes we found men participating in washing in a selective way. They would take on the washing of, say, towels and the children's jeans but leave the rest to the woman for fear of 'making mistakes'. Such men preferred a sporadic involvement, avoiding commitment while giving an impression of being cooperative.

In general it was the younger men in our small sample who were to some extent – if spasmodically – participating in household laundry. Perhaps we were seeing a generational change in the way men relate to housework. If so, the shift was not one from non-participation to full sharing, but rather one from non-participation to 'showing an interest' in learning a few skills to 'help' the woman, whose sphere the household continued to be. At best men's participation was unreliable and they continued to give priority to activity outside family and home.

There was an age difference in the washing practices of the women in the sample too, cut across by other factors, such as engagement or otherwise in outside work, and the skill level of that work. The older women were unshaken in their belief that washing is women's work. 'Men don't know how to.' They were therefore not eager to ask their menfolk for more help. In answer to our question whether they would welcome more collaboration from their husbands, they might answer 'yes', but it would be with a smile of disbelief that said 'that'll be the day!' When women, and it was mainly the younger women, did demand of their partners, directly or subtly, more participation in housework, men were not unresponsive. They would 'help' more, though irregularly, and not to the extent of equal sharing. For that they would require a willingness they do not show to learn the finer arts of laundry skill.

On the other hand, women themselves impede such a transformation in the gender relations of housework by their own inflexibility. Many women would like more involvement from their partners but are themselves unwilling to see the household laundry practices modified. They are unwilling to negotiate their sense of propriety, their standards of cleanliness and their preferences for a certain order in domestic work. For instance, many women will wash a man's underwear but not expect him to wash hers, apparently feeling it an intrusion into an intimate and personal feminine space. The woman in the young couple cited above, albeit abetted by her partner's carelessness, could be seen as actively impeding his involvement by her protectiveness over her silk blouses. Again, men usually arrive home later in the evening than women, even when both work. Women often use this as a reason to be the one to start the wash, when objectively it would not suffer from a small delay.

Willingness to negotiate seems to be lowest when the woman's external work is non-skilled, low paid or low in satisfaction. We found women in that situation to be the ones tending to take their housework more seriously and to be more possessive about it, as if they were compensating thereby for the minimal responsibility and self-respect accorded them in the world outside the home.

Men's power and women's bodies

This sketch of an artefact pursuing its course from conception through to use has highlighted the class and gender relations in technological processes. The interrelation between class and technology is clear enough. Class relations involve a dynamic opposition between two forces with contrary intentions. What capital seeks in technological innovation is greater profitability. Women and men of the workforce look to it for an improvement in their working conditions. We saw evidence of both these motivations in the company described.

The interrelationship of technology and gender is more subtle and less obvious, but no less profound. Technological innovation occurs within and reinforces existing, traditional gender relationships. We saw several gendered phenomena in the workplace that add up to systematic forms of control and physical domination of women that can only be interpreted as manifestations of male power.

There was the dominant position of men as a sex in the design and development of the artefact. There was the actual display of physical strength by men, and an affirmation of their physical superiority through association with machines that symbolized strength. There was the size of controls and levers on certain machines and tools, explicable only by the masculinity of the intended user. Simply by virtue of being men, men occupied not only management and professional positions in the firm, but the better paid manual jobs evaluated and graded according to masculine criteria of what is arduous work and what is technical work. Technology presents itself as an instrument in the hands of men that dramatizes and augments masculine supremacy.

Then again, we saw women excluded from jobs that, though once they called for a man's strength, no longer did so. Instead, women were performing jobs that needed manual dexterity or care in handling parts. Skills and characteristics learned in their lives as girls and women, assumed to be 'natural' attributes of the female sex (Kergoat 1990), were being used to confine them to some jobs and exclude them from others. The effect was again, in a workforce where women were entirely absent from supervisory, professional or management positions, a clear advantage for men in pay, status and control. To compound women's disadvantage, male solidarity and dominance in the trade union combined with that in the plant to prevent them from organizing in support of their own demands. These are not incidental phenomena, but active affirmations of male supremacy through technology and organization.

Male dominance and female subordination persist in both public and private spheres, and the gender relations of workplace and home are mutually reinforcing. We saw how women's workload in the home deprives them of the time they need to be involved in negotiating their rights at work. Besides, as other researchers have pointed out, women's domestic responsibilities, so often cited by employers as an explanation of their unequal treatment at work, might just as well be seen as equipping them (precisely by tying their hands) as a supremely desirable, super-exploitable labour force (Chabaud-Rychter *et al.* 1985). Conversely, dissatisfied with their paid work, women tend to overcompensate with domestic chores – which in turn holds them back from making cogent demands on men to share them.

We found too that women were active participants in patterns of relationship that perpetuate their oppression. In the circumstances in which they are employed, women themselves are often obliged to define their physical needs relative to the work load, which inevitably involves stressing their own physical *limitations*. Such demands cannot help but play into the image of women as relatively weak. They do not force men to acknowledge them as equal and valuable. They are therefore well enough received by the men who hold power – just so long as they do not involve them in much expenditure.

Women occupied relatively less space, and less prominent space, in the factory than men. This too reflected women's own reticence: we found the majority of women eating their meal at their work station, leaving the dining room to men. A cycle is generated in which women come to feel like intruders in spaces into which they seldom venture. It is likely that this withdrawal from space nominally shared by both sexes is partly due to women's avoidance of sexual harassment.

The tale of the social life of this innocent artefact, the washing machine, then, uncovers a painful reality in which men can be seen to control women, not just through symbolic manipulation of difference but also through quite material bodily positioning and inferiorizing. We might hypothesize that the continual reaffirmation of men's physical superiority serves to keep alive a fear in women of actual physical aggression by men – the ultimate weapon of male supremacy.

Note

1 This research was financed by the Women's Institute (Ministry of Social Affairs, Madrid) and CICYT (Inter-Ministry Commission of Science and Technology, Madrid, Reference SEC92-0465). It was carried out at the Centre for Studies on Women and Society, Barcelona.

146 *Bringing technology home*

References

Bianchi, Patrizio and Forlai, Luigi (1988) The European domestic appliance industry 1945–87, in de Jong, H.W. (ed.) *The Structure of European Industry*. Dordrecht: Kluwer Academic Publishers.

Callon, Michel (1989) *La Science et Ses Reseaux: Genèse et Circulation des Faits Scientifiques [Science and Its Networks]*. Paris: La Decouverte.

Callon, Michel and Latour, Bruno (1988) Recherche, Innovation, Industrie [Research, innovation, industry], special issue of *Culture Technique* edited by these authors, No. 18, March. Neuilly sur Seine: Centre de Recherche sur la Culture Technique.

Chabaud-Rychter, Danielle (1987) La division sexuelle des techniques [The sexual division of technique], in *Les Rapports Sociaux de Sexe [Gender Relations]*, Cahiers de l'APRE, No. 7, Vol. 1. Paris: Centre National de la Recherche Scientifique.

Chabaud-Rychter, Danielle, Fougeyrollas-Schwebel, Dominique and Sonthonnax, Françoise (1985) *Espace et Temps du Travail Domestique [The Space and Time of Domestic Work]*. Reponses sociologiques [Sociological answers]. Paris: Librarie des Meridiens.

Cockburn, Cynthia (1985) *Machinery of Dominance: Women, Men and Technical Knowhow*. London: Pluto Press.

Foucault, Michel (1979) *Microfisica del Poder (Microphysics of Power)*. Madrid: La Piqueta.

Kergoat, Danièle (1978) Ouvriers = ouvrières? [Male workers equal women workers?] in *Critiques de l'Economie Politique [Political Economy Review]*, new series, No. 5, October–December, pp. 65–97.

Kergoat, Danièle (1990) *Qualification et rapports sociaux de sexe (Skill and Gender)*. Paper presented at the World Congress of Sociology, Madrid.

Latour, Bruno (1989) *La Science en Action (Science in Action)*. Paris: Editions La Decouverte.

Owen, Nicholas (1983) *Economies of Scale, Competitiveness and Trade Patterns within the European Community*. Oxford: Clarendon Press.

Woolgar, Steve (1991) *Abriendo la Caja Negra (Science: The Very Idea)*. Barcelona: Editorial Anthropos.

8

Women, technology and societal failure in former Yugoslavia

ANDJELKA MILIĆ

This story is, and has to be, qualitatively different from others in this book. It emerges from a unique, and uniquely terrible, situation. The country in which I began research for our joint project was among those aspiring to development and modernity, one that saw itself as constituting a successful paradigm between socialist and market systems, and was seen by other Europeans as a beautiful place to enjoy sun and sea. That country no longer exists. At the time of writing I live in a land of disintegrating communities, of torture, rape and killing.

At a certain point I felt it impossible to continue. The war brought political priorities to the fore and made empirical research on 'gender and technology' practically difficult and emotionally irrelevant. For a moment I abandoned the project. Then it dawned on me that our very theme was one way into the story of a society that had failed. There was, however, a prerequisite for the telling: the tale had to be simultaneously on two levels, the personal and the societal. The research findings and analysis had to be bracketed with my own life narrative.

It all began so innocently. It was in July 1988 in Zagreb, torpid and lazy in the summer heat, on the eve (I recall) of a major international meeting, the World Congress of Anthropology, that our own little group of women sociologists met for the first time. We discussed and set a framework for this cross-comparative project on 'technology and gender relations'. I decided I would contribute research on one of the newest of domestic technologies in Yugoslavia: the personal computer. There was something in the air at that time that promised a new era and I felt both a personal and professional excitement about our project.

About a decade previously, Yugoslavia had experienced its epidemic of 'computer fever'. Computers swept into industrial, commercial and financial organizations. Particularly interesting for our research, a household market had opened up for the personal computer. The technology I chose could thus meet the criteria for our joint project. It would enable me to study the technology–gender relation in two separate but related segments of everyday life: work and home. I could research gender relations both where the sexes meet in the process of production of personal computers and in the family setting where they meet as consumers.

In the following two years I completed the production phase of the research, while participating in our occasional team meetings, sharing our research experiences and deepening our friendships. Then, for me, a hiatus occurred. Disintegration of my country, which became an anomaly on the map of Europe: ex-Yugoslavia. War in Slovenia, war in Croatia, war in Bosnia Herzegovina. As the horizons darkened and we were plunged into general and individual uncertainty, the first reaction was to hide from the horror, refuse to accept the reality unfolding all around. Then followed a period of apathy, of getting used to being in a war situation, being subjected to sanctions, a gradual acceptance of an infinite extension of the given moment.

As I write I find myself trying to stop time, to turn it back to the beginning of the story, to collect together the broken fragments of the research and with them the pieces of my very existence. More re-examination, more self-re-examination. All the time new perspectives keep opening up, new questions pose themselves, fresh insights about the research and its social protagonists keep occurring to me. Can I continue as though the interruption never happened? Where to begin from? How to continue? Which story is the true one, the one I started telling before the war, or the one I tell now? Is it possible to establish some link between my choices and findings as a researcher 'before' and the realities I confront 'now'? Perhaps there are causalities and connections we can see now – things that were buried so deep they could be brought to the surface only by an explosion so terrible it tore open the very fundament of Yugoslav society and unleashed this pent-up torrent of discontent and antagonism, passion and violence.

If I look at the whole concept of my research project from the perspective of 'now', I can see that its main actors – computer technology, women and men – are still there as before. Now however they occupy different roles, their relations have changed and they exert different influences on each other. Computers are no longer produced or purchased to achieve greater efficiency in business or administration, nor to provide home entertainment for girls and boys. Instead they are being produced and applied to devices that will achieve greater efficiency in destruction and killing, by and of those same girls and boys. The women and the men whom I saw before, negotiating with each other in the production and use of computers, struggling with gender relations in the process, I see today defined exclusively by an atavistic sexual division of labour. In an affirmation of unmoderated patriarchal gender relations, men are warriors whose purpose is defence and attack; women are mothers, wives and sisters whose task is to protect and renew life.

There is, however, an important continuity. 'Before', the traditional gender roles against which women struggled were always represented as unchangeable, as given by nature. In the same way, 'now', the war, and the reconstruction of women and men for their particular war assignments, appears as an ineluctable necessity. It is seen as something in which people have no choice, something dictated by a higher, unquestionable will. This constant conservative evocation of the 'naturalness' of relations and events does constitute a link between then and now, and in it, I believe, lies the key to our story. It is the reason we fail to break out of the vicious circle, the current that pulls us continually backwards.

If this connection I now see between the time 'before' and 'now' is real, not just an artefact of my desire to restore a disrupted sequence, I can take up the tale of the research. I can start over anew, writing a story founded on a clear-eyed critique, one that strips away the veil cast over things by this persisting discourse of 'naturalness' by means of which so many of the social actors make meaning of the events in which they are caught up and of their part in them.

The new story that I shall now tell is a tale about a tale and has to take into consideration a wider range of actors, factors and relations than the one I originally had in mind. It will deal with three matters. The first is the *modernization process* in former Yugoslav society that was the background to the maturing of today's actors. I shall explore this through two signally important phenomena within it: *technology* and *education*. The second is the *gender relations* of that modernization and in particular women as actors in this process that was supposed to have been bringing them social equality and personal emancipation. The third is the relations of gender and technology seen in two contrasted contexts – *the rural household*, at one extreme, and *the high-technology enterprise*, at the other. Those two poles bring into view two contrasted groups of women: the rural housewife-cum-agricultural labourer; and the woman engineer. We shall be able to see, in their 'before' worlds, how gender and technology were among the social relations in which the 'now' breakdown of modernization and the retreat to the so-called natural state were already being prepared.

Socialist industrialization or modernization?

If the country could collapse, as it did, from one moment to the next into chaos and war it makes sense to ask: just what had been going on in Yugoslav society during the last half century? Was development, despite the fact that we lived it in our own lives, saw it with our own eyes, and read it reflected in the eyes of the world, no more than illusion? Was technology not in fact the agent of modernization we thought it to be, but merely a machine mass-producing cheap plastic decoration, a veneer that hid an unchanged structure? Was education not the guarantor of modernity after all? Were the changes brought about by industrialization too rapid, were its objectives mistaken, or perhaps incomprehensible to people who not long before had lived in constant dread of shortages and poverty? Were the generation born between two wars fated, though they did not know it, to be all along in preparation for another?

Such enormous themes can hardly be addressed in an essay of this scope. Yet some answer must be attempted at least to the question of what precisely 'socialist industrialization' was. It was identified as the path to progress and development. But what kind of progress and development occurred in practice? What means were used to stimulate them? And what criteria were used to evaluate them?

Many scholars have identified and analysed the fundamental weaknesses and biases, the 'great leaps' and harder falls, in the industrialization of 'actually-existing socialist societies' (Gorz 1976; Feher *et al.* 1986). Yugoslavia was often congratulated for saving itself from the disastrous outcomes of some other socialist countries by opting early on for a middle path between state and market. With hindsight, however, we have to ask ourselves more candidly whether we blundered in this unique project.

To our credit, in the early 1960s in Yugoslavia we did measure socialist industrialization by the criterion of a higher standard of living, both for the individual and in the social domain (Berković 1977). The alternative common in other Eastern countries, 'tons of steel per capita', would have been intolerable, even for the hardest-headed among us. This choice of social criteria was important, a radical break in the concept and practice of socialist development. What happened however was that this promising first step never led to the next. Despite renouncing the vulgar formula 'socialism = electrification + industrialization', we never fully embraced the alternative: radical *social* modernization.

Modernization has been defined as, first and foremost, an 'ability to develop and support the institutional structures capable of absorbing changes which transcend its own initial assumptions' (Eisenstat 1973: 210). If we accept that as a defining characteristic of modernization, as I believe we should, we must admit that it was not modernization we had in Yugoslavia. In not a single major institution or sector was that essentially *social* process embarked upon, that capability for self-transcendent change brought into being. In this chapter I will illustrate the failure to modernize through two of the most important spheres, those of technology and education.

Technology

To take technology first. It would be incorrect to say that no relevant technological progress took place in Yugoslav society and economy. Even superficial evidence clearly shows that Yugoslavia had, in a number of areas, technologically highly-developed systems of production (Bakić 1984).

We cannot therefore truly say we were a technologically backward coun-try or that our economic leaders had an anti-technological attitude. We can however question two things: the social and political goals to which technological development was yoked, and the institutional pattern that was decisive in selecting objectives and the methods and means of achieving them.

Technological modernization took place under the auspices of state and para-state political structures. It was these that controlled economic investment decisions, the flow of funds, the credit raised at home and abroad. Once the initial impetus of the country's post-Second World War industrialization was spent, a malign pattern developed. The elite at all levels in these official structures, at local, regional (republic) and national levels, directed development policy towards the fulfilment of two simple goals: enhancement of their individual and institutional monopolies; and legitimation of this state of affairs.

Investment in each new production project, every industrial plant updated, materially strengthened the political decision-makers in their dominant role in society and, at the same time, legitimated their power by appearing to confirm their 'progressive' reputation and ability to keep abreast of the latest world achievements. The elite thus controlled the system's reproduction as a whole and more precisely the manner in which technology and production interacted.

In this context modernization became a process of attempting to har-monize two irreconcilable principles: on the one hand, new technologies applied to production organized on technological principles; and, on the other, unchanged authoritarian management structures, labour relations and work practices. In other words, the prevalent perception of techno-logy was a reifying one: technology was seen as row upon row of shiny new machines, quite divested of their potential for generating new social actors, roles and relations.

The elite of each republic congratulated itself on its achievements and boasted of its enterprises as technological 'giants', regardless of the losses that accrued in place of the anticipated gains. The losses were compen-sated by milking already-drained national budgets and social resources. In self-justification these rival elites of the various republics played on dif-ferences between regional and national interest in development. Eventually the differences so constructed grew into irreconcilable confrontation In such circumstances the initial impetus for social change through tech-nological development stalled. What rolled on, still misleadingly carrying the label 'development', was no more than the preservation, the ossifi-cation, of obsolete structures of management in production and monopoly in politics.

Education

This prompts the question: what happened to those young, professional, educated women and men from all walks of life in Yugoslavia? Why were they not able to lift development onto other tracks? Could they not have exploited the spaces within Yugoslavia's relatively decentralized and open structure to achieve a change of direction? The answer lies in the second sphere I selected for analysis: education.

There is no denying that the high percentage of young people afforded a complete secondary, higher and professional education is one of the great civilizing achievements of the socialist countries. Yugoslavia's record in this respect, throughout the country and from early in the post-War period, must be acknowledged. Women made the greatest relative gains. The large gap in educational achievement between the sexes before the socialist period was quickly narrowed and during the 1980s it all but disappeared (Blagojević 1992). Of course, gender inequalities did not vanish overnight, and in particular differences in subject preference emerged, leading in time to feminization of certain vocations and professions. Even this, however, could be read in a positive light, since what it meant was an opening for large numbers of women into majority and even dominating positions in formerly masculine occupations, often with high social standing. Yugoslavia had many women doctors, lawyers and university professors (Milić 1984).

The new generations of educated young people of both sexes however never had a chance to make proper use of their knowledge, either for themselves or for society. Education should have been a source of knowledge to modernize society and transform its social relations. Instead it was instrumentalized, harnessed to three quite other social purposes.

The first was social integration. Achievement in education came to assure a loyal individual, thoroughly involved in the system and in accord with its values. Educational achievement and professional excellence were not of themselves guarantors of career advancement. They did however afford access to decision-making positions for individuals who passed the system's real 'suitability test', loyalty to the self-management system the Communist Party was building, and visible participation in its activities.

The second was ranking. Educational attainment and grades became important criteria for defining the individual's status in a stratified and hierarchical society. This educational status system took hold the more easily since in Yugoslav society the real criteria of socioeconomic class differentiation were concealed by the dual effect of the monopoly of political power and the atomization of economic power in the self-management system.

The third purpose was legitimation. By providing mass education the regime won credibility for itself and its apparent social objectives. An inherently unequal system was made to seem one which educates its people and rewards educational merit.

Thus education in Yugoslavia was diverted from being the modernizing force it might have been. The young professional women and men with ideas that might have stimulated change could not play the part. Over time this selective recruitment to all sectors and at all levels of the hierarchy was increasingly pernicious. Cadres retained power, not by fostering the system's capability for change, but, on the contrary, by dint of preserving and wherever possible expanding their individual privileges.

The sociopolitical manipulation of the formal education system had several side effects. First, there was ever more ferocious competition for student places at all higher grades. Second, we saw inflation in educational institutions and diplomas – more and more of them, with lower and lower value. Another effect was parents' feverish ambition for their children to gain the desirable certification, even when it was no longer really able to deliver on its promise of employment or social advancement.

Both technology, then, as potential vehicle for modernization of the economy, and education as potential vehicle for social modernization, failed in Yugoslavia, degenerating into hollow symbolism and ideological rhetoric. Both have been cheated of their power to transcend and transform society. The importance of technology has been narrowed to its reified results: tools and machinery. The value of education has been reduced to its formal accomplishments: paper certificates.

In both cases it was the ruling institutional structure – narrow, self-referring and rigid – that blocked change and diverted development into conservation of the existing social order. The project of modernization in Yugoslavia has been distorted, delayed and, in the last analysis, derailed.

Women as 'symptom' in development

If the political system in Yugoslavia was perpetuation of the power monopoly of the Party, it was also an expression of patriarchy and continued to sustain male dominance in political and economic life.[1] As in other socialist countries, the equality of women was ascribed formal importance. Marx's dictum, adapted from Fourier, was well known and frequently quoted: 'the degree of emancipation of woman is the natural measure of general emancipation' (Marx and Engels 1975: 196).

The complete legal equality women were supposed to enjoy in socialist Yugoslavia, although not quite so complete in practice, was sufficient to ensure them educational opportunity at all levels equal to that of men. Women were encouraged to get an education, career opportunities were open to them and it was seen as desirable that they should be politically active. The socialist establishment therefore congratulated itself on having attained that 'general level of emancipation' projected by Marx. Without willing it, therefore, women became one of the main pillars of the social system: their 'emancipation' legitimated it as being as progressive as any before in history.

Of course, the reality belied the rhetoric. Male power, manifested both at the systemic level and in a widespread patriarchal culture, remained the main factor in gender relations in Yugoslavia. This unbridged gap between ideology and practice calls for new thoughts about that Marxist formula.

I would suggest that what we can do is to see the 'emancipation' of women as a *symptom* of social development, using the word 'symptom' in a very particular way (Žižek 1984). 'Symptom' has two subtly different meanings. On the one hand, it signifies a condition in process, a condition potentially capable of development, though prior to and without certainty of the development itself. In this sense we could suppose (an optimistic and generous supposition) that the gains women had already made under 'actually-existing' socialism were a symptom of, that is to say they promised, a coming radical transformation of gender relations and society as a whole.

The second meaning of symptom, however, though less cheerful, may well be more appropriate in our case. In clinical usage symptom means a visible external sign that does not necessarily have any direct or causal connection to the internal phenomenon or process to which it refers. Thus symptoms may be misleading and result in faulty diagnosis.

The first interpretation seems to be appropriate in Yugoslavia in one limited sense: it applies to women who are, and in so far as they are, incorporated into the paid labour force. In fact the Marxist formula of 'women's emancipation' as an index of general social development in socialist societies always meant the degree of women's integration into paid employment. The dictum envisaged 'employed women', with an emphasis on the attribute 'employed' rather than the subject 'women'. In the Yugoslav instance, however, with certain variations by region and ethnic group, employed women accounted for only a minority of the adult female population, around one-third in most areas, and nowhere more than 40 per cent.

The second interpretation of symptom is the one that applied to the remainder of Yugoslav women. Women's apparent 'emancipation' was a misleading sign that obscured the blocking of their progress to real equality and liberation. The majority of women, that other two-thirds who did not possess the attribute 'employed', had to be content with marginal and inferior status and to accept discrimination that negated their real achievements.

Half of this majority were women who, due to personal or social circumstance, were obliged to accept the traditional women's roles of spouse, mother and homemaker. The other half were rural women for whom that housewife role was combined with one of agricultural labourer on their private family holding. These women suffered a double marginalization. First, by working on family land they were invisible to the formal economy. Second, their modest education and their traditional subordination to the male family head kept them from active engagement in political life.

Only that third of women who were in the paid labour force, then, and had thereby obtained their pass into the system and its institutions, were in a position to realize their rights. And they now found themselves the bearers of a dual representational burden. On the one hand they stood for women's emancipation within society as a whole, and on the other they legitimated the system by giving some plausibility to its claim to be progressive. Under this weighty load, and for the most part lacking a feminist awareness or organization as women, this group paid a high price in effort and risk if they made demands or engaged in conflict to obtain their legal rights. Most never even allowed themselves awareness of the gap between their promised status and the painful reality. Those who were aware of the discrepancy, who perceived it in their daily lives, more often than not settled for their limited gains and tried to overlook the all-too-visible signs of social inferiority and subordination as a sex.

We can, then, go beyond the Marxist notion that 'women's emancipation is a measure of general emancipation' and, using our own concepts, say, rather, that transformation of gender relations is a measure of societal modernization. Bearing all this in mind, let us move on to consider the specific relationship between gender and technology in context of Yugoslav modernization, using the two promised groups of women, at their opposite poles in Yugoslav society, as particularly telling examples. They will show us, from their respective places on the edge and at the centre of technical modernization just how our gender relations are structured by male domination.

Women and technology in the rural household

From the early 1960s, coinciding with Yugoslavia's liberalization and shift towards a market economy, family agricultural holdings embarked on a process of technological modernization. The result was a significant growth in individual and overall productivity in agriculture and the generation of sizeable surpluses which permitted increased national capital investment (Mrkšić 1981). One impact this growth in agricultural productivity did not have however was social improvement for rural communities, agricultural households and, our particular concern, women within them. No reduction ensued in differences in the quality of work and life between individual members of farming households. The disparity between high productivity in the private sector of agricultural production and low state input in support of rural social development was balanced over women's backs, whether in their guise as housewives or farm workers.

The gains, however, accrued to men and passed women by. Men managed to ease, shorten or altogether obviate their traditional tasks by the use of advanced farm machinery. Women, however, saw little change in their traditional tasks and working methods. Their lot continued to be manual labour, often in response to seasonal demand. Rural women, socially marginalized by processes I have already mentioned, found the economic value of their labour power now reduced yet further by changes in production in small holdings consequent on new technology. On the other hand, their labour could not easily be replaced by hired hands since its very cheapness enabled important savings for reinvestment in the family enterprise.

Second, inside the home, where these women were also productive, contributing as housewife to the family's consumer power, yet again they had to wait for their needs to be addressed by new technology. The rural household was growing and new technologies were becoming available to aid housework but the modernization of rural houses and their domestic equipment moved slowly.

For farmers, equipping the farm came first. Acquiring certain highly-regarded items such as automobile and television came next. Research from the period when rural households were beginning to share increasingly in consumption of home appliances shows more owned record players (5.5 per cent) than electric stoves (4.7 per cent), refrigerators (2.2 per cent) or vacuum cleaners (0.1 per cent). The author explained this phenomenon by the fact that entertainment equipment brought its owners more social prestige than those appliances that might have lightened or dispensed with women's work (Pešić 1977).

When the moment did at last come for the household to be equipped for this purpose, it turned out that many of the infrastructural conditions for proper utilization of washing machines and dishwashers, flush toilets, freezers and electric food processors were missing. Power supplies were too often unreliable, electricity voltages too low, water supply and sewage inadequate, supportive services for repair and maintenance lacking. Besides, often the models of equipment available were unsuitable, there was little choice, prices were too high. Finally, of course, good access roads did not yet exist to generate a sufficiently fast and effective link between industrial centres and the rural consumer markets.

It was not surprising, then, that researchers uncovered behaviour that seemed irrational. In some homes smart new household appliances that in daily use could have greatly eased a woman's work were saved for special occasions. Sometimes they were given a prominent position, serving as decoration and proof of the family's purchasing power, boosting its standing in the rural community (Hodžić 1976).

So modernization in the rural areas passed women by in two senses, first in respect of their agricultural work and second in their housework. In neither sphere did new technology ease their burdens or increase their productivity in the way it might have done. A new generation of rural girls grew up seeing their mothers toiling in backward conditions in a way that contrasted painfully with the glitter of the modern home and the glamour of the modern housewife as seen on their television screens. What could be more detrimental to the development of a confident and self-respecting feminine identity?

The paradoxical result has been that, instead of striving to transcend the limitations of their traditional role and context, many young rural women have embraced 'housewifization' (to use Maria Mies' term (Mies 1986)). Swept by consumer fever, determined to have the things their mothers lacked, and seeing no available model for change in gender relations, they have settled in large numbers for an artificial domestic paradise. Wasting what education and qualifications they had obtained, they turned their back on dismal rural job opportunities and avoided exposure to the hard world outside. In doing so they have forfeited a wealth of social communication and relationship (Korać 1991).

Modernization, then, barely reached the first generation of rural women in Yugoslavia, even in the limited form of new technologies. Worse, when and as it came, technological change did not produce any modernization of social relations – let alone the gender relations of the male-dominant family – for rural women or even for their daughters.

Women engineers in computer technology

The previous section was based on the work of other Yugoslav researchers. I turn here to the research I myself contributed towards our group project. Interviews were conducted with 66 people, equal numbers of women and men, in two Belgrade-based companies engaged in advanced research and production in electronics, robotics and computer engineering.[2] All were university graduates with a decade or more of experience in employment. Today they were senior professionals in their field. In sharp contrast, then, to the rural women described above, we now encounter women engineers whose educational achievements have brought them almost to the pinnacle of the social and professional hierarchy. Yet even they, for all their advantages, have failed to transcend the inhibitions and restrictions with which gender surrounds their lives. These women and men engineers share the same initial qualification: a university engineering degree equipping them for high-level work at the leading edge in the new technology.

The divergence in truth began even during their professional education, when they often selected different kinds of specialist training. Women had more often chosen theoretical options – mathematics, physics or statistics. Men had tended towards practical, applied engineering. They further parted company as they embarked on their careers.

The gender difference was most marked in terms of grade. Only 12 per cent of our women occupied a management post, compared with 44 per cent of our men. Half of the women were still at the first level in the professional grade structure, while only 16 per cent of the men remained on that rung. There were consequent inequalities of income. Of the women 85 per cent were in the lowest salary bracket for employees with their level of qualification, 75 per cent of men were in the top bracket.

A closer look at the kinds of position in which the women characteristically worked can partly explain the grade difference by sex. We found women disproportionately in defined research projects, professionally interesting and rewarding perhaps, and demanding of high levels of professional ability, but to one side of the career ladder that alone led to managerial power and authority in the companies. Men, in the main, were the ones in a position to make decisions, for instance about what products the company would make, or what research would be done.

Women were the ones who would carry through the research and development initiated elsewhere. Other researchers in other countries have also noted this tendency for professional women to seek the relative seclusion of an 'individual oasis' in the organization (Stolte-Heisekenen 1988). Such locations attract women by permitting them a measure of responsibility, while affording a degree of independence. There are other implications, however, that we discuss further below.

These findings provide grounds for concluding that sex-disadvantage of some kind was operating in the companies we studied. However, in the Yugoslav context it did not spring from any legal inequity nor from any outright restrictions on women arising in the organization. What were its causes?

First, it became clear in interview that these women, no different from their less educated rural sisters, and notwithstanding their prestigious jobs, were the ones in their families to have and to feel responsibility for household and children.[3] The men we interviewed did not express themselves as being preoccupied with these things. More women were single or separated, more men were in conventional marriages. It seems family responsibilities often prevent women attaining to paid work in the first place. The men, precisely in having families, were being supported, emotionally and practically, by a woman in the home who, although certainly in a paid job, would subordinate that job to her domestic responsibilities. Women in the sample looked after themselves, and usually looked after others too.

It was not surprising, then, if women valued their 'individual oasis' jobs because they saved the time that would otherwise be expended on the organization itself – on business communication, coordinative activities and policy-work. Men, like women, often resented the tedium of the participative decision-making of Yugoslav enterprise culture. Women however, with domestic responsibilities eating into either end of the working day were more likely to face a choice between professionally-interesting activity and organizational involvement.

The combining factors of company structure and women's domestic handicap can be assumed to go some way towards explaining their position in these companies. It is not however the whole explanation. Equally important were the sociocultural processes observable within the organizations. We identified three relevant factors: the functioning of the formal hierarchy; the positioning of women and men in relation to the informal communication networks; and women's consciousness.

First, the position we described women as holding, in relative backwaters of research and development, left them poorly placed to compete for promotion up the grades. In these organizations the evaluation of an individual's output and contribution to the collective product was directly correlated with her or his prominence in the management hierarchy. Women were relatively invisible, overshadowed by the achievements of those, mainly men, in the organizational mainstream. Women were more likely to be collaborating with others, rather than managing others. For that reason too, their work was accorded less value, regardless of actual achievement. Women's marginality was hindering their professional progress since they were less likely to be identified for and entrusted with prestigious research assignments.

Second, women were less well connected. In professional terms, they were less likely to acquire the insider information and develop the contacts in Yugoslavia and abroad that could help a career along, and in the informal network of relations inside the company women and men were again differently situated. Women engineers were more often involved and active in a social network in which exchanges were primarily on private, personal and family problems. Men, on the other hand, were more often involved and active in those social networks focused on professional and business information, the lobbying of influential individuals or groups with whose support advancement in the hierarchy became more likely.

Third, women were not altogether pawns in these processes. Their own consciousness of their lives and situations caused them to adopt certain attitudes and select certain behaviours. Women's double marginalization, their outlying position relative both to the professional/management hierarchy and communication networks, was resulting in disaffection. More women than men expressed negative feelings about their working environment and relationships. The most frequent comment we heard from women about working relations in these companies was that they were 'saturated with' men's career ambitions and a feverish pursuit of top jobs. They felt this to be a culture in which real professional skill and achievement were low in the scale of values.

Women showed themselves less motivated than men to integrate themselves strategically into the hierarchy of professional/management structures, and they revealed more disillusionment with their own professional progress. While 38 per cent of men said their present employment matched up to the professional expectations they had had as a student, only 21 per cent of women felt this. More than half the women (56 per cent), as against 38 per cent of men, expressed disappointment, feeling they had underachieved professionally relative to their original expectations. Indeed, of the sample of 33 of each sex, seven women felt their professional life to be a complete failure against only two men.

Women's frustration at the lack of recognition they experience grows from year to year, eroding their will-power, harming their self-identity, generating insecurity and progressively isolating them within the formal and informal networks of the organization. Such processes explained why, though their educational achievements and professional qualifications represent no hindrance, so few women had reached the top professional, executive and management positions.

In order to understand better how attitudes were shaping women's chances, we probed in the interviews for evidence of stereotyping. We approached this in two ways, with rather different results. One set of questions required the informants to select from closed alternatives. We asked them to consider a list of the lower-level occupations within the computing field and to say whether they felt each job to be 'more suited to' a man, a woman, or neither sex in particular. The responses from both women and men clearly showed stereotyped images to exist. Computer hardware was represented as men's field, software as women's. Data input was either ascribed to women or to neither sex; it was never identified as men's work. Computer operation, however, was definitely associated with men (Milić 1992).

This was a depressing finding. The fact is that computer engineering is strongly characterized by a sexual division of labour, in Yugoslavia as elsewhere (Volst and Wagner 1988; Hacker 1989). Many of us had believed that, since women had been among the experts in computer technology from its inception in Yugoslavia, the field would escape the stereotyping of earlier kinds of engineering. Unfortunately we were wrong. And here, perpetuating these stereotypes, were high-level computer specialists of both sexes, people who had the influence to actualize them in developing new technologies and recruiting staff to the jobs they generate.

Yet, when we approached the stereotyping by another route, permitting our informants to choose their own words to elaborate their thoughts in the less structured part of our interviews, we found a surprising divergence between the sexes. From women, we heard many assertions of observable differences between women and men. They noted women's lower position in the organization, despite equal qualifications. They said women were obliged to prove themselves against a superior model: men. They were the ones to carry the burden of housework and children. We heard men and women's characters differentiated. For instance one woman said 'women have a more studious approach to everything. They waste a lot of energy analysing a problem, and it's harder for them to get the job completed.'

However, beliefs about sex difference in their work environment were *not* being directly or openly used by men to the detriment of women. When given the opportunity to select their words carefully, the men in our study chose to make little of the sex differences their answers to the structured questions had clearly revealed them to believe in. Women cited differences of approach to professional tasks. But when men mentioned them at all, it was with a degree of tolerance. This led us to conclude that the mechanism used by men to inferiorize women in the organization involved not the emphasis of sex difference but the assertion of sex *neutrality*. It was precisely by a denial of sex difference that men avoided admitting their superior position within the organization and evaded any guilt about their masculine behaviour in pursuit of career advantage.

This denial of difference however was little help to women, since it prevented the alternative practices preferred by the women being recognized and emerging to challenge male practices for legitimacy in the organization. It permitted masculine ways to remain the unquestioned norm in such a way that women had a perennial handicap: they had to fight for their advancement using not their own, but men's, rules.

To some extent the gender-stereotyped images these professionals hold of the work capabilities of the sexes and of jobs arise from observation of the actually-existing sexual division of labour in the industry. However, this is not the only, nor even the principal, source of stereotyping. The impulse comes from the relations of power in the organization. Men are the sex that occupy the upper ranks of the hierarchy of power, women the sex deprived of power. Gender stereotyping is a practice of power. Those who hold the power, mainly men, have no interest in recognizing the existence of a sex/gender system. Recognizing it would be to acknowledge inequalities and expose them as societally created. They could no longer be represented as stemming from natural differences, beyond the reach of individual or social regulation.

On the other hand, those deprived of societal power, mainly women, do have an interest in being clear-sighted about 'difference'. Even if we found in women's consciousness a confusion as to its significance, an uneasy slippage between the expressions of difference as (natural) cause and as (social) effect of gender disadvantage, there was no doubt they recognized its existence. This is important, because only if it is recognized can disadvantage be challenged.

Back to the beginning

Despite the social distance between the women engineers and the rural housewives they show marked similarities. Both groups are unrecognized, undervalued and excluded women, frustrated of opportunity to participate equally with men in public life. In rural family households we saw women left out of the modernization process, partly due to the neglect of investment in the agricultural sector but also due to the deeply rooted patriarchal culture. Women had recognition only 'indoors' and their social scope was limited to informal contacts with relatives and neighbours. In the case of the women engineers the mechanisms of subordination were different, and so therefore were the women's responses. They were located in the very centre of technological modernization and, therefore, potentially of social dynamism. Male-dominant gender relations, however, ensured their distancing to the periphery of this centre, where they were relatively unseen and unheard.

Not surprisingly, therefore, the two groups of women reacted in different ways. The farming women were marginalized from the outset and, when changing times in Yugoslavia made this a possibility, were prone to abandon work outside the home and choose the reduction of their role to that of housewife and mother in the nuclear family. It appeared to them a radical answer to the particularly intolerable over-exploitation of rural women in unrelieved and unmodernized manual labour inside and outside the home.

Women engineers also made a deliberate choice to exclude themselves – though it has to be said that alternatives were not always available to them. These women, unlike the rural women, had started by bravely and resolutely showing they could enter men's world as equals – only later to withdraw from a contest in which they found the odds stacked against them. Whether we should see this self-exclusion as acceptance of defeat or courageous resistance against the terms of the competition perhaps varies from woman to woman.

Overall, however, both instances represent a defeat for women and a perpetuation of male power in new circumstances. It was not women's fault, nor was it inevitable. It derived from the patriarchal socialist system's essentially flawed conception of modernization. The social forces that initiated and carried out the Yugoslav modernization project led it up a blind alley of history. As a result, today the promise of *technological* modernization has finally perished under the treads of a blazing war machine that has ravaged much, and threatens the remainder, of what was once Yugoslavia. And the promise of modernization through *education* has its bitter fruit in the self-exile abroad, fleeing the war, of hundreds of thousands of the young women and men it had educated.

The failure of the modernization project sprang in both cases from the nature of the country's state-Party authority structure. The system's governing elite directed all its efforts to ensuring exclusive access to modernization's benefits and perpetuation of a monopoly of power – thereby aborting its potential for new, transformed, social relations.

At this moment of crisis we have to return to fundamentals: the necessity to survive. It is tempting to forget what it was we had been trying to achieve, to stop asking the reasons for our failure. If we do so, however, we will be accepting as destiny developments that in reality were never ordained, but rather chosen by a powerful minority as its solution to 'our' problems. It will be to accept self-interest, malice and political manipulation as natural and inevitable.

To be strictly honest with myself and the reader, working on this chapter has been a way to protect my sanity. I returned to its reasoning again and again as a defence against irrationality and barbarism. Besides, remaining linked to our international group of women researchers, and the thought of reaching out to a still wider group of readers, strengthened me against the crescendo of nationalism, militarism and xenophobia around me. Our research did not directly address the destruction of Yugoslavia's federal state and society – which for all their shortcomings I believe represented the most rational form of cohabitation for the jumbled ethnicities of the Balkans – but it led me none the less to a better understanding of the reasons for the catastrophe.

Looking at technology and education, I saw how our one-dimensional and overbearing power structure had been inadequate to the modernization process it had itself initiated. Being the monopoly of an elite and essentially still an expression of male power, it sought not to overturn existing relations of domination of either kind, but only to conserve them.

Seeing how it failed women, I was able to see too how, in a time of nationalistic rivalry within its ranks, such a system was bound to destroy and self-destruct. Monopoly rule, posited on an inherent homogeny between state and Party, was incapable of transformation into authentic egalitarian pluralism. Instead it exploded into fragments. Each imbued with the same tyrannical one-dimensional logic, what could they do but drag each other into war?

Notes

1 I use the terms 'patriarchy' and 'patriarchal' in this chapter with some hesitation. Patriarchy has acquired specific and contested meanings in debates in countries with histories very different from our own. The term 'male power system' however is too general, and 'paternalism' and 'patrimony' inappropriate. The concept I seek would be one descriptive of a system in which political and economic power resides in the hands of 'the fathers'. It is such a system that Yugoslavia has had and that continues today. And that is the reason our system could be as easily swept into nationalism as it has been.
2 The research was funded by the Committee for Science of the former Republic of Serbia and carried out during May and June 1990 in the Institute for Sociological Research of the Faculty of Philosophy, University of Belgrade. The main instrument for data gathering was a questionnaire including both closed and open questions, personally introduced and followed by interview. The 66 subjects of interview (women and men in equal numbers) came from developmental departments of two engineering firms and all had a university degree and at least 10 years of work experience. Thirty-seven had higher qualifications (14 a specialized diploma, 13 a masters degree and 10 a doctoral degree). Of these, 20 were women and 17 were men.
3 Of the 66 interviewed, 90 per cent of the men were married, 76.5 per cent of the women. The average number of children was 1.03 for women, 1.56 for men. Of women 14.7 per cent were childless, against 9.4 per cent of men. Of men 81.3 per cent were living in a nuclear family household, against only 52.9 per cent of women.

References

Bakić, S. (1984) *Automatizacija i radnička klasa* [*Automation and the Working Class*]. Belgrade: Institut za sociološka i kriminološka istraživanja.

Berković, E. (1977) *Kvalitet životnog standarda* [*Quality of the Standard of Living*]. Belgrade: Ekonomski institut.

Blagojević, M. (1992) *Žene izvan kruga* [*Women Outside the Circle*]. Belgrade: Institut za sociološka istraživanja Filozofskog fakulteta.

Eisenstat, S. (1973) *Tradition, Change and Modernity*. New York: John Wiley.

Feher, F., Heller, A. and Markus, G. (1986) *Diktatura nad potrebama* [Dictatorship over Needs]. Belgrade: Rad.

Gorz, André (1976) *Tegobni socijalizam* [*Le Socialisme Difficile*]. Zagreb: Centar društvenih djelatnosti SSOH.

Hacker, S. (1989) *Doing It the Hard Way: Investigation in Gender and Technology*. Boston: Unwin Hyman.

Hodžić, A. (1976) Masovna kultura na selu [Mass culture in the countryside], *Sociologija sela*, No. 53–4, pp. 111–17 Zagreb.

Korač, M. (1991) *Zatočenice pola* [*Prisoners of their Sex*]. Belgrade: Institut za socioloska istraživanja Filozofskog fakulteta.

Marx, K. and Engels, F. (1975) *Collected Works*, No. 4. New York: International Publishers.

Mies, M. (1986) *Patriarchy and Accumulation on a World Scale*. London: Zed Books.

Milić, A. (1984) Obrazovanje žena i feminizacija obrazovnih profila u Jugoslaviji [Women, education and feminization of vocational choices]. Paper to the Seminar on Women and Work, Inter-University Centre, Dubrovnik.

Milić, A. (1992) Nove tehnologije i odnos polova – pogled iznutra na odnose moći [New technologies and gender relations – an inside perspective on power relations], *Sociologija*, No. 1, pp. 5–22, Belgrade.

Mrkšić, D. (1981) Uticaj politike raspodele na promenu materijalnog položaja osnovnih društvenih grupa, u: *Politika raspodele i ideologija* [Impact of distribution policy on changes in material status, in *Distribution Policy and Ideology*]. Belgrade: Institut za socioloska istraživanja Filozofskog fakulteta.

Pešić, V. (1977) Društvena slojevitost i stil života, u: *Društveni slojevi i društvena svest* [Social stratification and styles of life, in *Social Strata and Social Consciousness*]. Beograd: Institut društvenih nauka.

Stolte-Heiskenen, V. (1988) *Women's Participation in Positions of Responsibility in Career and Technology: Obstacles and Opportunities*. Working Paper No. 26. Tampere: University of Tampere, Department of Sociology.

Volst, A. and Wagner, I. (1988) Inequality in the automated office: the impact of the computer on the division of labour, *International Sociology*, Vol. 3, June, pp. 129–54.

Žižek, S. (1984) *Birokratija i uživanje* [*Bureaucracy and Pleasure*]. Belgrade: Studentski informativni centar (SIC).

9

A gendered socio-technical construction: The smart house

ANNE-JORUNN BERG

Technological innovation processes can be *gendered*. In this chapter I take one example – the so-called 'smart house'[1] – and show the way gender enters into the design of this supposed technological home of the future.

Everyday life and the home have been important arenas for feminist research and feminist politics but, as has been pointed out (Cronberg and Sangregorio 1983; Cronberg 1987; Gullestad 1987), technology has not been of central interest in that context. On the other hand, in the 1980s, popular scenarios of a future shaped by information technology did point to the home as one important field for change (Gorz 1981; Toffler 1981). The home is traditionally women's domain. Technology is traditionally men's domain. Consequently technological change in the home will be a gendered process. Does that mean we may anticipate change in gender relations and the domestic sexual division of labour? The research on which this chapter is based aimed to find out just what is forecast with regard to this in the case of the construction 'the smart house'.

It is a widely held popular belief that new technologies in the home have rationalized housework so that it is no longer an important source of inequality between the sexes. Time budget studies however show us another picture (Vanek 1974, 1978; Boalt 1983; Cowan 1983; Hagelskjær 1986). The average weekly hours spent on housework have not declined significantly with the introduction of modern equipment, and, since it is still primarily women who do it, it remains a significant source of inequality between the sexes (Berg 1988; Nyberg 1990). These two questions (how much work? who will do it?) were central to the study of the smart house on which this chapter is based.[2] Are there any time-saving appliances in the making? Is change in the sexual division of housework anticipated in the design of the house?

The popular technology-based scenarios of the 'new' everyday life perceive technology as an agent of change and a source of 'progress' in modern society. Critical studies of technology have opposed this view by emphasizing instead the degradation of work, increased political and social control, pollution and unemployment. These studies point to important aspects of technological change, but their political implications have left a feeling of political pessimism. Feminist technology studies are pessimistic too, finding little evidence of 'progress' in gender relations or women's lives (Zimmerman 1986; Lie *et al.* 1988).

In both cases, this pessimism stems from the theoretical approach adopted. Technology is too often described as a static independent variable which 'has impacts' on social relations. Few questions are asked about what technology really means and what part value conflicts play in technological innovation. In research on the smart house I posed such questions, hoping to throw light on some of the theoretical problems discussed in connection with the 'housework-technology paradox' (Vanek 1974; Cowan 1983; Berg 1988; Nyberg 1990), the curious fact that so much time continues to be spent on housework in modern households, despite the massive introduction of technology to the home. One of the most interesting aspects of this field of research is the encounter in domestic technology between technology as a masculine domain and the home as a feminine domain (Berg 1989). Can a focus on conflicting values between *design* and *use* of household appliances show us more of the development of domestic technology as a gendered process?

In the sociology of technology there is very little theorizing about gender in relation to innovation (Wajcman 1991). Inspiration may be gained from feminist studies of science, which reveal that masculine values, masculine practices and male domination enter significantly into the social construction of scientific facts (Harding 1986, 1991; Tuana 1989). What is true for science however is not necessarily true for technology. The construction of facts and artefacts may well differ, and it remains an open question how feminist studies of science and technology may benefit each other.

This chapter is one example of the latter. It is about the shaping of the innovative home of the future and the importance of gender in that process. For several reasons, my study concentrates on a specific version of the home of tomorrow – the 'smart house'. First, it has information technology, *the* new technology, at its heart. Second, as publicly projected it resembles the popular scenarios of the 1980s in presenting new technologies as gender neutral. Third, several of the big international electronic corporations are already creating prototypes. The smart house is interesting because it is beyond the stage of unbridled imagination. It is already at pre-production stage – a serious IT-home-in-the-making.

From the outset we noticed that the scenarios on which the smart house is based had an astonishing lack of concern with gender (Berg

1991). Information technology (IT) was perceived and represented as gender neutral. This is common enough, as others have shown, in debates about technology (Cockburn 1983, 1985; Sφrensen and Berg 1987; Lie *et al.* 1988). For women, however, IT in the home is not just any technology: it proposes to transform the home and everyday life – and what are these if not women's traditional concern?

In our research project on the smart house I gathered information through the 'snowball' method, one source of information leading to another. The lack of empirical and theoretical social research on gender and innovation, particularly on the smart house,³ made such an exploratory approach appropriate. I interviewed designers and producers, systematically analysed advertisements and other kinds of written material and visited the three North American test houses described here.

I formulated three main questions, answers to which I hoped might reveal the relationship between gender and technology in the design of the smart house. These questions have their origins in the existing sexual division of labour. First, what material appliances are actually in the making today? Scenarios are not always to be trusted as a guide to the future. Second, what kind of household activities are the new artefacts or appliances meant for? Concretely, is housework taken into consideration during the design process? Third, who are the consumers the designers and producers see as their target group? For whom, exactly, are they making this new home? These three topics are addressed in the research in various ways with the aim of exposing to analysis how innovation can be said to be a gendered process, how the smart house can be seen to be a gendered socio-technical construction.

Smart house prototypes: modelling our futures

Two of the three smart house prototypes I analysed are laboratory houses financed respectively by Honeywell and the National Association of Home Builders (NAHB). The third is a commercial show-case named Xanadu, owned by private investors.⁴

The Honeywell house

Honeywell is a multinational corporation producing control systems and services, including thermostats, air cleaners, burglar and fire alarms. The home is not Honeywell's only market, but its various control appliances are already installed in more than 60 million one-family houses in the United States.

Honeywell has been interested in home automation since 1979. Its first laboratory house was built in natural surroundings in a residential area, but it proved too difficult to test and change the infrastructure of the house in such a location. The current Honeywell test house is therefore built inside a laboratory. It embodies the Honeywell products and services linked together through one central programmable communication network: the integration system. Honeywell aims to develop a flexible package that can be adjusted to individual homes to suit different life situations and life styles.

The house, as it was when I visited it, is a life-sized model of a typical North American detached house. The 'Home Automation Test Laboratory' (the house together with two environmental test chambers) is a large research and development project within Honeywell Corporate Systems Development Division. The six-room house is the test site for prototypes of home automation products and the integrated house control systems Honeywell are developing. Apart from the fact that the walls are 'open' to simplify access by the engineers, the house looks like any ordinary house. No fanciful details suggest that this is the home of the future. The R&D team says this is deliberate: Honeywell plan to present home automation as nothing out of the ordinary. Only the control panel, affording central control of all electronic systems, reveals this to be a somewhat special house.

The interior of the house is decorated in a studiedly 'ordinary' style. People from the neighbourhood are sometimes invited along to consumer-test Honeywell technologies. To make the test situation as natural as possible, say the producers, the house must resemble a typical home. Of course, they have not fully achieved this, because the many small details and decorations that go to make a house a home are missing.

NAHB smart house system

The National Association of Home Builders (NAHB) is an association of producers and suppliers of different products for the home. The Association has about 150,000 members which makes them an organization to reckon with in the struggle over standardization to which we shall refer below. It has its own National Research Foundation which fostered the idea of developing a smart house. From 1986 they intensified and restructured their research effort, turning smart house R&D into an independent business, The Smart House Development Venture Inc. (SHDVI).

The NAHB demonstration house is located in a large long-distance truck, so that it can be moved from place to place. From the outside, it resembles less a house than a large caravan. The associated R&D work is carried on in a nearby building, where the house is also modelled in miniature. The house consists of entrance hall, kitchen, living room and bedroom. The rooms, to natural size, are arranged in a linear plan, one adjacent to the next. Each is in fact only half a room, but together they embody all the functions found in a normal house.

The main focus in the NAHB smart house system is on the communication network. The whole infrastructure of the home is going to change, say its designers. Their cable system integrates all kinds of power, independent of the energy source. NAHB are particularly competing to influence standards for signal transmission in networks made for homes.

Xanadu

Xanadu is located in Orlando, Florida. It is owned by private investors and used as a show-case for different suppliers to display and demonstrate their various products.

Unlike the other two houses, Xanadu embodies architectural innovations: its external appearance is unique. The unconventional form is supposed to express symbolically the novel thinking in the infrastructure of the house. One of its founding fathers, the architect Roy Mason, invented the term 'architronics', to signify the designed integration of building structure and information technology (Mason 1983).

Xanadu too has a central control unit that integrates various appliances. It is described as an analogue of the human brain, emphasizing differences in function between left and right hemispheres. The interior of the house seems unfinished; it has no comprehensive style. Each application stands alone and fails to blend into the futuristic unity promised in the brochures. Whereas in the Honeywell and NAHB houses the control network is designed for application to an existing structure, in Xanadu the net is integral with its innovatory structure and is thought of mainly as applicable to new construction.

Technological developments: what do designers have in mind?

Leaving aside the appliances designers liked to tell us about in futuristic terms, I chose to concentrate on new technologies actually visible or simulated here and now in the smart house prototypes.

Technologies in the Honeywell house

The substance of the Honeywell smart house concept is *integration*, the central programming of diversified control and regulation systems. The main R&D effort is directed towards a control system integrating: remote registration of outdoor temperature and humidity, regulation of indoor air quality, temperature and environmental control in specified zones and light regulation. It includes control of an advanced security system, with motion detectors. For instance, a video camera scans the main entrance and shows visitors on a monitor. It also involves service/diagnosis equipment and makes use of voice recognition and voice information. A safety device, for example, detects smoke and alerts the inhabitants, indicating on a video screen both the source of the fire and the appropriate action.

Honeywell pay particular attention to means of reducing energy consumption. With this in mind, they have invested considerable effort in a motion-activated system of light control in which lights switch on and off in response to information from motion detectors as to where people are currently located. (Besides, all lights are automatically switched on if the security alarm sounds.) Honeywell are not very happy with the results so far, however. To try out the system in a natural situation they had invited several people to the test house for dinner. As the guests entered the dining room, the lights obligingly went on. But when everyone had settled around the table and all was still the room was suddenly plunged in to darkness. The Honeywell engineers had to ask their guests to flap their arms to activate the lights again. On consideration, Honeywell now feel voice activation may have more potential, in combination with infrared remote control.

To sum up, the technologies in the Honeywell version of the home of tomorrow are applied to light and heat regulation, to security control and alarm systems. Technologies that have anything to do with *housework* are notably absent.

Technologies in NAHB's smart house

In today's home we have different cables for different types of power or energy. In 1988 NAHB directed their R&D efforts to the development of a system to make all sources of power available with the same cable and through identical power-points. In such a multi-cable system the microwave oven, the washing machine, the home computer and the telephone may all be plugged into the same socket. This calls for purpose-designed appliances, of course, for only those equipped with the correct microchip will access the new power source. Signals from the microchip in each appliance will be sanctioned by a chip in the control unit.

SHDVI does not see its role as developing new appliances as such. They are, rather, projecting a future in which domestic technology is adjusted to their own project: the new network. The washing machine will signal on the television screen when the washing is ready to be moved to the tumble-dryer. The vacuum cleaner will be programmed to stop when someone is at the door or when the phone rings. When the temperature in the microwave indicates that dinner is almost ready it will signal to the hot-plate to warm the soup and to the stereo to provide the right background music for the meal. In addition to integrating in-house appliances in this way, the house net will also be connected to outside communication networks. It will support telework, telebanking and teleshopping as such services become available to private households.

The appliances displayed in this second smart house, then, are familiar technologies. The only thing that is new is their integration. Again we have to emphasize: the technological changes envisaged here are a long way from being consciously concerned with routine housework.

Technologies in Xanadu

As we saw, Xanadu has rooms with traditional functions: kitchen, bedroom, bathroom, etc. In every room appliances are presented that, claim the designers, are innovatory. In the book about the house, the new appliances are presented in a 'hi-tech' style, and to a certain extent this is carried through in the house itself. Xanadu is represented as a house you can talk to, a house that answers in different voices, where every room can be adjusted to your changing moods, a house that is servant, adviser and friend to each individual member of the household. Controlling all the functions in the home is Xanadu's house-brain.

Xanadu's technologies, with certain exceptions, are not dissimilar from those in the two prototypes already described, though their applications encompass a wider range of activities. These applications, however, have not all yet reached the stage of being prototypes. Some are simulations anticipating future possibilities.

Dreaming of integration

Our first question concerned the appliances in the home of the future. The list of what we found as testable prototypes – disregarding mere future possibilities – is neither extensive nor impressive. The innovations discussed above amount to control of:

- energy (heating and lighting);
- safety (security and fire alarms);
- communication (information and messaging, within the home and between the home and the outside world);
- entertainment (television, compact disc player, video recorder, computer games);
- environment (temperature, air pollution).

None of the technologies on this list differ radically from technologies already in existence (Miles 1988). All are available – albeit unintegrated – on the market today. All that is new about these 'smart houses' is the *integration* itself, linking different appliances in a central local network, variously called a 'small area network' (SAN), 'homebus', *'domotique'* or 'house-brain'.

This is the designers' dream, therefore – integration, centralized control and regulation of all functions in the home. This is the core of the smart home as a socio-technical construction. Many different companies and organizations today are engaged in R&D projects for such home networks, and the battle over standards is preoccupying all the big electronic firms and other contenders such as the NAHB. Whoever wins the standardization battle will have a clear advantage in the future market for networks and new appliances.

Housework: out of sight, out of mind

Women and men traditionally have distinct and different work in the home. Housework, still mainly women's unpaid work, comprises the most repetitious and time-consuming tasks in the household – cooking, washing, cleaning, tidying, mending. Turning to the second topic in our research, then, the precise activities preoccupying the designers of smart houses, we must ask: Does housework feature in their thinking about the smart house? What do they seem to know about housework?

Honeywell: the house will 'do the job for you'

For Honeywell the main idea about the smart house is, to quote an R&D manager, that 'it does more things for you, the way you would like to have them done, than today's houses'. This means the overall purpose of the smart house is to help the owner so that he (I use the pronoun advisedly) will 'no longer have to think about how things are done'. All he has to be concerned with is 'whether the technologies are simple to use, increase comfort, are pleasant and affordable'. Housework is not mentioned in any way here – though one could imagine that technological solutions that increase comfort could relate to housework somehow. The designers responded to our question as to the *advantages* of the smart house with the following words – listed in order of the priority they felt they would have in the market: comfort, security, convenience, energy saving and entertainment. Labour-saving was not mentioned. Neither was it mentioned when they were asked about any *disadvantages* in the smart house. The main problem pointed out was a new kind of hazard: vulnerability to the 'housebreak'. With all appliances integrated in a single electronic network, a failure due to technical breakdown or human interference would bring down the entire system.

It seems strange that in talk about 'a house that will do the job for you', 'job' does not refer to the actual work that is carried on in a house. Housework is no part of what this house will 'do' for you. This anomaly became yet more obvious when one of our informants went on to tell us how their prototype differed from Japanese home automation. According to him, Japanese systems are designed to leave the finishing of jobs to manual intervention. Japanese culture, he explained, is extremely service-minded. In Japanese households women render service to men. Even when technologically possible to eliminate it, the Japanese do not want to change this service relationship. North Americans, he said, by contrast, see the optimal use of technology as full automation of as many activities as possible. Yet he did not see the paradox of Honeywell's own lack of concern with housework.

NAHB: a house that will 'take care of me'

We found the same tendency at the NAHB. They present their smart house as, primarily, 'a house which will take care of me'. This implies the house will do 'anything you want to be done in your home today – and in the future'. Such a general concept could, of course, well include housework. On asking for more detail however we were told that it is first necessary to develop a communication network to modernize the basic infrastructure of the house. This network would then act as an invitation to suppliers of domestic technology to intensify their product development with the new network in mind. Housework as such was not NAHB's concern.

When asked more precisely what it means that a house will do 'anything you want done', the NAHB designers signalled as important that the house will be more comfortable, safer and easier to live in. Other advantages cited were better communication with the surrounding world, saving on energy, and enhanced entertainment. Things are vaguely glimpsed as being 'done' in a home, but housework as such is invisible and it has not occurred to the NAHB designers that users might like the house to carry out the time-consuming activities of housework.

Xanadu: a house to serve you

Xanadu is somewhat different. Integration in a house network is important here too, but in addition this more social, more imaginative version of the smart house does accommodate (albeit rather elliptical) references to housework. The title page in the book about Xanadu, for example, has a picture of a robot serving mother breakfast. The accompanying text reads: 'We are not replacing Mommy with a robot. We are presenting ideas on how to design, build and use a home in new ways that can reduce drudgery while increasing comfort, convenience and security' (Mason 1983: 1). Housework is not mentioned explicitly, but it is easy to interpolate: drudgery will be reduced. The robot serving mother is a technical solution that serves the traditional server.

Family life is often mentioned, and the house is designed to be a place in which people can live happily together. 'What is really futuristic about an architronic house like Xanadu . . . is not the way it looks but the way it works. In this sense, the house of the future will be more like the houses of the past than like the houses of today' (Mason 1983: 43). The house is intended to work in such a way as to give the family more opportunity to spend time together, but the designers say nothing about how work time can be saved to make this a possibility.

Xanadu's message is therefore ambiguous. Women as mothers and housewives are shown as playing an important role in the home. But we are left unclear as to whether it is women's work they mean when claiming the house will reduce drudgery.

Ignorance of housework

During the interviews we pressed the housework issue. When making appointments with informants we told them explicitly that housework would be our main focus. Nevertheless, when it came to it, they seemed surprised to be asked about it, and their answers were imprecise. NAHB said housework was not their concern – they left that to the white goods producers. At Honeywell they said they had paid some attention to housework, but when prompted they gave unconvincing examples such as the automatic light switch. They justified this as facilitating housework by arguing that a housewife entering a room with her hands full of wet clothes would not have to put them down to turn on the light.

In Xanadu one example of a housework appliance was the 'robutler'. This device was said to serve drinks. In fact, someone had to fill the glasses first and place them on exactly the right spot for the robutler to collect them. The machine then required guidance by remote control in serving them. There seemed to be little saving in manual intervention and, besides, serving drinks can hardly be said to be a burdensome task in the average home.

Another instance of Xanadu's insubstantial inventions is the 'gourmet autochef'. It sounds interesting and looks fancy but on closer inspection is found to do nothing except suggest a menu for the dinner party. The housewife (a woman is shown in the picture) is still responsible for planning, shopping, cooking and all the rest of the work that goes into preparing a meal. The gourmet autochef, when the chips are down, is no more than a computer program.

When reflecting on what goes on in a home the Xanadu designers say 'today home is often little more than a place to sleep, eat a meal or two and store possessions' (Mason 1983: 16). This is a highly misleading description of what takes place in a home (Cowan 1983). A housewife would certainly ask 'Does nobody change the sheets? Is that meal not cooked and are the dishes not washed up afterwards? Are those possessions never dusted?'

The designers' knowledge of such material realities of housework is scanty indeed. First, the variety and necessity of today's housework is quite overlooked. 'Once household chores were regarded as inescapable duties – like tending animals or crops on a farm. But today they are more often resented as impositions that everyone in the family would like to avoid.' They continue: 'As a result a host of new household appliances are appearing that require less time and physical effort to do unpleasant jobs.' Yet they clearly have no idea of housework's centrally time-consuming tasks for they cite quite peripheral appliances: 'the toilet-bowl cleaner that fits inside the tank, the in-sink garbage disposal, trash compactor etc.' (Mason 1983: 19–20).

What is more, many of the appliances described in connection with Xanadu, technologies that might seem to promise to reduce household labour, are as yet no more than future possibilities. There are plans, for instance, for a closet that could make the washing machine superfluous. Vapour is distributed inside the closet during the night to clean the clothes where they hang. Despite the fact that a woman, Frances GABe, pioneered such a concept some years ago in her 'self-cleaning house' (GABe 1983), this cleaning-cupboard does not exist in Xanadu even as a prototype – its control panel is no more than a simulation, the innovation no more than a thought.

In printed publicity about these smart homes, the housewife is some-times pictured with new technologies. She smiles happily by the computer in her kitchen. Our interviews with the men behind the publicity, how-ever, convinced us that they did not know much about this woman's work and visions for the future.

Women as a social group: relevant but absent

I move now to the third question to ask: just whom, then, do the designers have in mind as their target consumer? 'Relevant social group' is a term used by Trevor Pinch and Wiebe Bijker to denote 'institutions and organ-izations . . . as well as organized or unorganized groups of individuals' for whom an artefact has a shared 'set of meanings'. They emphasize specifically that the social group of 'consumers' or 'users' fulfils such a requirement and should be included in the analysis of a technological development (Pinch and Bijker 1987: 30).

Women are a relevant social group in the development of the smart house in at least two ways. First, women possess important skills for and knowledge about the home that should be a resource in the design pro-cess. Second, since the home is women's traditional domain, women could be seen as an important target in the marketing of the smart house.

Often, when the user–producer relationship is discussed in connection with technical design it refers to a relation where the user's competence, based on task-related experience, knowledge and skills, could guide the development of a new tool or machine for factory or office. In a similar way women's competence in housework could constitute an important innovative resource for the development of home-oriented information technology.

When asked about the relevance of users in the design process, producers said they found it 'an interesting idea'. Such an interest would seem self-evident: after all, how can one expect a product to sell except by ensuring it corresponds to consumer needs and demands? Yet we found evidence of only one actual contact by these designers with potential users: the instance already described when Honeywell invited guests to dinner and left them in the dark. Women's housework skills are being entirely neglected as a design resource.

Who exactly do the producers see as the target purchaser of their smart house? It proved difficult to pin them down. 'Anyone and everyone' seemed to be the answer. NAHB was the most specific: they had at least decided to concentrate on the one-family house. The others had only vague pic-tures of potential consumers. Honeywell see the user as 'the owner', synonymous with the man of the house. It is 'the owner' who will no longer have to think about 'how things are done'. The 'things' they rank as potentially most important in the house market are male activities and the most important consumer group (they say when pressed) is the technically-interested male.

In Xanadu too the user/consumer is difficult to identify. When the *user* is discussed at all it is in connection with specific appliances. Alleviation of household labour is mentioned as a potential demand in the market but the robutler and the gourmet autochef typify the lightweight response.

When we asked about the *consumer* the designers had in mind, we were answered several times with rather similar stories of individuals that had built and equipped their own houses with new technologies. One example was a Norwegian engineer living in Texas who had built his own private smart house. A detail that fascinated the storytellers was the lighting system he had devised: the lights would dim along the corridor when, for example, the children went to their rooms to sleep. This was the kind of consumer the producers liked and speculated about, one who would share their fascination with electronic or technological gadgets. That this man had been unsuccessful in his attempt to sell his house seemed not to dampen their enthusiasm. It is the technology-as-such, the way artefacts function in technical terms, that fascinates the designers. Again, the target consumer is implicitly the technically-interested man, not unlike the stereotype of the computer hacker.

In summary, then, the men (and it is men) producing prototypes of the intelligent house of the future and designing its key technologies have failed to visualize in any detail the user/consumer of their innovation. In so far as they have one in mind, it is someone in their own image. They have ignored the fact that the home is a place of work (women's housework) and overlook women, whose domain they are in effect transforming, as a target consumer group.

Gendered innovation process, gendered technology

Smart house prototypes resemble their literary forerunners, those scenarios of the 1980s that presented home-oriented information technologies as gender neutral. We have seen just how far from reality this is. Nothing could be clearer evidence of the gendering of the technological innovation process than the absence of women we have uncovered in this design and development process – their invisibility, the waste of their housework knowledge.

Smart house prototypes are one of several kinds of attempt to create today the technological home of tomorrow. The nature of that future home has serious implications for women. Technology as an element in social action has the power to change, or to preserve, today's gender relations, including the sexual division of labour. This particular sociotechnical construction is transparently not intended to change gender inequality.

To say the smart house is a masculine construct and leave it at that, however, is unnecessarily defeatist. I argued in Chapter 5 that technology should not be understood as ready-made artefacts whose use is non-negotiable. A technology's impacts are never entirely determined by its designers' and producers' intentions or inscribed visions (Akrich 1992). Rather, technology should be seen as *process* – open to flexible interpretation by its various user groups. To look at the eventual application of a technology, to see what users make of it for themselves, is often to dissipate the pessimism. Unfortunately, in the case of the smart house, still at prototype stage, we cannot yet see it in use.

Despite the non-fixed nature of a technology, however, to observe its gendering in those early stages before it reaches the user is of vital importance for understanding what happens subsequently. The smart house is a typical case of 'technology push', in contrast to 'consumer pull'. Its inspiration lies not in the practices of everyday life but in a fascination with what is technically possible.

The gender implications of this are clear. Technology is traditionally a masculine domain and an interest in technology is seen as constitutive of masculinity (Lie 1991). When technological possibilities lead, as they do in the socio-technical construction of the smart house, the house that results is somewhat like Corbusier's 'machine for living' – a highly masculine concept.

Conversely, decor and style are traditionally a feminine domain, and creative flair in home-making has been described as an important part of feminine identity (Prokopi 1978; Gullestad 1989). There is a crucial difference between a house and a home. It is women, in the main, whose work and skills make the former into the latter. Decor and style have no place in these prototypes. The smart house is no home (Miles 1991).

As we saw, historical studies of housework and domestic technology have disproved the idea that new technologies have reduced the time spent on housework (Boalt 1983; Cowan 1983; Hagelskjær 1986). None the less, the popular conception of domestic technology remains one of 'time-saving' (Vanek 1974, 1978), and it seems reasonable to expect to find such a conception among the designers of the smart house. Instead, they manifest neither interest in nor knowledge of housework. The home is acknowledged as an important area of everyday life, yet the work that sustains it is rendered invisible.

To summarize, then, the integrative technology that is the core of the smart home project appears unlikely to initiate any developments that would substitute or save time in housework. As a result we may anticipate that the producers will experience serious difficulties in selling their ideas. This socio-technical construct reflects a male idea of the home and responds to male activities in it. It is gendered in what it leaves out – its lack of support for changes in the domestic sexual division of labour.

There has been no actual user participation in the innovation process of the smart house to date, nor is the anticipated user described in more than hazy outline. Behind the shadowy notion however we can see the consumer these designers really have in mind: a technically-interested man in their own image. Women and men could, at different stages in the development process, 'negotiate'. Here such a negotiation has not taken place. And in women's exclusion from the imagination of its designers, as a 'relevant social group' we see how deeply gendered the nature of an innovation process can be.

Is our finding on the smart house cause for hope or fear? For women who may have reckoned on saving themselves time and labour the smart house looks like being a cheat. For techno-freaks who hope for some really interesting and significant inventions the smart house will likewise be a disappointment. On the other hand, for those who may have feared 'technology is taking command' the evidence assembled here should be reassuring. Nothing much, it seems, is going to change because of the smart house – at least not in terms of gender.

Notes

1 'Smart home', 'intelligent home', 'home automation' and 'computerhome' are synonyms for 'smart house'. The term denotes the extensive application of information technology (IT) to the dwelling of the future. Here, for simplicity, I limit myself to the term 'smart house'.
2 The research project, *From the Home Computer to the Computer Home*, was financed by the Norwegian Research Council (NAVF) programme on *Technology and Society* and was carried out in the Institute of Social Research in Industry (SINTEF-IFIM), Trondheim, during 1988–90. The planning of the project and collection of data were undertaken in cooperation with my late colleague Elin Hagelskjær, who died in February 1990.
3 The existing literature on the smart house is mainly concerned with the functions of appliances in technical terms.
4 These three North American houses were chosen because in 1987 when I applied for money for this project they were the ones I knew about. Later I learned of several other prototypes being built in European countries (including a joint project in the European Community) and in Japan, as well as others in the United States. Information about the European houses, and permission to visit them for research purposes, proved difficult to obtain.

References

Akrich, Madeleine (1992) The de-scription of technical objects, in Bijker, W.E. and Law, J. (eds) *Shaping Technology/Building Society: Studies in Sociotechnical Change*. Cambridge, MA: MIT Press.

Berg, Anne-Jorunn (1988) Husarbeid som et trekkspill om teknologi [Stretch-to-fit housework, adjusts to all technologies], in Lie, M. *et al.* (eds) *I menns bilde: Kvinner-teknologi-arbeid* [*In the Image of Men: Women-Technology-Work*]. Trondheim: Tapir.

Berg, Anne-Jorunn (1989) Informasjonsteknologi i hjemmet – den nye hjemmefronten [IT in the home – old or new forms of resistance], in Sørensen, K. and Espeli, T. (eds) *Ny Teknologi en Utfordring for Samfunnsforskning* [*New Technology – A Challenge to Social Science*]. Oslo: NAVF-NTNF-NORAS.

Berg, Anne-Jorunn (1991) He, she, and I.T. – designing the technological home of the future, in Sørensen, K. and Berg, A.-J. (eds) *Technology and Everyday Life:*

Trajectories and Transformations. Report No. 5: Proceedings from a Workshop in Trondheim, May 1990. Oslo: NAVF-NTNF-NORAS.

Boalt, Carin (1983) Tid för hemarbete. Hur lång tid då? [Time for housework, but how much time?], in Åkerman, Brita (ed.) Den okända vardagen – om arbetet i hemmen [Unknown Everyday Life – On Housework]. Stockholm: Akademilitteratur.

Cockburn, Cynthia (1983) Brothers: Male Dominance and Technological Change. London: Pluto Press.

Cockburn, Cynthia (1985) Machinery of Dominance: Women, Men and Technical Know-how. London: Pluto Press.

Cowan, Ruth Schwartz (1983) More Work for Mother. The Ironies of Household Technology from the Open Hearth to the Microwave. New York: Basic Books.

Cronberg, Tarja (1987) Teknologi og Hverdagsliv [Technology and Everyday Life]. Copenhagen: Nyt fra samfundsvidenskaberne.

Cronberg, Tarja and Sangregorio, Inga-Lisa (1983) Fagre nye Hverdag [Brave New Everyday Life]. Copenhagen: Delta.

GABe, Frances (1983) The GABe sclf-cleaning house, in Zimmerman, J. (ed.) The Technological Woman: Interfacing with Tomorrow. New York: Praeger.

Gorz, André (1981) Farvel til Proletariatet [Adieux au prolétariat]. Copenhagen: Politisk Revy.

Gullestad, Marianne (1987) Kitchen-Table Society. Oslo: Universitetsforlaget.

Gullestad, Marianne (1989) Kultur og Hverdagsliv [Culture and Everyday Life]. Oslo: Universitetsforlaget.

Hagelskjær, Elin (1986) Teknologiens Tommeliden: Moderne Tider i Husholdningen [The Tom Thumb of Technology Modern Times in Households]. Aalborg: Aalborg Universitetsforlag.

Harding, Sandra (1986) The Science Question in Feminism. Ithaca: Cornell University Press.

Harding, Sandra (1991) Whose Science? Whose Knowledge? Milton Keynes: Open University Press.

Lie, Merete (1991) Technology as Masculinity. Trondheim: SINTEF-IFIM.

Lie, Merete, Berg, A.-J., Kaul, H., Kvande, E., Rasmussen, B. and Sørensen, K. (1988) I menns bilde: Kvinner-teknologi-arbeid [In the Image of Men: Women-Technology-Work]. Trondheim: Tapir.

Mason, Roy (1983) Xanadu: The Computerized Home of Tomorrow and How It Can Be Yours Today! Washington, DC: Acropolis Books.

Miles, Ian (1988) Home Informatics. Information Technology and the Transformation of Everyday Life. London: Pinter Publishers.

Miles, Ian (1991) A smart house is not a home?, in Sørensen, K. and Berg, A.-J. (eds) Technology and Everyday Life: Trajectories and Transformations. Report No. 5: Proceedings from a Workshop in Trondheim, May 1990. Oslo: NAVF, NTNF, NORAS.

Nyberg, Anita (1990) Hushallsteknik – mødrars møda och mäns makt [Household technology – mothers' toil and men's power], in Beckman, S. (ed.) Teknokrati, Arbete, Makt [Technocracy, Work, Power]. Stockholm: Carlsons.

Pinch, Trevor and Bijker, Wiebe E. (1987) The social construction of facts and artefacts: or how the sociology of science and the sociology of technology might benefit each other, in Bijker, W.E., Hughes, T.P. and Pinch, T. (eds) The Social Construction of Technological Systems. Cambridge, MA and London: MIT Press.

Prokopi, Vlrike (1978) Kvindelig livssammenherg [Female Life Situations]. Copenhagen: GMT.

Sørensen, Knut and Berg, A.-J. (1987) Genderization of technology among Norwegian engineering students, *Acta Sociologica*, Vol. 30, No. 2, pp. 151–71.
Toffler, Alvin (1981) *Den tredje bølge* [*The Third Wave*]. Copenhagen: Politisk Revy.
Tuana, Nancy (ed.) (1989) *Feminism and Science*. Bloomington: Indiana University Press.
Vanek, Joann (1974) Time spent in housework, *Scientific American*, Vol. 231, No. 5.
Vanek, Joann (1978) Housewives as workers, in Stromberg, A. and Harkess, S. (eds) *Women Working: Theories and Facts in Perspective*. Palo Alto.
Wajcman, Judy (1991) *Feminism Confronts Technology*. Cambridge: Polity Press.
Zimmerman, Jan (1986) *Once Upon the Future*. London: Pandora.

Index

MAKING VIOLENCE SEXY
FEMINIST VIEWS ON PORNOGRAPHY
Diana E.H. Russell (ed.)

A crucially important collection of feminist voices challenging the pornocrats. Even if you read nothing else on the subject, read this.

(Robin Morgan)

Making Violence Sexy is a courageous book that chronicles women's resistance to pornography over the last twenty years. It does this in a collection of feminist articles, including testimonies by victims/survivors of pornography that together make a convincing case for the view that pornography (as distinct from erotica) causes harm to women, including acts of violence.

This book will appeal to students and lecturers of women's studies and sociology, political activists, public officials, social scientists, legal and medical professionals – those who consider it a form of discrimination against women. Women's studies teachers will find it a welcome addition to their required reading lists, and those working against sexual violence will appreciate it as a primary, up-to-date, and comprehensive source and inspiration.

Contents
Introduction – Part I: Survivors of pornography – Part II: Overview – Part III: Feminist research on pornography – Part IV: Feminist strategies and actions against pornography – Notes – References – Index.

320pp   0 335 19200 9 (Paperback)

THE SOCIAL SHAPING OF TECHNOLOGY
HOW THE REFRIGERATOR GOT ITS HUM

Donald MacKenzie and Judy Wajcman (eds)

Technological change is often seen as something that follows its own logic – something about which we may protest, but which we are unable to alter fundamentally. This reader challenges that assumption. In it, a collection of distinguished authors demonstrate that technology is affected at a fundamental level by the social context in which it develops.

The first section introduces the reader to general arguments about the relation of technology to society. In subsequent sections the editors examine three types of technology in particular: the technology of production, domestic technology and military (especially nuclear) technology. In each case a variety of examples is used to demonstrate how technologies reflect such features of the social and economic environment as the social relations of the workplace, gender divisions in society, or the dictates of the state. The editors argue that social scientists have devoted disproportionate attention to the effects of technology on society, and have tended to ignore the more fundamental question of what shapes technology in the first place. Drawing both on established work in the history of technology and on newer feminist and marxist perspectives they show how important and fruitful it is to try to answer that deeper question.

These readings, supplemented throughout by helpful editorial introductions and suggestions for further reading, will be invaluable to all students of science, technology and society and the place of technology in the modern world.

Contents
Part 1: Introductory essay and general issues – Part 2: The technology of production – Part 3: Domestic technology – Part 4: Military technology – Other areas of study – Bibliography – Index.

Contributors
Michael H. Armacost, Jane Barker, Marc Bloch, Harry Braverman, Tine Bruland, Cynthia Cockburn, Mike Cooley, Ruth Schwartz Cowan, Moyra Doorly, Hazel Downing, James Fallows, Thomas P. Hughes, Mary Kaldor, William Lazonick, Donald MacKenzie, William H. McNeill, David F. Noble, Alan Roberts, Judy Wajcman, Langdon Winner.

336pp   0 335 15026 8 (Paperback)   0 335 15027 6 (Hardback)

WOMEN IN BRITAIN TODAY

Veronica Beechey and Elizabeth Whitelegg (eds)

In recent years the impact of feminist approaches has revolutionized almost all aspects of the study of women's role in society, challenging previous assumptions about the nature of gender roles. This book draws on a wealth of current materials to provide an introduction to and an analysis of women's situation in British society. In a series of coordinated essays, the authors examine four key issues – the family, employment, education and health – challenging existing stereotypes of women's role, discussing contemporary research and providing alternative explanations.

Adapted from the popular and innovative Open University course U221: *The Changing Experience of Women*, this book is an invaluable introduction to feminist analyses which will be relevant to students and teachers of women's studies and to all others interested in the position of women in contemporary Britain.

Contents
Introduction – Women in the family: companions or caretakers? – Women's employment in contemporary Britain – State education policy and girls' educational experiences – Women, health and medicine – Index.

Contributors
Madeleine Arnot, Veronica Beechey, Lesley Doyal, Mary Ann Elston, Diana Leonard, Mary Anne Speakman.

224pp   0 335 15137 X (Paperback)   0 335 15138 8 (Hardback)